An Ecological Atlas of Grassland Plants

For Jean and Sheila

An
Ecological Atlas
of Grassland Plants

J. Philip Grime

Philip S. Lloyd

*Nature Conservancy (N.E.R.C.) Unit of Grassland
Research, Botany Department, Sheffield University*

Edward Arnold

FIRST PUBLISHED 1973
BY EDWARD ARNOLD (PUBLISHERS) LIMITED
25 HILL STREET,
LONDON, WIX 8LL

ISBN 0 7131 2397 4

PRINTED IN GREAT BRITAIN BY
FLETCHER AND SON LTD, NORWICH

Preface

Increasing public sympathy and support are placing new responsibilities upon those who carry out research in ecology. It is now generally accepted that considerable effort is needed in the various fields of applied ecology and, as we explain in the Introduction, it is our hope that the information in this book, in addition to being of intrinsic value, may be of use in connection with landscape design, nature conservation and the management of marginal land. However, the responsibilities of the ecologist affect not only the nature of the work he undertakes but also the way in which he carries it out. Research contributions in ecology, no matter how successful individually, are notoriously disparate, each tending to apply to a unique permutation of environments, species and methods of study.

It may be argued that each field situation *is* unique and that for this reason ecological data cannot attain the coherence and predictive power of those generated in the physical sciences. It is this viewpoint as much as any technical difficulty which has perhaps tended to discourage ecologists from a fundamental activity characteristic of science—the standardized description of the properties of matter. However, while it cannot be maintained that the units with which the ecologist deals—ecosystems, communities, species, populations —have an integrity comparable to that of atoms or molecules, there seems to be no good reason to ignore the systematic approach which has served physics and chemistry so adequately and which is also the basis of taxonomy. Accordingly, this book is an attempt to introduce the concept of greater standardization into the collection and presentation of ecological field data.

The information refers to species. In view of the widespread occurrence of genetic variation in plant species there is need to justify this approach. In the first place, the species seems likely to continue to be the most readily recognizable unit in the field and, for this reason, information relating to species is most easily utilized for practical purposes. Secondly, delimitation of the ecology of the species is a necessary preliminary to the systematic study of intraspecific variation. Thirdly, as the effects of man upon vegetation become increasingly disruptive and diverse, data referring to phytosociological units are likely to decline in general applicability and it may be more judicious to base our attempts to understand new or disturbed plant 'communities' upon knowledge of the ecology of the component species rather than to extrapolate from existing synecological data. Finally, as our knowledge of plant physiology expands, the possibility arises that the ecology of a species may be predicted on the basis of measurements carried out in the laboratory. Quantitative descriptions of the ecological range of each species will be needed in order to measure and improve the accuracy of such predictions.

In focusing upon species we are consciously ignoring opportunities to follow a synecological approach. Although it is more difficult to apply rigorous standardization in the presentation of plant sociological data, that alternative is necessary and complementary to the approach adopted in this book. It is our experience that the same field data can be used profitably for both purposes.

Many people have taken part in the collection and processing of the field data on which this book is based. For their contribution to the planning of the survey work and for their active participation in 1965, we are indebted to Dr. I. H. Rorison, Dr. M. B. Dale and Dr. D. J. Anderson. In the subsequent stages of the field-work, we have been fortunate in having the assistance of Dr. J. G. Hodgson and Mr. S. R. Band, whose skill and enthusiasm have played a major part in the completion of the project. In addition, we wish to thank Mr. Band for his help in analysing the data. We are grateful also to Miss E. Cox and Mr. R. Law for their assistance in certain parts of the work.

Figure 3 was prepared following a discussion with Dr. G. C. Evans and we are indebted to him for his continuing interest in the project.

Mrs. N. Ruttle patiently and carefully typed the manuscript, Mr. H. Walkland drew a majority of the histograms and Professor A. J. Willis did much to see the book through the press. To all these we offer our sincere thanks.

J.P.G.
P.S.L.

Sheffield, 1973

Contents

I

Introduction

If maximum use is to be made of our knowledge of the relations of individual species to factors of the environment, it is essential that comparisons between species of similar or contrasted ecology should be possible. Such comparisons are valid only where the procedures of sampling, measurement, analysis and presentation have been standardized.

Autecological data meeting these requirements are not readily available, although the pioneer work of Hundt (1966) in Central Europe is a notable contribution. Articles in the *Biological Flora of the British Isles*, published in the Journal of Ecology, have been designed to provide an account of the ecology of a species over a large geographical area and it has not been found practicable or perhaps desirable to standardize in detail the collection and presentation of field data. In particular, little or no account has been taken of the field situations in which a given species *fails* to occur. Perring (1958, 1959, 1960) has studied the effect of climate and topography on the distribution of individual species in a way which allows comparisons, but the detailed observations on which his conclusions were based have not been published.

In 1966, during the processing of data collected both for a descriptive survey of the semi-natural grasslands of the Sheffield area and for certain autecological purposes, it became apparent that the field records could be summarized in a standard way so as to display basic information on the ecology of individual grassland plants. The frequency of each species, together with measurements of certain environmental characteristics, had been recorded at more than three hundred (eventually 630) sites. The sites had been selected at random; hence the information for any one species could be abstracted to give an indication of the performance and ecological amplitude of the species (within established grassland) which was nearly independent of 'observer bias' and which was directly comparable with those obtained for other species encountered in the survey. This book is an account of the results which were obtained for ninety-five common grassland plants when this form of analysis was carried out on the survey data.

An outcome of the essentially random method of sampling is that, inevitably, rarer plant species or communities are unlikely to have been encountered. The data presented may nevertheless give some indication of the ecology of rarer species, by providing information on associated but commoner species.

It should perhaps be emphasized that in some species at least there is considerable genetic variability and it is as yet uncertain to what extent the success of wide-ranging species is due to the existence of distinct ecotypes. The possibility of ecotypic variation and of subtle but important differences in environment places an obvious limitation on the degree to which conclusions based on this regional work may be extended to other areas in Britain or abroad. However, by virtue of its position in central England, the area from which the samples have been drawn is unusually representative of the geological, topographical, climatic and floristic diversity encountered within the British Isles. This is reflected in the range of species and types of grassland encountered during the course of the survey.

The work provides a basis for direct comparison of the ecology of a majority of the commoner grassland species of Britain and it is hoped that the data will be useful in the study of a number of distributional problems of long-standing interest to plant ecologists. One such problem is that of explaining the restriction of certain species or ecotypes either to calcareous or to strongly acidic soils (the calcicole-calcifuge problem). Another concerns the frequent occurrence of abrupt northern or southern boundaries of plant distribution.

Both these problems are well illustrated by the grassland flora of the Sheffield region and the form of presentation adopted allows quite small differences in distribution to be recognized between species usually regarded as similar in ecology. Such differences may provide a clue to the mechanisms involved and in some cases they suggest that, in different species, similar patterns have different explanations.

Further investigation will be necessary before it is clear to what extent the 'comparative autecological approach' can provide an insight into mechanisms of plant competition and the determination of vegetation structure. However, as with the distributional problems, the approach may be expected to assist in a stricter formulation of hypotheses and in the choice of species for experimental study.

It is our hope that the information presented here may be useful also in the field of applied ecology. The data provide opportunities to assess the value and reliability of common grassland plants as field indicators of environmental features such as geological substratum and soil acidity or of effects of management likely to affect the economic value of grassland or the status of rarer species of plants and animals. In addition, the information can serve as a guide to the circumstances in which particular native species may be used in the construction of new landscapes.

2

The survey area

The area around Sheffield from which samples were obtained extends from Castleton in the west to Bawtry in the east and from Doncaster in the north to Matlock in the south (Fig. 1) (p. 5). Aspects of the geography, geology and vegetation of the region are described by Linton (1956), Edwards (1962), Neves and Downie (1967), Moss (1913), Clapham (1969), and Lloyd, Grime and Rorison (1971). The notes which follow in this section give a brief outline of the geology, topography and land use of the area.

From east to west across the survey area successively older geological strata are exposed. The distribution of the five major formations is shown in Fig. 1. A sixth formation is composed of the Toadstones (Table 1). These occur in the Carboniferous Limestone as local volcanic intrusions which give rise to distinctive soils of intermediate base status.

The Carboniferous Limestone crops out in the south-west of the survey area and on its northern and eastern sides is overlain by Millstone Grit. With this exception the strata run north–south throughout the region. The plateau of the Carboniferous Limestone, which averages about 300 m (1000 ft) above sea level, is dissected by steep-sided valleys, or dales, the majority of which no longer hold permanent water courses. The Millstone Grit hills attain 600 m (2000 ft) in the north-west, but become progressively lower further south, scarcely reaching 300 m near Matlock. To the east of the Millstone Grit the country becomes considerably lower, falling to 60 m (200 ft) in the valley of the river Don in Sheffield (Coal Measures). A low scarp marks the outcrop of the Magnesian Limestone (reaching 180 m (600 ft) in the south but only 90 m (300 ft) in the north). The Bunter Sandstones to the east rarely exceed 60 m above sea level.

Table 1 Geological formations within the survey area

Abbreviations are those used for the formations in tables throughout the book.

Age	Formation	Rock types
Triassic	Bunter Sandstone (BS)	Sandstones and pebble beds
Permian	Magnesian Limestone (ML)	Soft limestones and marls
Carboniferous	Coal Measures (CM)	Sandstones, shales and coal seams
	Millstone Grit (MG)	Gritstones, sandstones and shales
	Carboniferous Limestone (CL)	Hard limestones and volcanic rocks (Toadstones, TS)

The prevailing winds are west to south-west and, associated with the variation in topography just described, there is high rainfall, 1300–1500 mm (50–60 in), in the west and low rainfall, 530–630 mm (21–25 in), in the east, with inversely correlated sunshine and temperature records (Table 2). Thus to the west and east of Sheffield there are two rather distinct climatic and topographic areas, each of which includes one stratum giving rise to soils of high pH (Carboniferous or Magnesian Limestone) and one to soils of low pH (Millstone

Grit or Bunter Sandstone). There is a pronounced leaching sequence on the soils of the Carboniferous Lime-stone so that plateau soils may be strongly acidic while adjacent dale-side soils are basic (see Balme 1953 Pigott 1962, 1970 and Bryan 1967 for further details). A similar but less pronounced leaching sequence is locally evident in the low rainfall area of the Magnesian Limestone.

The vegetation survey for which the data were collected was restricted to natural and semi-natural grass-land communities and so the availability of potential sites was strongly influenced by the pattern of land use in each part of the region.

On the Carboniferous Limestone the plateau is almost fully exploited for agricultural purposes and semi-natural grassland is more or less confined to the steep dale sides. A few uncultivated areas on the plateau still remain and were available for sampling. On the Millstone Grit most of the arable farming is confined to the valley bottoms, but the tops of the hills are extensively covered by moorland dominated by *Calluna vulgaris* or *Eriophorum vaginatum*. In consequence suitable grassland sites are mainly located on the hill slopes between the upper limit of arable farming and the lower limit of the moorlands.

Table 2 Climatic data for the Survey area

Buxton is approximately 13 km south-west of Castleton (Fig. 1). Altitudes of the three stations are: Buxton 300 m (1000 ft), Sheffield 137 m (450 ft), Bawtry 10 m (30 ft). All figures are means for the period 1943–65, with the exception of temperature records for Buxton (1931–60). Data by courtesy of the Meteorological Office.

	J	F	M	A	M	J	J	A	S	O	N	D	Total
(a) Mean daily maximum temperature (°C)													
Buxton	4.2	4.5	7.2	10.1	13.5	16.7	17.9	17.7	15.2	11.3	7.6	5.4	
Sheffield	5.8	6.3	9.0	12.5	15.7	18.6	19.8	19.4	17.2	13.6	9.2	6.8	
Bawtry	5.5	6.4	9.7	13.4	16.5	19.4	20.8	20.5	18.2	14.3	9.2	6.7	
(b) Mean daily minimum temperature (°C)													
Buxton	−0.5	−0.4	0.8	2.8	5.4	8.4	10.6	10.3	8.5	5.5	3.2	1.1	
Sheffield	1.3	1.3	2.4	4.9	7.3	10.2	12.2	11.8	10.2	7.4	4.4	2.2	
Bawtry	0.9	0.9	1.9	4.2	6.7	9.7	11.5	12.9	9.5	6.8	4.0	2.1	
(c) Monthly and annual rainfall (mm)													
Buxton	140	96	76	86	79	88	104	116	115	103	129	153	1285
Sheffield	82	62	52	50	56	59	59	73	66	62	85	82	788
Bawtry	48	36	35	34	42	47	53	61	48	44	55	44	547

At their western edge, the Coal Measures carry moorlands continuous with those of the Grit, but at lower altitudes they are either farmed or subject to extensive urban or industrial development. Intensive farming is characteristic of the Magnesian Limestone and also of much of the Bunter Sandstone, and in some areas railway cuttings are the only source of suitable sites. (In passing it may be noted that railway cuttings, in common with the dales of the Carboniferous Limestone, usually possess opposing faces with comparable angles of slope, a feature of particular value to survey work of this kind.) Grassland sites on the Bunter Sandstone are almost entirely restricted to open areas in Sherwood Forest in the south of the region and to neglected parts of golf courses elsewhere.

The differences between the areas east and west of Sheffield are characteristic of the two distinct geographical regions, Lowland and Highland Britain. Within the area selected for study there are grasslands which, although in close proximity, provide marked contrasts with respect to topography, soil development, climate and management. Thus the region is peculiarly suitable for the study of plant distribution and its causative factors.

3
Collection of the data

The methods of data collection were planned to enable the grassland vegetation of the region to be described in an objective, statistical way (Lloyd, Grime and Rorison 1971, Lloyd 1972). Initial field work was completed in 1965 and 1966, but when it became apparent that the data could be used to provide standardized information about individual species it was realized that the coverage of slope and aspect on the different strata was far from uniform. Further sampling using the same procedures as before was therefore carried out during the summer of 1968.

The sampled localities provide a tolerably uniform coverage of the whole region (Fig. 1). To the west of Sheffield these localities are representative of much more extensive grassland, but to the east of Sheffield undisturbed grasslands are rather scarce and on the Magnesian Limestone and Bunter Sandstone almost all the available sites were sampled.

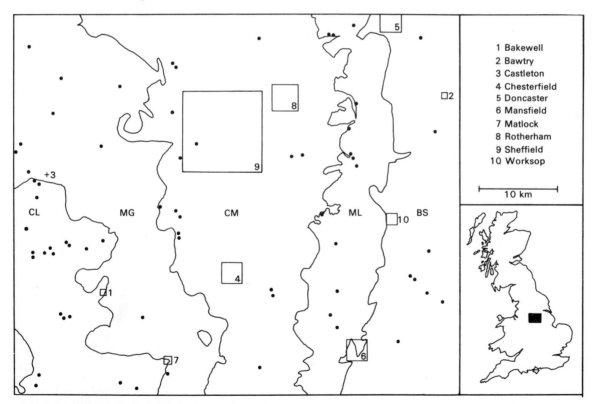

Fig 1 The survey area. The approximate extent of urban development is shown by squares and the distribution of sampling localities by circles (●). Abbreviations of geological strata as in Table 1. The position of the survey area in Britain is shown by the inset.

5

Within each locality quadrats were positioned by means of random co-ordinates and were allocated at a density of one per 200 square metres of grassland. The area of each quadrat was one square metre, which was considered to be the maximum advisable in view of the small-scale variation in soil type and vegetation cover known to occur widely in the daleside grasslands on the Carboniferous Limestone (Balme 1953, Grime 1963b).

For each species present in the quadrat a figure of percentage frequency was obtained, being the number of 10 × 10 cm subdivisions of the quadrat in which the species was rooted. Though a laborious technique, this minimizes 'observer error' and is a more constant value through the summer than is an estimate of cover. In practice, the metre square quadrat was divided into four quarters of 25 subdivisions, each quarter being examined by a single observer. Comparison of the four sub-totals provided a rough guide to the homogeneity of the area. At least two observers worked on each quadrat.

The slope and aspect were recorded at each quadrat site and soil samples were taken from 0–3 cm ('surface') and 9–12 cm ('10 cm') depth for subsequent pH determinations on the fresh soil saturated with distilled water, using a glass electrode. The soils encountered rarely exceeded 50 cm in depth and were frequently much shallower.

Grassland sites were excluded from sampling if there were signs of recent disturbance of any kind, such as mining activity or excessive treading or picnicking by man or trampling by cattle. Level ground was rejected if there were any signs that it had been ploughed in the past. An outcome of these restrictions was that, on the Carboniferous Limestone, flat ground was sampled only from the leached plateau grasslands and not from the base-rich grasslands of the dale floors, which are usually heavily trampled by cattle.

4

Presentation of the data

A standard format has been adopted in the presentation of the data for each species. On the left-hand page there are notes to assist interpretation of the figures and tabular data illustrating the distribution of the species with respect to geological stratum, soil pH, grazing and burning. Below the notes, one histogram illustrates the constancy of the species within classes of soil pH and the other illustrates the range of frequency records encountered. On the right-hand page there are figures which describe the distribution of the species in relation to slope and aspect. A brief synopsis of the ecology of each species is incorporated in the index (p. 190). Nomenclature follows that of Clapham, Tutin and Warburg (1962).

The notes provide some background information about the species and summarize the main features of the tables and diagrams. The value following 'Occurrence' gives the percentage of the 630 samples in which the species was recorded. The brief description of the life form of the plant and its height range is based upon Clapham, Tutin and Warburg (1962), amended where necessary in the light of our experience. The notes also draw attention to the general ecology of the species. This is of particular interest where the species concerned is a plant more usually associated with habitats other than grassland. The major headings in the notes refer to the tables and diagrams, with the exceptions of **B.S.B.I. Atlas**, which summarizes the distribution of the species in Britain as given by Perring and Walters (1962) or Perring (1968), and **Biological Flora**, which gives reference to the Biological Flora account, where available, of the species (see p. 16). *Unless otherwise specified, statements about the local distribution and ecology of the species refer only to the data presented. Although many of the species occur in a wide range of habitats the notes refer in detail only to grasslands.*

The pH tables record the number of occurrences of the species within classes of one pH unit on each geological stratum. Results based on pH determinations on surface soil and on soil at 10 cm depth are tabulated separately. In order to interpret these tables in detail a comparison is necessary with Table 3 which gives the total number of samples in each class. As a rapid guide to the relationship with stratum, for each geological formation the percentage of the sites in which the species occurred is recorded as its 'Constancy', a value based on the 'stratum totals' given in Table 3. In these constancy figures bold type indicates that the species shows a positive association with the stratum (P > 95%), italic type indicates a negative association and normal type indicates no significant association.

The grazing/burning table shows for separate strata the occurrence of the species in relation to the prevalence of grazing and burning. Each site has been assigned to one of four categories: ungrazed and unburned, grazed, burned, or grazed and burned. On certain strata, representation of one or more categories is inadequate (Table 4); the percentage of the sites occupied has been calculated only for categories containing at least ten sites. In general all quadrat sites at one locality were assigned to the same category, the main exception being some Carboniferous Limestone sites on open scree which were classed as ungrazed and unburned irrespective of the classification of the surrounding grassland.

The pH histogram illustrates the relative frequency of the species in half-unit pH classes over the range 3.0–8.0. The diagram is based on surface soil pH only and includes data from all strata. The smallest total number of sites in any class is twenty-nine and the number of sites containing the species in each class is expressed as the percentage of all sites in that class.

The frequency histogram illustrates the range and distribution of frequency values recorded for the species at all its sites. Three major patterns are recognizable:

CLASS 1. That in which almost all records are restricted to the left-hand side of the histogram, the lowest frequency classes (e.g. *Senecio jacobaea*).

CLASS 2. That in which the species has a wide range of frequency values with or without a peak in the lowest classes (e.g. *Poterium sanguisorba*).

CLASS 3. That in which there is a peak of records towards the right-hand side of the frequency distribution, the highest frequency classes (e.g. *Brachypodium pinnatum*).

Records from grazed sites (black) are distinguished from those from ungrazed sites (open). This makes it possible to recognize species in which the higher frequency values tend to be correlated with grazing, either directly (e.g. *Galium sterneri*) or inversely (e.g. *Lotus corniculatus*).

Table 3 The distribution of soil pH at two depths with respect to geological formation (number of sites)

At certain sites on screes or rock outcrops only one soil sample could be collected. This accounts for differing totals in corresponding columns of the two parts of the table.

pH range	TS	CL	Geological formation MG	CM	ML	BS
0–3 cm depth						
3.0–4.0	1	15	152	99	0	32
4.1–5.0	8	28	10	21	4	4
5.1–6.0	18	39	3	3	12	0
6.1–7.0	9	37	0	0	13	0
7.1–8.0	2	59	0	0	57	0
9–12 cm depth						
2.8–4.0	0	15	152	83	0	24
4.1–5.0	16	16	7	31	2	12
5.1–6.0	15	25	5	8	2	0
6.1–7.0	6	37	0	0	14	0
7.1–8.1	1	84	0	1	66	0
Stratum Totals	38	182	165	123	86	36

The slope-aspect polargraph displays the pattern of occurrence of the species in relation to slope (concentric axes) and aspect (radial axes). The range in slope extends from 0° at the centre to 50° at the circumference. Thus a 50° east-facing slope is represented at the extreme right-hand end of the radial axis at the 'three o'clock' position. On the individual diagrams radial axes have been drawn only to the four cardinal points and concentric axes are indicated only by their intersection on these radial axes. The **transparent overlays** in a pocket in the end cover have the concentric axes of 10° interval of slope (to 50°) drawn in full, with intersections at 15° interval of aspect. These overlays show the distribution of all sampled sites on the separate geological formations. On the overlays the appropriate slope and aspect of each site is marked by a square, the size of which indicates the pH of the surface soil in one of ten classes, from pH 3.1–3.5 (smallest square) to pH 7.6–8.0 (largest square).

In the polargraphs drawn for each species, the sites at which the species occurred are marked by circles, the size of which show the frequency value recorded at that site; the smallest circle represents a frequency of 1–10%, the largest 91–100%. Hence a slope or aspect preference may be apparent from the distribution of the sites (e.g. *Medicago lupulina*) or from the pattern of frequencies (e.g. *Briza media*). Distribution of the species with respect to aspect is further analysed in the diagrams above the polargraph and with respect to slope in the histograms below the polargraph.

The aspect analyses To aid recognition of the aspect preferences, the occurrence and abundance of the species are summarized for the north-facing and south-facing quadrants of the polargraph. All records of the species in the aspect ranges 315–360–45° and 135–225°, on slopes equal to or greater than 5°, are given in the left-hand diagram (**Presence**) as a percentage of all sites sampled in those quadrants. The right-hand diagram (**Abundance**) shows the percentage of those records of presence in which the frequency value of the species exceeded 40%. In both diagrams bold type is used to indicate significant (P > 95%) positive association with aspect in terms of either presence or abundance.

Table 4 The distribution of grazing and burning with respect to geological formation (number of sites)

Values in brackets refer to categories omitted from the tables for individual species.

	Geological formation					
	TS	CL	MG	CM	ML	BS
Ungrazed, unburned	(7)	31	28	61	(8)	36
Grazed, unburned	15	94	137	37	10	(0)
Ungrazed, burned	16	37	(0)	21	67	(0)
Grazed, burned	(0)	21	(0)	(4)	(0)	(0)

The slope histograms. The construction of the polargraph is such that the area representing unit change of slope and aspect increases considerably towards steeper slopes. Except where there are marked discontinuities, changes in the density of records with slope are correspondingly difficult to interpret. To assist recognition of slope preferences, histograms at the foot of the polargraph illustrate the percentage occurrence of the species in five 10° classes of slope, on acidic formations (Millstone Grit, Coal Measures and Bunter Sandstone) to the left (A), and on basic formations (Toadstone, Carboniferous Limestone and Magnesian Limestone) to the right (B).

PAIRED SPECIES

Many species of ecological interest were recorded with insufficient frequency to warrant presentation in the standard format. However data on a few of the less common species, for which there are sufficient records for distribution patterns to emerge, have been presented at the end of the main series of diagrams. These latter species are presented in pairs, the criteria for pairing being that the species either should be related, but with contrasting ecology, or should be unrelated, but with similar ecology. *Taraxacum officinale* and *T. laevigatum* have been paired because of the difficulty of certain determination of some vegetative specimens. (*Poa pratensis* ssp. *pratensis* and ssp. *angustifolia* have been paired because of incomplete separation of the two subspecies, but this pair is included in the main series of diagrams.)

On the polargraph the sites and frequencies of the second species are represented by squares of sizes comparable to the usual circles. In general the data available for the paired species are inadequate for pH or frequency histograms, but an indication of the type of distribution can be obtained by inspection of the pH tables and the polargraph.

9

5

Interpretation of the data

Synopsis of primary autecological data in one- or two-factor diagrams or tables inevitably masks the possible significance of co-related variables and the existence of local and exceptional circumstances. The notes provided for individual species draw attention to some of these complications, but certain underlying or recurring features of the diagrams and tables deserve a further explanation at this point.

The pH tables contain values for two depths in the soil and hence provide a crude index of soil stratification. On most strata leaching is such that the pH at 10 cm depth is higher than that at the soil surface. This is particularly true on the Carboniferous Limestone where there may be a difference of more than 1 pH unit between the two depths. On occasion however the pH value of the surface soil may be higher than that at 10 cm. For example, at one locality on the Toadstone the surface soil is strongly influenced by wind-blown dust from a nearby limestone quarry. Stratification of the soil chemical properties is frequently associated with cohabitation by calcicole and calcifuge plants and may explain apparently anomalous records for individual species.

The grazing/burning tables do not distinguish between the different methods, intensities and seasonal distributions of grazing and burning which occur within the sampled area and which may give rise to different responses. In particular it should be noted that the forms of grazing and burning differ markedly between the upland and lowland parts of the region and between individual strata. Certain generalizations about the grazing and burning regimes on the various strata can, however, be made and may assist interpretation of the tables. **Grazing** on the Magnesian Limestone is almost entirely by cattle, whereas both sheep and cattle graze on the Carboniferous Limestone and sheep are more important than cattle on the Millstone Grit. **Burning** is sporadic on the Carboniferous Limestone (Lloyd 1968), but is a frequent and often annual event at many localities on the Magnesian Limestone and at certain localities on the Toadstone. Grazing reduces fire-risk through the removal of potential fuel by the grazing animal and in consequence the 'grazed and burned' category is uncommon except on the Carboniferous Limestone where both phenomena are of low intensity and burning is infrequent.

The pH histograms are based on all sites without reference to stratum. The contribution of the different strata to each pH class is illustrated in Fig. 2 where, in addition, screes are separated from the rest of the Carboniferous Limestone sites. The relative importance of grazing and burning regimes in each pH class is indicated in Table 5.

Apart from the distributions shown by extreme calcicoles such as *Scabiosa columbaria* and extreme calcifuges such as *Deschampsia flexuosa*, the most notable recurring feature of the pH histograms is the sharp 'cut-off' below pH 4.0 (e.g. *Festuca rubra*). This curtailed distribution appears to coincide with the change from 'mull' to 'mor' in humus type and to be characteristic of species which are sensitive to the toxic effect of aluminium, which shows a substantial increase in solubility below pH 4.0 (Grime and Hodgson 1969).

A second recurring feature is the appearance of two peaks on the right-hand side of the histogram. In certain species (e.g. *Dactylis glomerata*) this feature appears to be related to the occurrence of calcareous mineral

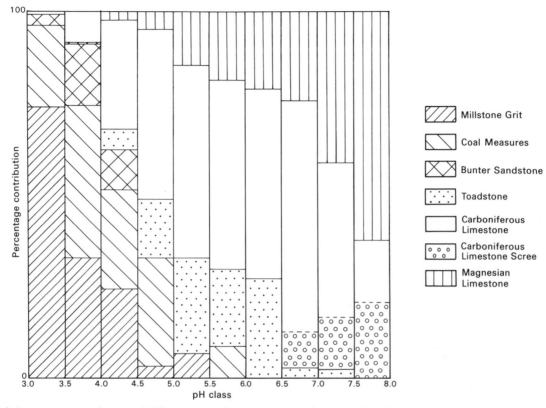

Fig 2 Percentage contribution of different geological strata to the classes of the pH histogram.

soils which are concentrated about pH 6.0 on the Carboniferous Limestone and are most frequent above pH 7.0 on the Magnesian Limestone. This explanation cannot, however, be applied to all the species which show a bimodal distribution. In *Hieracium pilosella*, for example, the pattern appears to be associated with the distribution of sites with short or open turf over the pH range 5.0–8.0.

The frequency histograms, by showing the pattern of frequency records of the species, indicate the role of the species in the sampled vegetation. Species with a Class 1 distribution are those which occur as isolated individuals and contribute little to the structure of the vegetation. Species with a Class 2 distribution attain high frequency values on occasion, but often provide minor contributions to the vegetation elsewhere. Species with a Class 3 distribution are those which are normally major components of the vegetation and frequently occupy large areas of ground probably to the exclusion of many other species. This may be either because of their competitive ability in environments potentially favourable to the growth of many other species (e.g. *Brachypodium pinnatum*) or because of specific adaptation to an unfavourable environment (e.g. *Deschampsia flexuosa*).

Table 5 The frequency of grazed and burned sites within the classes of the pH histogram
(percentages of each pH class)

	pH Class									
	≤ 3.5	3.6–4.0	4.1–4.5	4.6–5.0	5.1–5.5	5.6–6.0	6.1–6.5	6.6–7.0	7.1–7.5	≥ 7.6
Ungrazed, unburned	31	37	32	41	7	9	10	19	23	21
Grazed, unburned	63	51	45	35	43	39	45	34	41	18
Ungrazed, burned	3	12	18	19	45	46	42	38	27	56
Grazed, burned	3	0	5	5	5	6	3	9	9	5

For the great majority of species the 1 m² quadrat subdivided into 10 cm squares appears to give a realistic indication of the contribution of the plant to the vegetation. However, the absolute values recorded for a species in this histogram are a reflection of the interaction between quadrat size and plant morphology and are not a reliable index of biomass. At one extreme small or short-lived plants (e.g. *Linum catharticum*) may show high frequency values without making a major contribution to the total bulk of the vegetation, while at the other extreme tall plants may truly dominate the vegetation with frequency values of less than 100%. For example, had more samples been taken from areas dominated by *Pteridium aquilinum*, there is reason to think that its peak frequency would fall in the range 60–70%.

It should be re-emphasized that the diagrams show the frequency distribution of the species in natural or semi-natural grassland and they do not provide a guide to the performance of the species outside that habitat. *Mercurialis perennis*, for example, would undoubtedly show a Class 3 distribution in woodlands and *Arrhenatherum elatius* would probably attain Class 3 status in roadside vegetation.

The slope–aspect diagrams. At temperate latitudes it is to be expected (Geiger 1966) that considerable differences in insolation will be found on different slopes and aspects and that air and soil temperature, atmospheric humidity and soil moisture will all vary in concert with radiation, although local features of topography or substratum may disrupt the general pattern. In Fig. 3, an estimate of the daily duration of direct radiation for January and July for Latitude 53°N is plotted on the polargraph and may be used as an indication of the amplitude and pattern of microclimatic variation due to slope and aspect.

Another factor to be taken into account in explaining specific patterns is the distribution of soil types (as reflected by the pH of the surface soil) with respect to slope and aspect. Overlays 1–6 incorporate pH measure-

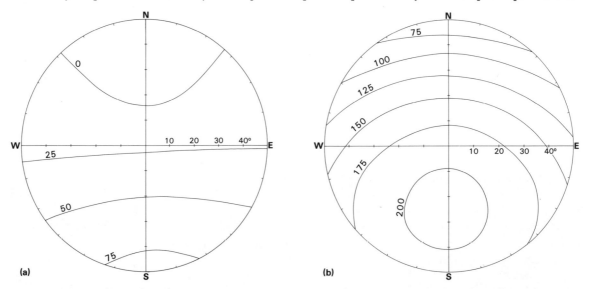

Fig 3 Estimated mean daily duration (min) of direct radiation received on slopes of < 50° of all aspects for **(a)** January and **(b)** July.

    The mean daily distribution of bright sunshine (min/h) was calculated for each month for the period 1966–8 from the cards of a Campbell-Stokes recorder sited at Finningley, near Bawtry. In order to allow for the effect of topography on the intensity of insolation, the angle of incidence of the sun on to all required angles of slope and aspect was measured on a globe for each hour of the day, using solar tracks appropriate for the 15th day of the month at Latitude 53° N. The products of the cosine of the angle of incidence and the hourly duration of bright sunshine were totalled to give the daily duration for each point on the polargraph (5° or 10° intervals of slope, 15° intervals of aspect).

    Equivalent records from Buxton indicated a similar daily distribution of sunshine, but lower totals particularly in January. Diffuse radiation has been omitted from the calculations, but would provide a background pattern of distribution (uniform with aspect, decreasing with increasing angle of slope) on which the pattern of direct radiation is superimposed.

ments for the sites on the separate strata. The overlay for the Carboniferous Limestone (2) shows that, on this stratum, surface pH rises with increasing angle of slope and, to a lesser extent, towards slopes of southern aspect. This is a reflection both of the accumulation of leached horizons on soils of level ground and on gentle north-facing slopes and of the presence of non-calcareous loessic deposits on the limestone plateau (Pigott 1962). It should be added that no attempt is made here to distinguish between substrata of different origin or composition within the six broad headings listed in Table 1 (p. 3).

In addition to providing information on the relationship between soil pH and topography, the overlays may be used to identify the distribution of a species on separate strata and hence to give information of local variation in topographic relationships.

The species examined provide a wide range of distribution patterns with respect to slope and aspect, and these patterns are undoubtedly determined by a variety of factors (climatic, edaphic and biotic) affecting either vegetative growth or reproduction. This statement is consistent with the results of pioneer autecological studies in the Sheffield region (Balme 1954, Pigott 1958, 1968, Ratcliffe 1961). In the following notes, four basic patterns of response to slope and aspect are distinguished and an attempt is made to explain them by reference to particular examples.

(a) *Restriction to or concentration on north-facing slopes.* Examination of the list of species in this group (see Ecological synopsis, p. 190) shows that while a few are more common in the north than the south (e.g. *Galium saxatile* and *Molinia caerulea*) all are widespread in the British Isles. Also, many are species most commonly found in habitats other than grassland. It is clear that grasslands on north-facing slopes are comparatively cool and moist and especially where steeply sloping they experience relatively low light intensities (Fig. 3, p. 12). It is not surprising therefore to find that the group includes both familiar woodland plants (e.g. *Mercurialis perennis*, *Anemone nemorosa* and *Oxalis acetosella*) and species frequent in marshes (e.g. *Carex flacca*, *Succisa pratensis* and *Cirsium palustre*).

In a small number of plants the bias towards north-facing slopes is peculiar to the Magnesian Limestone (e.g. *Chrysanthemum leucanthemum*, *Leontodon hispidus* and *Prunella vulgaris*). All are low-growing rosette species and it is suggested that the pattern is at least in part determined by competition from *Brachypodium pinnatum*, a species which tends to deposit a thick layer of persistent litter on the ground surface and which is especially abundant on south-facing slopes on the Magnesian Limestone.

(b) *Restriction to or concentration on south-facing slopes.* Of the twenty-five species (Ecological synopsis, p. 190) which are more abundant on south-facing slopes half this number are plants of southern distribution in Britain (Perring and Walters 1962) and it is likely that, in some at least, the pattern is imposed by direct effects of climate upon the plant. However, since several are small annuals or biennials (e.g. *Arenaria serpyllifolia* and *Medicago lupulina*) or xeromorphic perennials (e.g. *Hieracium pilosella* and *Thymus drucei*) it is also possible that the southern bias in the distribution of some of these plants arises from their exclusion by competition from all except open communities, which are most frequently encountered on dry south-facing slopes.

(c) *Restriction to or concentration on flat ground and/or gentle slopes.* The small number of species in this group are mainly calcifuges and their distribution is correlated with the absence of acidic soils from the steep dalesides of the Carboniferous Limestone. It would be dangerous, however, to ascribe these patterns to mineral nutritional factors alone. Soils on plateaux and gentler slopes are of greater depth and have a lower incidence of droughting in addition to being more podsolized than soils on steeper slopes. The need to consider moisture stress as a possible factor in the failure of these species on slope soils is emphasized by the fact that certain of the calcifuges (e.g. *Agrostis tenuis*, *Galium saxatile* and *Potentilla erecta*) are less common on steeper slopes, especially where these are south-facing, even over non-calcareous strata such as the Millstone Grit.

(d) *Restriction to or concentration on steep slopes.* Many of the plants in the group are strongly calcicolous species (e.g. *Scabiosa columbaria* and *Galium sterneri*) which are restricted to immature limestone soils in which the effects of leaching are nullified by solifluction. The remainder include small-seeded wind-dispersed weeds (e.g. *Chamaenerion angustifolium* and *Senecio jacobaea*) which presumably establish in openings in the turf on the unstable soils of steeper slopes.

13

References

BALME, O. E. (1953). Edaphic and vegetational zoning on the Carboniferous Limestone of the Derbyshire Dales. *J. Ecol.* **41**, 331–44.

BALME, O. E. (1954). Biological Flora of the British Isles: *Viola lutea. J. Ecol.* **42**, 234–40.

BRYAN, R. (1967). Climosequences of soil development in the Peak District of Derbyshire. *E. Midld Geogr.* **4**, 251–61.

BURNETT, J. H. (ed.) (1964). *The vegetation of Scotland.* Oliver & Boyd, Edinburgh.

CAMERON, E. (1935). A study of the natural control of ragwort. *J. Ecol.* **23**, 265–322.

CLAPHAM, A. R. (ed.) (1969). *Flora of Derbyshire.* County Museum, Derby.

CLAPHAM, A. R., TUTIN, T. G. and WARBURG, E. F. (1962). *Flora of the British Isles.* 2nd edn. University Press, Cambridge.

DAVIES, M. S. and SNAYDON, R. W. (1970). Adaptation of a plant species to a mosaic of contrasting environments. *Br. Ecol. Soc., Bull.* **1**, 26.

DE SILVA, B. L. T. (1934). The distribution of 'calcicole' and 'calcifuge' species in relation to the content of the soil in calcium carbonate and exchangeable calcium, and to soil reaction. *J. Ecol.* **22**, 532–53.

EDWARDS, K. C. (1962). *The Peak District.* Collins, London.

GEIGER, R. (1966). *The climate near the ground.* 4th edn. Harvard University Press, Cambridge, Mass.

GRIME, J. P. (1963a). Factors determining the occurrence of calcifuge species on shallow soils over calcareous substrata. *J. Ecol.* **51**, 375–90.

GRIME, J. P. (1963b). An ecological investigation at a junction between two plant communities in Coombsdale on the Derbyshire Limestone. *J. Ecol.* **51**, 391–402.

GRIME, J. P. and HODGSON, J. (1969). An investigation of the ecological significance of lime-chlorosis by means of large-scale comparative experiments. In *Ecological aspects of the mineral nutrition of plants* (ed. I. H. Rorison), pp. 67–99. Blackwell, Oxford.

GRIME, J. P. and JEFFREY, D. W. (1965). Seedling establishment in vertical gradients of sunlight. *J. Ecol.* **53**, 621–42.

HUNDT, R. (1966). *Ökologisch-geobotanische Untersuchungen an Pflanzen der mitteleuropäischen Wiesenvegetation.* Fischer, Jena.

HUTCHINSON, T. C. (1967). Ecotype differentiation in *Teucrium scorodonia* with respect to susceptibility to lime-induced chlorosis and to shade factors. *New Phytol.* **66**, 439–53.

LINTON, D. L. (ed.) (1956). *Sheffield and its region.* British Association for the Advancement of Science, Sheffield.

LLOYD, P. S. (1968). The ecological significance of fire in limestone grassland communities of the Derbyshire Dales. *J. Ecol.* **56**, 811–26.

LLOYD, P. S. (1972). The grassland vegetation of the Sheffield region. II. Classification of grassland types. *J. Ecol.* **60**, 739–76.

LLOYD, P. S., GRIME, J. P. and RORISON, I. H. (1971). The grassland vegetation of the Sheffield region. I. General features. *J. Ecol.* **59**, 863–86.

MOSS, C. E. (1913). *Vegetation of the Peak District.* University Press, Cambridge.

NEVES, R. and DOWNIE, C. (ed.) (1967). *Geological excursions in the Sheffield region.* Northend, Sheffield.

PERRING, F. H. (1958). A theoretical approach to a study of chalk grassland. *J. Ecol.* **46**, 665–79.

REFERENCES

PERRING, F. H. (1959). Topographical gradients of chalk grassland. *J. Ecol.* **47**, 447–81.

PERRING, F. H. (1960). Climatic gradients of chalk grassland. *J. Ecol.* **48**, 415–42.

PERRING, F. H. (1968). *Critical supplement to the Atlas of the British Flora.* Nelson, London.

PERRING, F. H. and WALTERS, S. M. (1962). *Atlas of the British Flora.* Nelson, London.

PIGOTT, C. D. (1958). Biological Flora of the British Isles: *Polemonium caeruleum. J. Ecol.* **46**, 507–25.

PIGOTT, C. D. (1962). Soil formation and development on the Carboniferous Limestone of Derbyshire. I. Parent materials. *J. Ecol.* **50**, 145–56.

PIGOTT, C. D. (1968). Biological Flora of the British Isles: *Cirsium acaulon. J. Ecol.* **56**, 597–612.

PIGOTT, C. D. (1970). Soil formation and development on the Carboniferous Limestone of Derbyshire. II. The relation of soil development to vegetation on the plateau near Coombs Dale. *J. Ecol.* **58**, 529–41.

RATCLIFFE, D. (1961). Adaptation to habitat in a group of annual plants. *J. Ecol.* **49**, 187–203.

RATCLIFFE, D. A. (1964). in BURNETT (1964).

SNAYDON, R. W. (1962). The growth and competitive ability of contrasting natural populations of *Trifolium repens* L. on calcareous and acid soils. *J. Ecol.* **50**, 439–47.

VALENTINE, D. H. (1941). Variation in *Viola riviniana* Rchb. *New Phytol.* **40**, 189–209.

WATT, A. S. (1950). Contributions to the ecology of Bracken (*Pteridium aquilinum*). V. Bracken and frost. *New Phytol.* **49**, 308–27.

WILLIS, A. J. and YEMM, E. W. (1961). Braunton Burrows: Mineral nutrient status of the dune soils. *J. Ecol.* **49**, 377–90.

YEO, P. F. (1964). The growth of *Euphrasia* in cultivation. *Watsonia* **6**, 1–24.

References to the
Biological Flora of the British Isles

ADAMS, A. W.	(1955)	*Succisa pratensis*	*J. Ecol.* **43**, 709–18
BEDDOWS, A. R.	(1959)	*Dactylis glomerata*	*J. Ecol.* **47**, 223–39
BEDDOWS, A. R.	(1961)	*Holcus lanatus*	*J. Ecol.* **49**, 421–30
CHADWICK, M. J.	(1960)	*Nardus stricta*	*J. Ecol.* **48**, 255–67
GIMINGHAM, C. H.	(1960)	*Calluna vulgaris*	*J. Ecol.* **48**, 455–83
HARPER, J. L.	(1957)	*Ranunculus acris* and *R. bulbosus*	*J. Ecol.* **45**, 289–342
HARPER, J. L. and WOOD, W. A.	(1957)	*Senecio jacobaea*	*J. Ecol.* **45**, 617–37
HOWARTH, S. E. and WILLIAMS, J. T.	(1968)	*Chrysanthemum leucanthemum*	*J. Ecol.* **56**, 585–95
HUTCHINSON, T. C.	(1968)	*Teucrium scorodonia*	*J. Ecol.* **56**, 901–11
LODGE, R. W.	(1959)	*Cynosurus cristatus*	*J. Ecol.* **47**, 511–18
OVINGTON, J. D. and SCURFIELD, G.	(1956)	*Holcus mollis*	*J. Ecol.* **44**, 272–80
PFITZENMEYER, C. D. C.	(1962)	*Arrhenatherum elatius*	*J. Ecol.* **50**, 235–45
PIGOTT, C. D.	(1955)	*Thymus drucei*	*J. Ecol.* **43**, 369–79
PROCTOR, M. C. F.	(1956)	*Helianthemum chamaecistus*	*J. Ecol.* **44**, 683–8
RITCHIE, J. C.	(1956)	*Vaccinium myrtillus*	*J. Ecol.* **44**, 291–9
SAGAR, G. R. and HARPER, J. L.	(1964)	*Plantago lanceolata*	*J. Ecol.* **52**, 211–21
SCURFIELD, G.	(1954)	*Deschampsia flexuosa*	*J. Ecol.* **42**, 225–33
TAYLOR, F. J.	(1956)	*Carex flacca*	*J. Ecol.* **44**, 281–90

Key to polargraph symbols

Frequency class (%)		pH class (for overlays)	
○	1–10	▫	<3.6
○	11–20	▫	3.6–4.0
○	21–30	◻	4.1–4.5
○	31–40	◻	4.6–5.0
○	41–50	◻	5.1–5.5
○	51–60	◻	5.6–6.0
○	61–70	◻	6.1–6.5
○	71–80	◻	6.6–7.0
○	81–90	◻	7.1–7.5
○	91–100	◻	>7.5

In the diagrams of paired species the frequency values of the second species are indicated by squares equivalent in size to the circles used elsewhere.

Achillea millefolium Yarrow

Rhizomatous perennial herb, 8–45(–60) cm.

Occurrence 8%

Pastures and waste places

Substratum   On all formations but very scarce on the three acidic strata. Characteristically found on soils in the pH range 4.0–6.5.

Slope and aspect   Absent from the steepest slopes; attaining local abundance on slopes of less than 25°.

Grazing and burning   The proportion of sites occupied by the species is consistently greater in grazed sites than in burned sites.

Frequency distribution   Class 1. The few high frequency values are from closely grazed sites.

B.S.B.I. Atlas   Ubiquitous.

			Geological formation			
	TS	CL	MG	CM	ML	BS
pH (0–3 cm)						
3.0–4.0	—	—	—	—	—	1
4.1–5.0	5	6	1	1	1	2
5.1–6.0	8	6	—	—	3	—
6.1–7.0	5	1	—	—	2	—
7.1–8.0	1	2	—	—	8	—
pH (9–12 cm)						
2.8–4.0	—	—	—	—	—	1
4.1–5.0	11	2	—	1	1	2
5.1–6.0	7	6	1	—	1	—
6.1–7.0	1	2	—	—	4	—
7.1–8.1	—	5	—	—	8	—
Constancy (%)	**50**	8	*1*	*1*	**17**	8
Ungrazed, unburned	—	6	0	0	—	8
Grazed, unburned	67	12	1	3	30	—
Ungrazed, burned	31	5	—	0	15	—
Grazed, burned	—	0	—	—	—	—

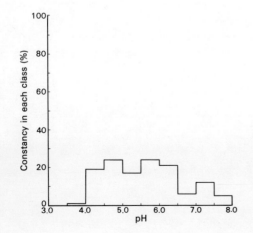

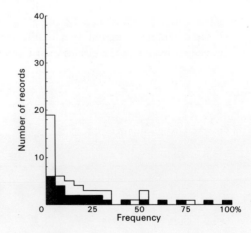

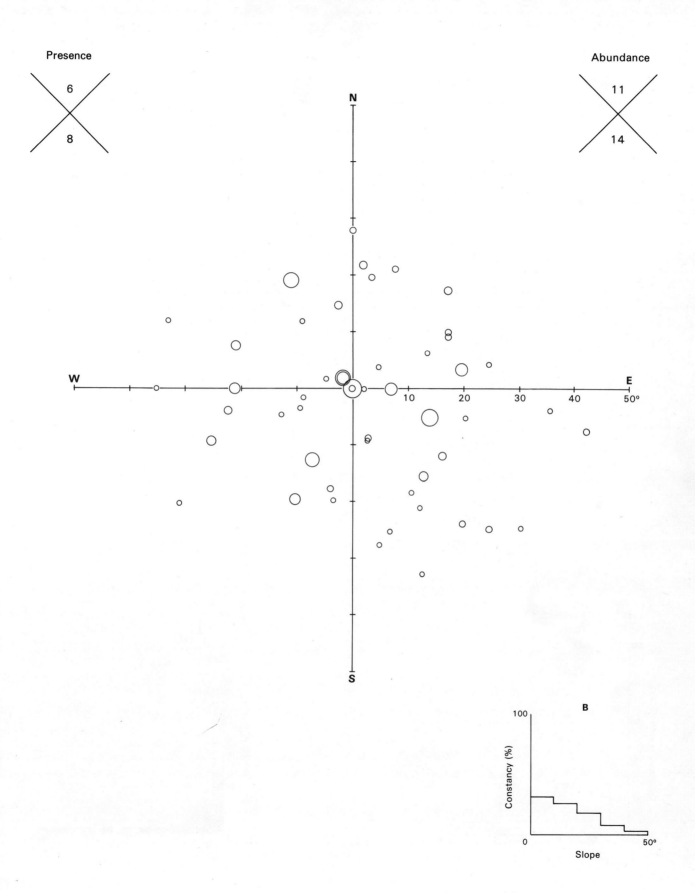

Presence

6

8

Abundance

11

14

N

W   E

10   20   30   40   50°

S

100   B

Constancy (%)

0   50°

Slope

Agrostis canina Brown Bent-grass

Occurrence 13%

Rhizomatous perennial grass, 10–60(–80) cm.

Grassland, heathland and bog

The records are almost certainly all for ssp. *montana* and not for ssp. *canina*.

Substratum Locally abundant on Toadstone and Bunter Sandstone with scattered occurrences on the remaining strata. Histogram shows a shallow but roughly normal distribution extending over the full range in soil pH.

Slope and aspect *A. canina* occurs over the range in slope 0–40° but on slopes greater than 10° the species scarcely appears in the south-facing (150–210°) sector.

Grazing and burning No consistent relationships apparent.

Frequency distribution Class 2.

B.S.B.I. Atlas Widespread but with a northern and western emphasis.

	Geological formation					
	TS	CL	MG	CM	ML	BS
pH (0–3 cm)						
3.0–4.0	1	4	22	2	—	9
4.1–5.0	6	10	1	—	—	2
5.1–6.0	—	8	—	—	—	—
6.1–7.0	3	5	—	—	—	—
7.1–8.0	2	5	—	—	2	—
pH (9–12 cm)						
2.8–4.0	—	3	22	2	—	9
4.1–5.0	9	5	1	—	1	2
5.1–6.0	3	7	—	—	—	—
6.1–7.0	—	7	—	—	—	—
7.1–8.1	—	10	—	—	1	—
Constancy (%)	**32**	**18**	14	2	2	**31**
Ungrazed, unburned	—	26	4	2	—	31
Grazed, unburned	13	22	16	0	10	—
Ungrazed, burned	31	3	—	5	1	—
Grazed, burned	—	10	—	—	—	—

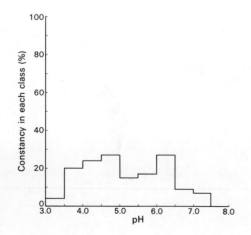

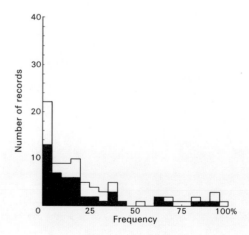

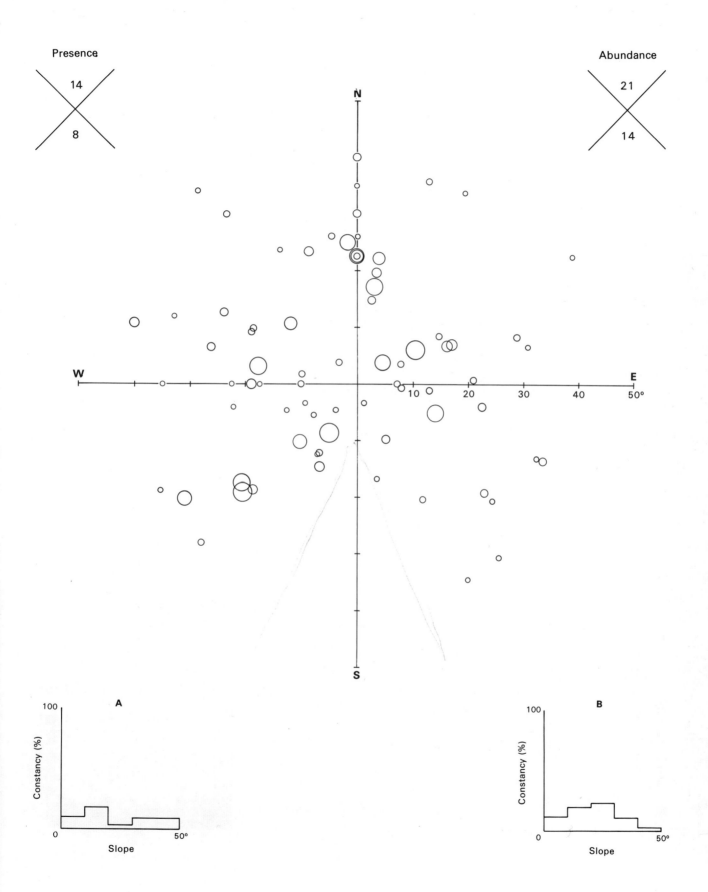

Agrostis tenuis Common Bent-grass

Rhizomatous perennial grass, (2–)20–50(–100) cm.

Occurrence 41%

Grassland, heathland and waste places

Substratum Frequent on all strata except the Magnesian Limestone. The species occurs most frequently on soils which are moderately acidic at the surface and is scarce on soils of very high pH. This is consistent with the low constancy on Magnesian Limestone.

Slope and aspect Common on flat ground and on gentle slopes. Previously distinguished as a species characteristic of the leached soils of plateau edges on the Carboniferous Limestone (Moss 1913, Balme 1953). There is a tendency for the species to have lower frequency values on south-facing slopes.

Grazing and burning The most consistently abundant grass occurring at grazed sites on the Toadstone.

Frequency distribution Class 3, but often a subsidiary component.

B.S.B.I. Atlas Ubiquitous.

	Geological formation					
	TS	CL	MG	CM	ML	BS
pH (0–3 cm)						
3.0–4.0	—	8	40	45	—	8
4.1–5.0	7	26	8	18	2	4
5.1–6.0	18	30	2	3	4	—
6.1–7.0	6	12	—	—	6	—
7.1–8.0	2	6	—	—	3	—
pH (9–12 cm)						
2.8–4.0	—	7	38	36	—	7
4.1–5.0	14	15	7	21	1	5
5.1–6.0	15	24	5	8	1	—
6.1–7.0	4	21	—	—	6	—
7.1–8.1	—	15	—	1	7	—
Constancy (%)	**87**	46	*30*	**53**	*18*	33
Ungrazed, unburned	—	29	3	56	—	33
Grazed, unburned	100	54	36	43	0	—
Ungrazed, burned	69	41	—	67	22	—
Grazed, burned	—	33	—	—	—	—

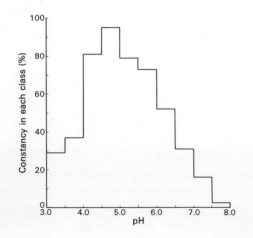

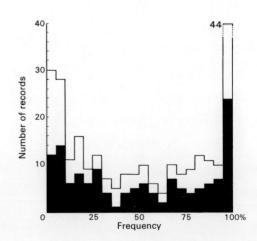

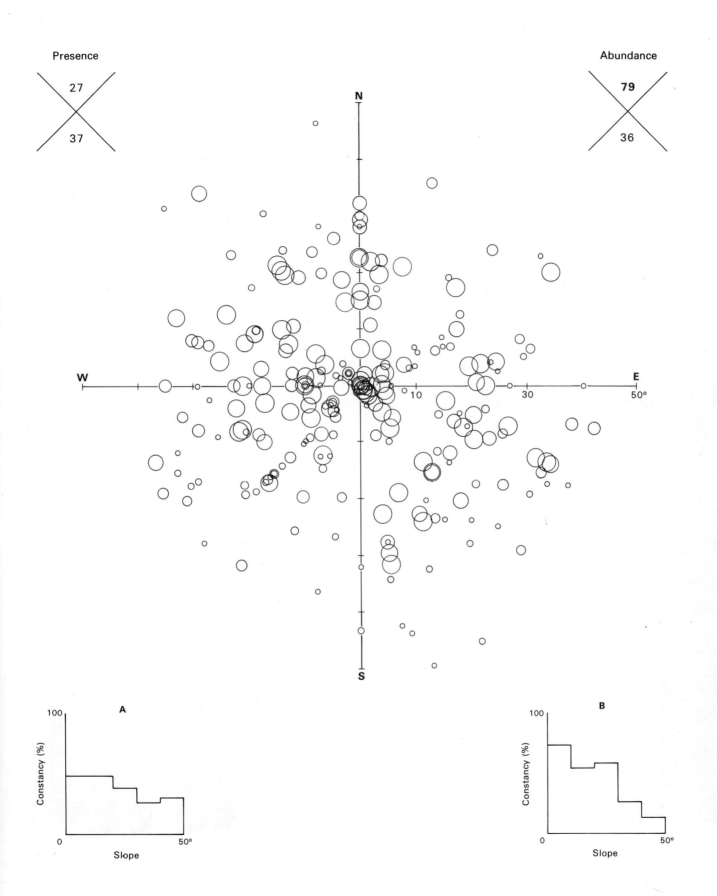

Presence

27
37

Abundance

79
36

A

B

Anemone nemorosa Wood Anemone

Rhizomatous perennial herb, 6–30 cm.

Occurrence 4%

Woodland and scrub

Substratum　Recorded only on the Toadstone and Carboniferous Limestone. Most frequent on soils of intermediate pH.

Slope and aspect　*A. nemorosa* is a woodland plant of common occurrence in the region. Where the species occurs in grassland, the sites are almost all of northern aspect; at some of these sites *A. nemorosa* may be a relic of former woodland.

Grazing and burning　Virtually absent from burned sites.

Frequency distribution　Class 1.

B.S.B.I. Atlas　Ubiquitous.

		Geological formation				
	TS	CL	MG	CM	ML	BS
pH (0–3 cm)						
3.0–4.0	—	2	—	—	—	—
4.1–5.0	1	5	—	—	—	—
5.1–6.0	2	6	—	—	—	—
6.1–7.0	1	4	—	—	—	—
7.1–8.0	—	5	—	—	—	—
pH (9–12 cm)						
2.8–4.0	—	—	—	—	—	—
4.1–5.0	2	4	—	—	—	—
5.1–6.0	2	4	—	—	—	—
6.1–7.0	—	3	—	—	—	—
7.1–8.1	—	11	—	—	—	—
Constancy (%)	11	12	0	0	0	0
Ungrazed, unburned	—	13	0	0	—	0
Grazed, unburned	20	18	0	0	0	—
Ungrazed, burned	0	0	—	0	0	—
Grazed, burned	—	5	—	—	—	—

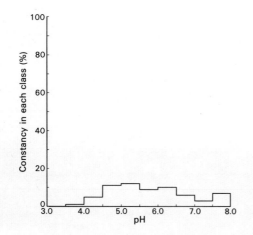

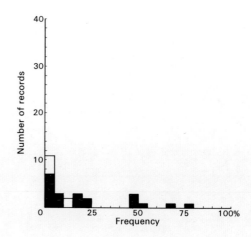

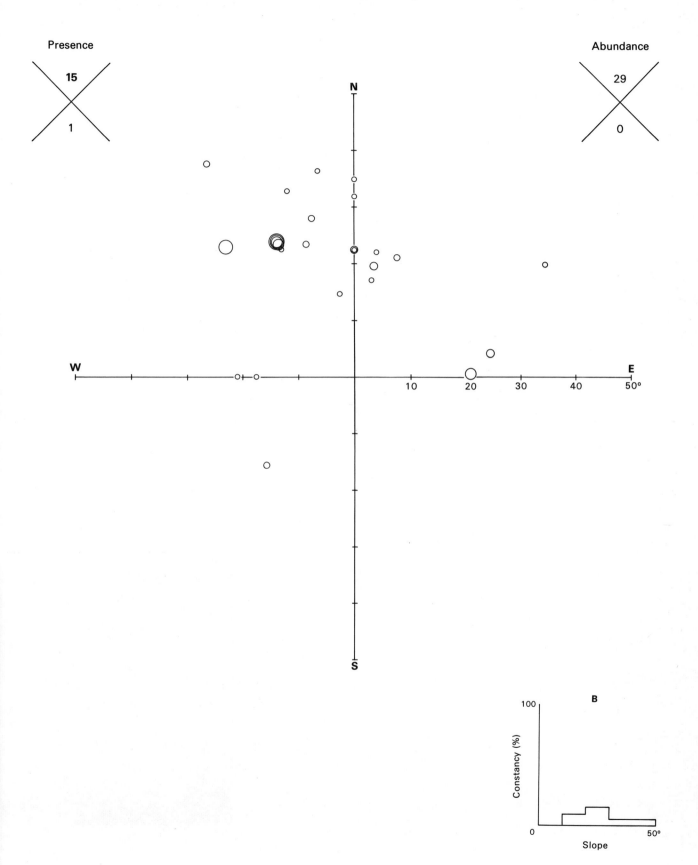

Anthoxanthum odoratum   Sweet Vernal-grass   *Occurrence* 27%

Tufted perennial grass, 20–50 cm.   Grassland, heathland and open woods

Substratum   Of frequent occurrence on the Carboniferous Limestone and Toadstone on soils of inter-mediate base-status. Normally distributed over the pH range 3.0–8.0 with a slight displacement in favour of soils of high pH. Edaphic ecotypes are known to exist (Davies and Snaydon 1970).

Slope and aspect   Occurrences more numerous on north-facing slopes. Common over the range in slope 0–40°.

Grazing and burning   No evidence of a marked response to either factor.

Frequency distribution   Class 2.

B.S.B.I. Atlas   Ubiquitous.

	TS	CL	Geological formation MG	CM	ML	BS
pH (0–3 cm)						
3.0–4.0	—	2	20	4	—	—
4.1–5.0	4	25	4	6	—	—
5.1–6.0	11	35	—	—	3	—
6.1–7.0	6	27	—	—	2	—
7.1–8.0	1	17	—	—	1	—
pH (9–12 cm)						
2.8–4.0	—	1	20	1	—	—
4.1–5.0	11	14	2	5	—	—
5.1–6.0	9	25	2	4	1	—
6.1–7.0	2	28	—	—	5	—
7.1–8.1	—	37	—	—	—	—
Constancy (%)	**58**	**58**	*15*	*8*	7	*0*
Ungrazed, unburned	—	36	7	13	—	0
Grazed, unburned	60	61	16	5	10	—
Ungrazed, burned	56	62	—	0	8	—
Grazed, burned	—	68	—	—	—	—

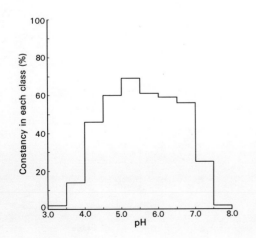

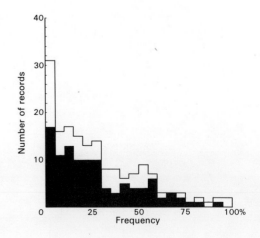

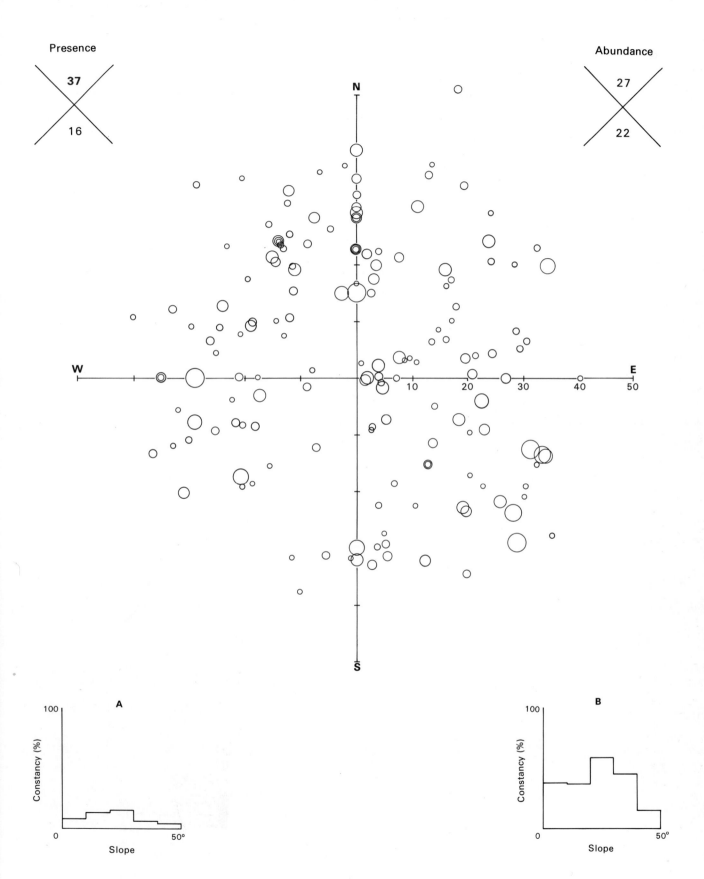

Presence
37
16

Abundance
27
22

N

W   10   20   30   40   50   E

S̄

A
100
Constancy (%)
0   50°
Slope

B
100
Constancy (%)
0   50°
Slope

Arabis hirsuta Hairy Rock Cress
Biennial herb, 10–60 cm, forming a compact rosette.

Occurrence 4%

Rock outcrops and walls

Substratum Confined to limestone and strongly calcicolous.

Slope and aspect The majority of records are on south-facing slopes. It seems likely that the pattern is related to the survival of the species in the more 'open' turf to be found on south-facing dalesides.

Grazing and burning No marked correlations although the species is restricted to burned sites on the Magnesian Limestone. *A. hirsuta* has been found to increase in abundance following burning of grassland on shallow calcareous soils (Lloyd 1968).

Frequency distribution Class 1.

B.S.B.I. Atlas Scattered but widespread occurrence on calcareous formations throughout the British Isles.

	TS	CL	MG	CM	ML	BS
			Geological formation			
pH (0–3 cm)						
3.0–4.0	—	—	—	—	—	—
4.1–5.0	—	—	—	—	—	—
5.1–6.0	—	1	—	—	—	—
6.1–7.0	—	6	—	—	2	—
7.1–8.0	—	14	—	—	2	—
pH (9–12 cm)						
2.8–4.0	—	—	—	—	—	—
4.1–5.0	—	—	—	—	—	—
5.1–6.0	—	—	—	—	—	—
6.1–7.0	—	6	—	—	1	—
7.1–8.1	—	13	—	—	2	—
Constancy (%)	0	**12**	*0*	*0*	5	0
Ungrazed, unburned	—	16	0	0	—	0
Grazed, unburned	0	9	0	0	0	—
Ungrazed, burned	0	16	—	0	6	—
Grazed, burned	—	10	—	—	—	—

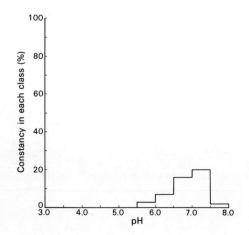

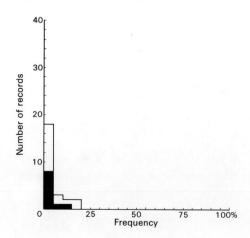

28

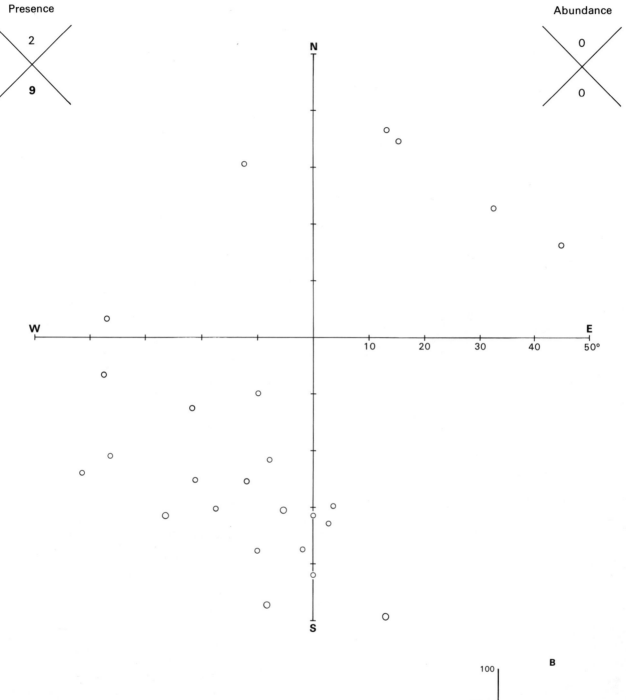

Presence

2
9

Abundance

0
0

N

W   E
                    10   20   30   40   50°

S

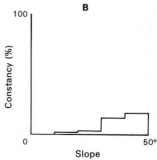

B

100

Constancy (%)

0   50°

Slope

Arenaria serpyllifolia Thyme-leaved Sandwort

Winter-annual herb, 2.5–25 cm.

Occurrence 3%

Rock outcrops, walls and open, sandy places

Substratum   Confined to limestone. Calcicolous.
Slope and aspect   Occurs on south-facing slopes, some of which are steeply sloping.
Grazing and burning   Insufficient records.
Frequency distribution   Class 1.
B.S.B.I. Atlas   Widespread but most common in SE England.

	TS	CL	MG	CM	ML	BS
			Geological formation			
pH (0–3 cm)						
3.0–4.0	—	—	—	—	—	—
4.1–5.0	—	—	—	—	—	—
5.1–6.0	—	1	—	—	—	—
6.1–7.0	—	2	—	—	2	—
7.1–8.0	—	11	—	—	4	—
pH (9–12 cm)						
2.8–4.0	—	—	—	—	—	—
4.1–5.0	—	—	—	—	—	—
5.1–6.0	—	—	—	—	—	—
6.1–7.0	—	2	—	—	1	—
7.1–8.1	—	11	—	—	5	—
Constancy (%)	0	**8**	*0*	*0*	**7**	0
Ungrazed, unburned	—	3	0	0	—	0
Grazed, unburned	0	11	0	0	0	—
Ungrazed, burned	0	11	—	0	9	—
Grazed, burned	—	0	—	—	—	—

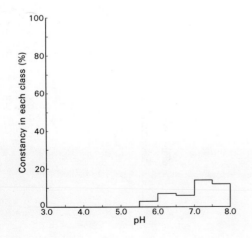

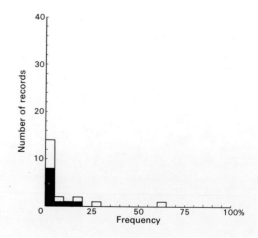

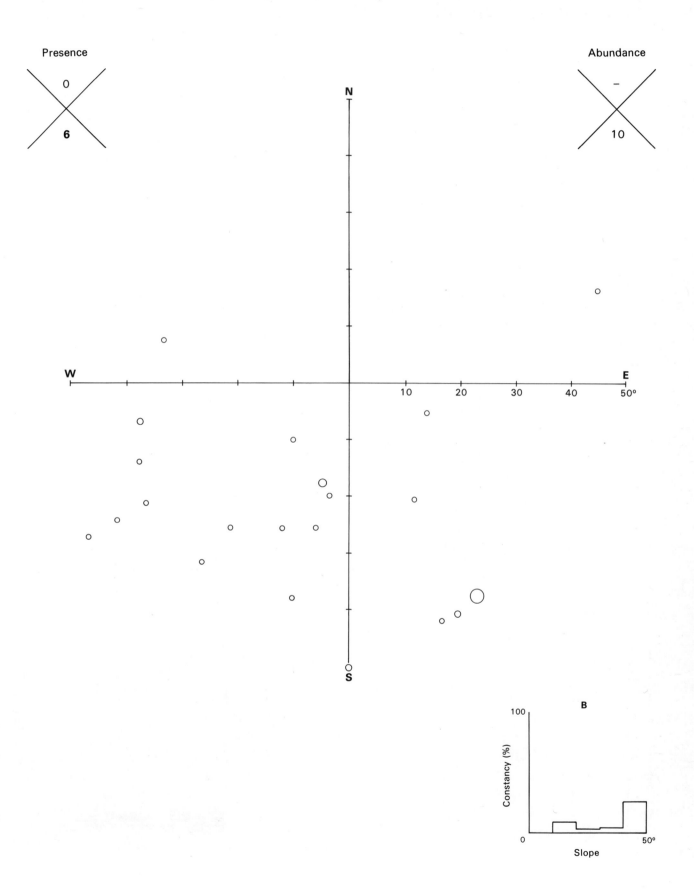

Presence

0

6

Abundance

−

10

N

W

E

10   20   30   40   50°

S

B

100

Constancy (%)

0   50°

Slope

Arrhenatherum elatius Oat-grass

Rhizomatous perennial grass, 60–120 cm.

Occurrence 22%

Meadows, roadsides and waste places

Substratum Absent or extremely scarce on acidic strata, frequent on the Magnesian Limestone and Toadstone, abundant on the Carboniferous Limestone. A distinct calcicole.

Slope and aspect Frequent on steep slopes of all aspects. In the Derbyshire dales a pioneer, with *Geranium robertianum*, of open limestone scree. High frequency values are rather more common on south-facing slopes.

Grazing and burning Particularly common in tall vegetation in ungrazed sites, whether burned or unburned. A high proportion of the 'grazed' sites at which the species was recorded were from semi-derelict sheep pasture on the Carboniferous Limestone.

Frequency distribution Class 2.

B.S.B.I. Atlas Ubiquitous.

Biological Flora Pfitzenmeyer (1962).

	TS	CL	MG	CM	ML	BS
			Geological formation			
pH (0–3 cm)						
3.0–4.0	—	—	—	4	—	—
4.1–5.0	2	4	—	3	1	—
5.1–6.0	8	13	—	1	3	—
6.1–7.0	4	23	—	—	4	—
7.1–8.0	—	51	—	—	10	—
pH (9–12 cm)						
2.8–4.0	—	—	—	—	—	—
4.1–5.0	1	2	—	4	—	—
5.1–6.0	9	7	—	4	1	—
6.1–7.0	3	15	—	—	5	—
7.1–8.1	1	66	—	—	12	—
Constancy (%)	**37**	**51**	*0*	*7*	21	*0*
Ungrazed, unburned	—	77	0	12	—	0
Grazed, unburned	0	34	0	0	30	—
Ungrazed, burned	75	57	—	5	18	—
Grazed, burned	—	90	—	—	—	—

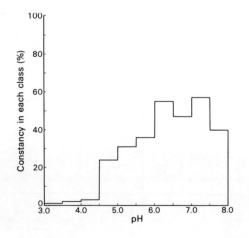

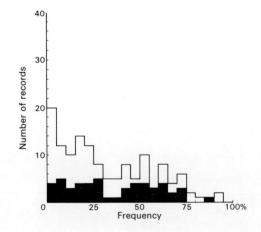

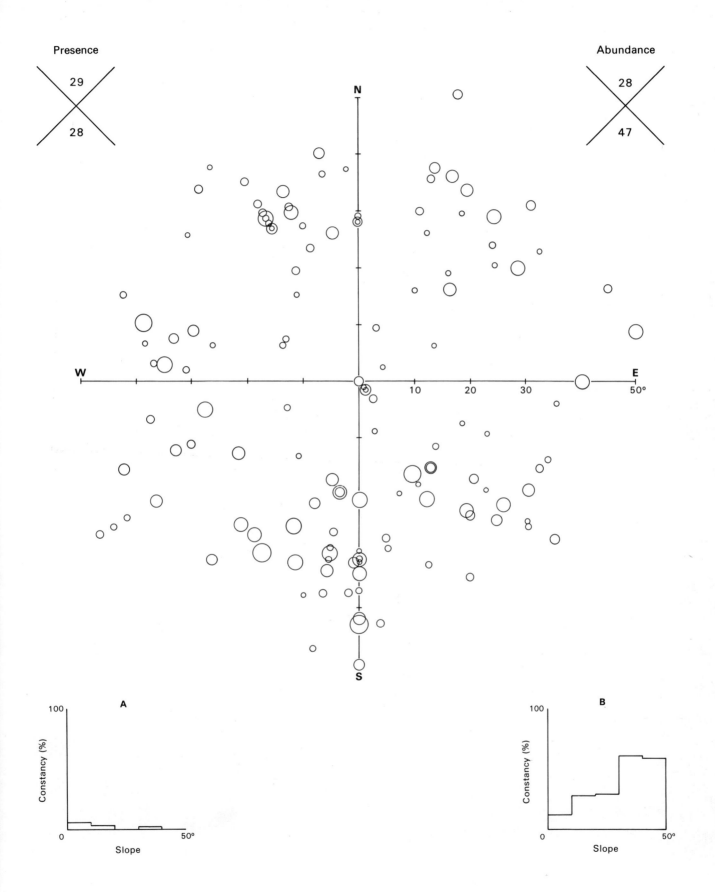

Presence

29

28

Abundance

28

47

N

W   10   20   30   50°   E

S

A

100

Constancy (%)

0   50°

Slope

B

100

Constancy (%)

0   50°

Slope

Bellis perennis Daisy

Perennial herb, 2–4(–8) cm, with compact rosettes.

Occurrence 4%

Closely grazed or mown grassland, grassy paths

Substratum   Restricted to limestone and the Toadstone. Calcicolous.

Slope and aspect   No consistent relationship with slope or aspect.

Grazing and burning   Confined to grazed sites on Toadstone and Carboniferous Limestone. Occurs very frequently in grazed Magnesian Limestone grassland.

Frequency distribution   Class 1–2.

B.S.B.I. Atlas   Ubiquitous.

	TS	CL	MG	CM	ML	BS
			Geological formation			
pH (0–3 cm)						
3.0–4.0	—	—	—	—	—	—
4.1–5.0	—	—	—	—	—	—
5.1–6.0	1	3	—	—	—	—
6.1–7.0	1	1	—	—	1	—
7.1–8.0	—	9	—	—	8	—
pH (9–12 cm)						
2.8–4.0	—	—	—	—	—	—
4.1–5.0	1	—	—	—	—	—
5.1–6.0	—	1	—	—	—	—
6.1–7.0	1	3	—	—	1	—
7.1–8.1	—	7	—	—	8	—
Constancy (%)	5	7	0	0	11	0
Ungrazed, unburned	—	0	0	0	—	0
Grazed, unburned	13	13	0	0	70	—
Ungrazed, burned	0	0	—	0	3	—
Grazed, burned	—	5	—	—	—	—

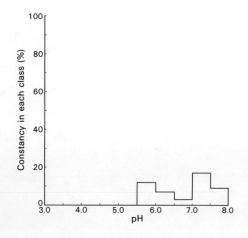

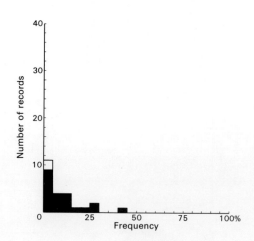

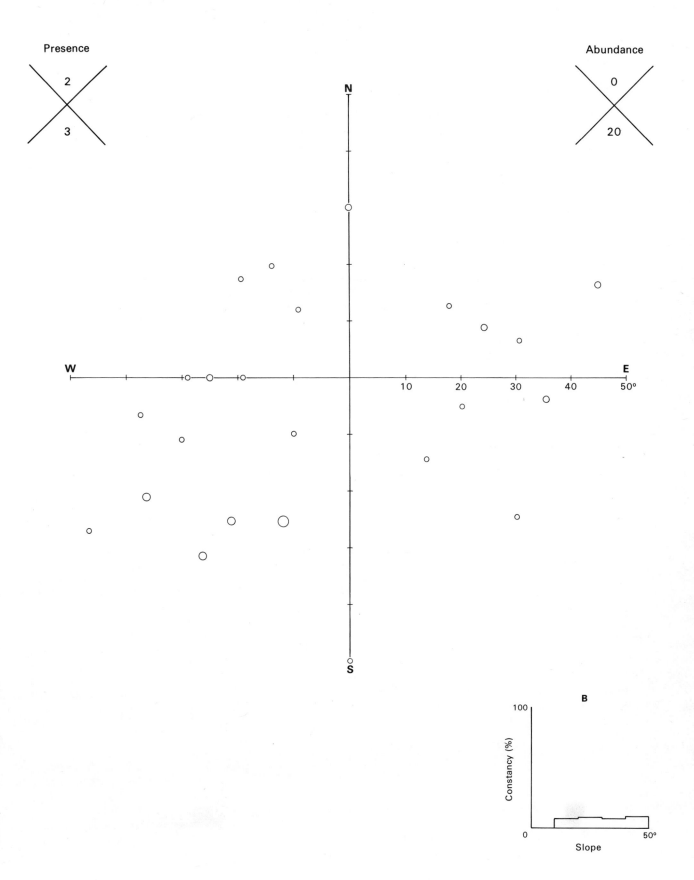

Presence

2
3

Abundance

0
20

N

W   E
          10   20   30   40   50°

S

B

100

Constancy (%)

0   50°
          Slope

Betonica officinalis Betony

Rhizomatous perennial herb, 15–60 cm.

Occurrence 4%

Grassland and the margins of woodland

Substratum Of frequent occurrence on the Toadstone. Restricted to brown earths and calcareous soils with a high content of clay minerals (mull-rendzinas). Most commonly found in association with *Agrostis tenuis* and *Lathyrus montanus* on soil profiles which are mildly acidic, at least in part of the rooting depth. It is only on the Magnesian Limestone that the species was recorded on unleached calcareous soil.

Slope and aspect Insufficient data.

Grazing and burning On the Toadstone the species is restricted to grazed sites.

Frequency distribution Class 2.

B.S.B.I. Atlas Widespread in England and Wales except for East Anglia. Virtually absent from Scotland and Ireland.

| | Geological formation | | | | | |
	TS	CL	MG	CM	ML	BS
pH (0–3 cm)						
3.0–4.0	—	—	—	—	—	—
4.1–5.0	1	2	—	—	—	—
5.1–6.0	4	3	—	—	3	—
6.1–7.0	4	—	—	—	2	—
7.1–8.0	1	—	—	—	3	—
pH (9–12 cm)						
2.8–4.0	—	—	—	—	—	—
4.1–5.0	8	1	—	—	—	—
5.1–6.0	2	3	—	—	1	—
6.1–7.0	—	1	—	—	4	—
7.1–8.1	—	—	—	—	3	—
Constancy (%)	26	*3*	*0*	*0*	9	0
Ungrazed, unburned	—	0	0	0	—	0
Grazed, unburned	53	5	0	0	0	—
Ungrazed, burned	0	0	—	0	12	—
Grazed, burned	—	0	—	—	—	—

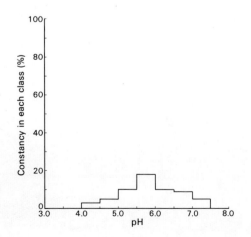

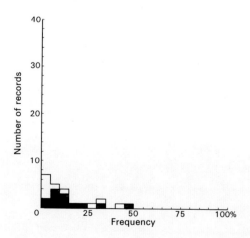

Presence

3

3

Abundance

0

0

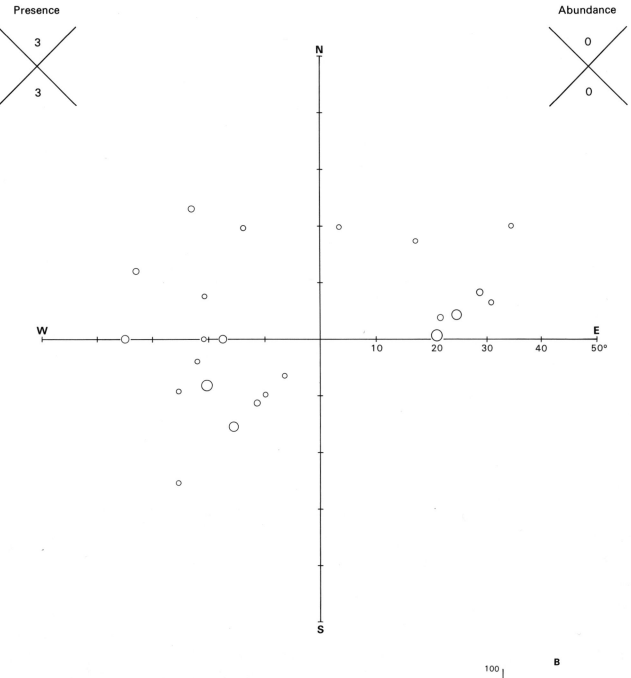

N

W · · · · · · · · · E
10 20 30 40 50°

S

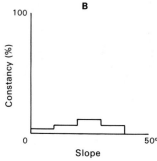

B

100

Constancy (%)

0 50°

Slope

Brachypodium pinnatum Heath False-brome

Strongly rhizomatous perennial grass, 30–60 cm.

Occurrence 11%

Grassland and waste places

Substratum   Present at 79% of the Magnesian Limestone sites but nowhere else. *B. pinnatum* is known to occur very rarely on the Carboniferous Limestone of Derbyshire but was not recorded in the present study. The pH distribution largely reflects the range found in the Magnesian Limestone sites, but in contrast to *Zerna erecta* the species occurs with high frequency at the majority of the leached Magnesian Limestone sites.

Slope and aspect   Of more constant occurrence on south-facing slopes.

Grazing and burning   Most of the Magnesian Limestone sites are burned periodically. Because of its strongly rhizomatous habit, the species is relatively insensitive to fire (cf. *Zerna erecta*).

Frequency distribution   Class 3.

B.S.B.I. Atlas   SE England, but mainly on the older Limestones.

| | Geological formation | | | | | |
	TS	CL	MG	CM	ML	BS
pH (0–3 cm)						
3.0–4.0	—	—	—	—	—	—
4.1–5.0	—	—	—	—	3	—
5.1–6.0	—	—	—	—	12	—
6.1–7.0	—	—	—	—	10	—
7.1–8.0	—	—	—	—	42	—
pH (9–12 cm)						
2.8–4.0	—	—	—	—	—	—
4.1–5.0	—	—	—	—	2	—
5.1–6.0	—	—	—	—	2	—
6.1–7.0	—	—	—	—	14	—
7.1–8.1	—	—	—	—	49	—
Constancy (%)	*0*	*0*	*0*	*0*	**79**	*0*
Ungrazed, unburned	—	0	0	0	—	0
Grazed, unburned	0	0	0	0	80	—
Ungrazed, burned	0	0	—	0	85	—
Grazed, burned	—	0	—	—	—	—

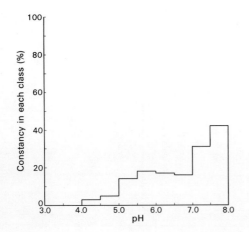

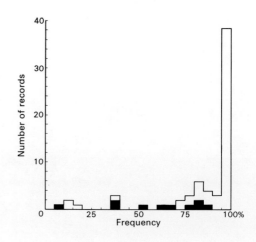

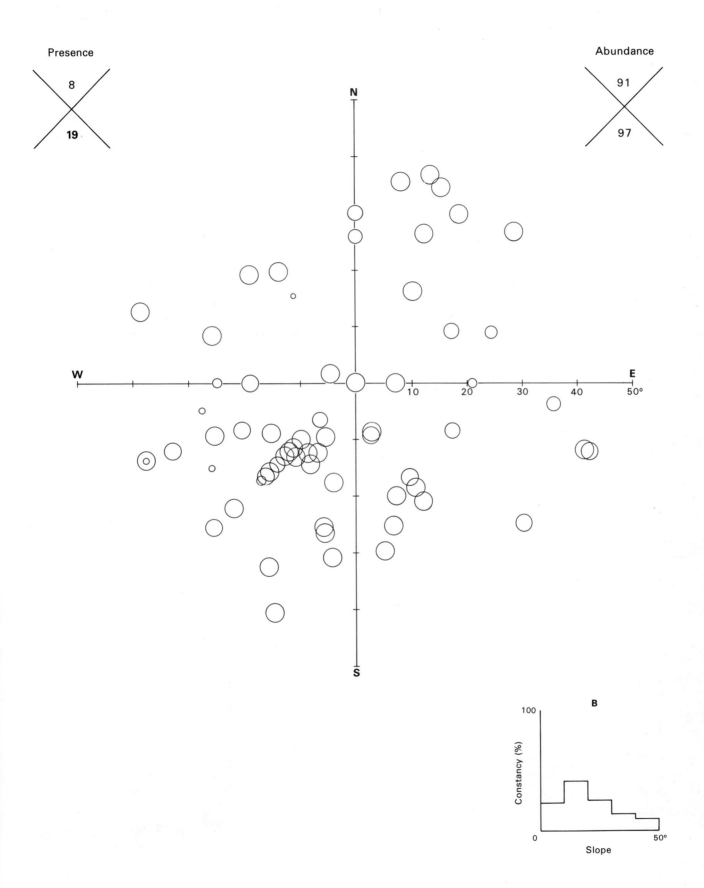

Brachypodium sylvaticum Slender False-brome

Tufted perennial grass, 30–90 cm.

Occurrence 4%

Woodland and scrub

Substratum   Restricted to tall herbaceous communities on the Toadstone and to areas of steep slope on the Carboniferous Limestone. Absent from acidic soils. The high frequency of occurrence in the pH range 7.5–8.0 is related to the contribution of screes to this category.

   Slope and aspect   Insufficient data with which to examine the aspect preference of the species. The species is a common woodland plant in the region and it is of interest to note that a majority of the records are in partly shaded situations either of scree with scrub or beneath tall herbaceous communities.

   Grazing and burning   On the Toadstone, the species is confined to burned sites.

   Frequency distribution   Class 2.

   B.S.B.I. Atlas   Widespread throughout the British Isles, ubiquitous in Southern and Central England.

		Geological formation				
	TS	CL	MG	CM	ML	BS
pH (0–3 cm)						
3.0–4.0	—	—	—	—	—	—
4.1–5.0	—	—	—	—	—	—
5.1–6.0	7	3	—	—	—	—
6.1–7.0	3	3	—	—	—	—
7.1–8.0	—	10	—	—	—	—
pH (9–12 cm)						
2.8–4.0	—	—	—	—	—	—
4.1–5.0	—	—	—	—	—	—
5.1–6.0	7	2	—			
6.1–7.0	3	2	—	—	—	—
7.1–8.1	—	13	—	—	—	—
Constancy (%)	26	**9**	*0*	*0*	*0*	0
Ungrazed, unburned	—	23	0	0	—	0
Grazed, unburned	0	5	0	0	0	—
Ungrazed, burned	63	5	—	0	0	—
Grazed, burned	—	14	—	—	—	—

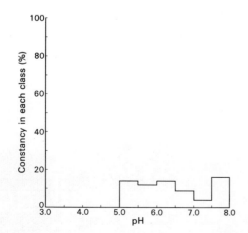

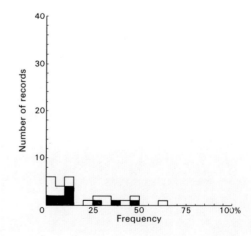

40

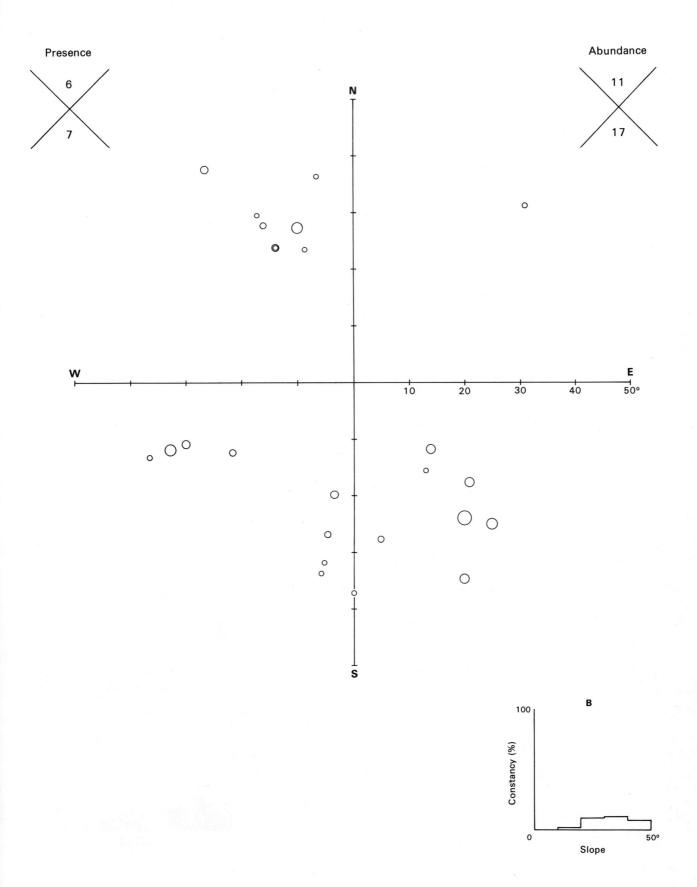

N

W · · · · · · 10 20 30 40 50° E

S

B

Constancy (%)

100

0   50°

Slope

Briza media Quaking Grass

Occurrence 14%

Tufted perennial grass, 20–50 cm.

Grassland

Substratum   A common plant of limestone grassland. The single record from the Toadstone is from a site strongly affected by dust from a nearby limestone quarry. In the survey area *B. media* was mainly restricted to well-drained calcareous soils, but elsewhere in Britain it is also to be found in eutrophic mire (e.g. Ratcliffe 1964).

Slope and aspect   Mainly on sites of moderate to steep slope. The distribution of high frequency values has a northern bias on both limestones.

Grazing and burning   Most common at grazed sites.

Frequency distribution   Class 1–2. Observations during the collection of data suggest that the highest values occur in open turf.

B.S.B.I. Atlas   Absent from N and W Scotland, common elsewhere especially over calcareous strata in S England.

	TS	CL	MG	CM	ML	BS
			Geological formation			
pH (0–3 cm)						
3.0–4.0	—	—	—	—	—	—
4.1–5.0	—	4	—	—	1	—
5.1–6.0	—	19	—	—	4	—
6.1–7.0	1	20	—	—	5	—
7.1–8.0	—	13	—	—	22	—
pH (9–12 cm)						
2.8–4.0	—	—	—	—	—	—
4.1–5.0	1	1	—	—	—	—
5.1–6.0	—	10	—	—	1	—
6.1–7.0	—	18	—	—	4	—
7.1–8.1	—	28	—	—	26	—
Constancy (%)	3	32	0	0	38	0
Ungrazed, unburned	—	26	0	0	—	0
Grazed, unburned	7	37	0	0	60	—
Ungrazed, burned	0	24	—	0	30	—
Grazed, burned	—	24	—	—	—	—

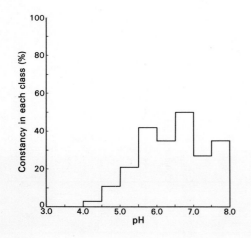

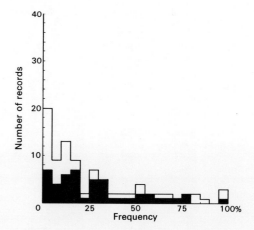

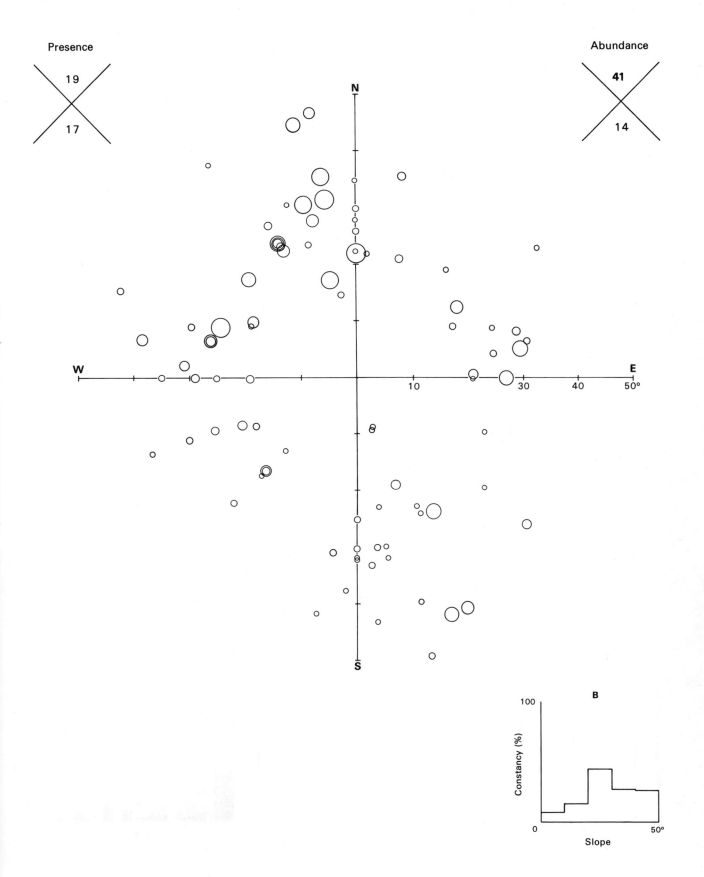

Calluna vulgaris Heather

Occurrence 10%

Evergreen shrub, up to 60(-100) cm.

Heathland and open scrub

Substratum A calcifuge of common occurrence on acidic soils irrespective of stratum. *C. vulgaris*, together with other calcifuges, e.g. *Vaccinium myrtillus*, occurs locally on shallow limestone soils. Where such sites were encountered in the survey the soil was found to be surface-leached; however, on the Carboniferous Limestone *Calluna vulgaris* is locally established on unleached rendzinas.

Slope and aspect The dominant species in heathlands of the Millstone Grit and the Coal Measures and recorded over a wide range of slope in the grasslands associated with heath. On calcareous strata grassheath is usually restricted to the acidic plateaux and in consequence *C. vulgaris* is confined to the slope range 0-20°.

Grazing and burning Tolerant of burning and grazing in heathland habitats (Gimingham 1960). No differential response evident in the grassland data.

Frequency distribution Class 2.

B.S.B.I. Atlas Scarce only in Eastern and Central England.

Biological Flora Gimingham (1960).

	TS	CL	MG	CM	ML	BS
			Geological formation			
pH (0–3 cm)						
3.0–4.0	—	8	24	24	—	2
4.1–5.0	—	1	—	1	—	1
5.1–6.0	—	1	—	—	—	—
6.1–7.0	—	—	—	—	—	—
7.1–8.0	—	—	—	—	—	—
pH (9–12 cm)						
2.8–4.0	—	9	24	24	—	3
4.1–5.0	—	—	—	1	—	—
5.1–6.0	—	—	—	—	—	—
6.1–7.0	—	1	—	—	—	—
7.1–8.1	—	—	—	—	—	—
Constancy (%)	*0*	*6*	**15**	**20**	*0*	8
Ungrazed, unburned	—	0	7	20	—	8
Grazed, unburned	0	11	16	16	0	—
Ungrazed, burned	0	0	—	14	0	—
Grazed, burned	—	0	—	—	—	—

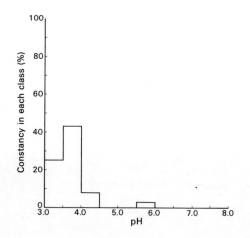

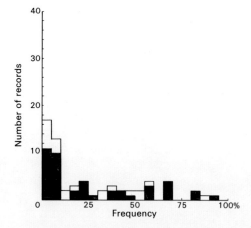

44

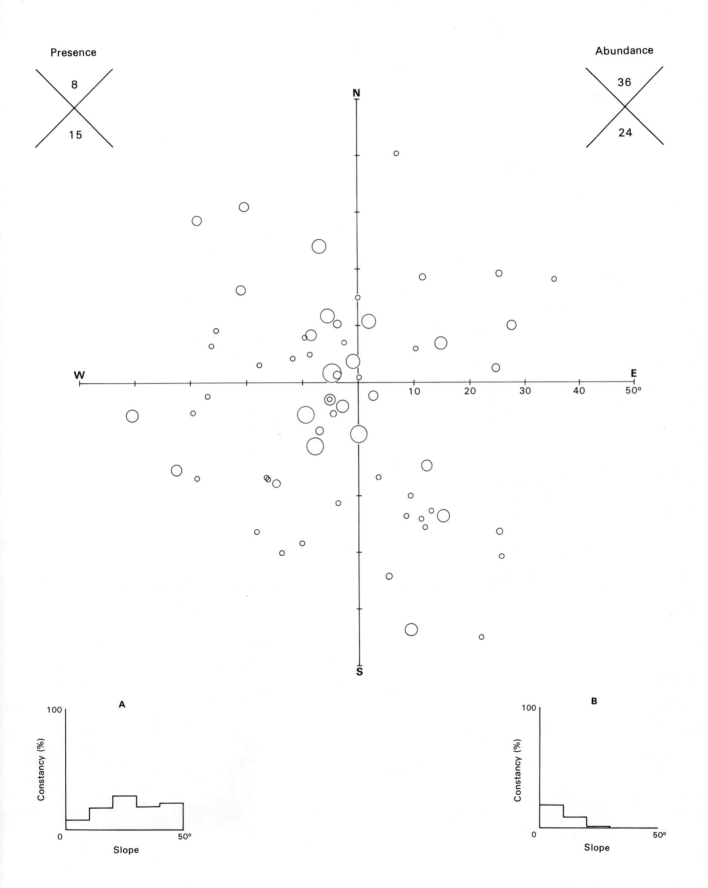

Campanula rotundifolia Harebell

Perennial herb, 15–40(–60) cm.

Occurrence 27%

Grasslands and rock outcrops

Substratum Widespread only on the limestones and the Toadstone. Two of the occurrences on the Millstone Grit were from an old limed pasture. Most abundant on circum-neutral soils and absent from strongly acidic soils.

Slope and aspect Virtually absent from level ground with some indication of slightly higher frequency values on N-facing slopes. In Dorset, Perring (1959) found *C. rotundifolia* to be widespread on all aspects but centred on flat ground or gentle NW- to E-facing slopes.

Grazing and burning Not noticeably influenced by the grazing or burning regime. *C. rotundifolia* has a rather variable growth form which may in part account for its survival in a wide variety of grassland habitats.

Frequency distribution Class 1.

B.S.B.I. Atlas Widespread, but absent from much of SW England, parts of the Midlands and from NW Scotland.

	Geological formation					
	TS	CL	MG	CM	ML	BS
pH (0–3 cm)						
3.0–4.0	—	1	—	1	—	3
4.1–5.0	4	12	3	—	1	—
5.1–6.0	7	23	—	—	8	—
6.1–7.0	6	30	—	—	7	—
7.1–8.0	2	42	—	—	23	—
pH (9–12 cm)						
2.8–4.0	—	—	—	—	—	3
4.1–5.0	10	4	2	1	—	—
5.1–6.0	7	17	1	—	1	—
6.1–7.0	2	25	—	—	7	—
7.1–8.1	—	60	—	—	30	—
Constancy (%)	**50**	**59**	**2**	*1*	**46**	*8*
Ungrazed, unburned	—	32	0	2	—	8
Grazed, unburned	40	68	2	0	60	—
Ungrazed, burned	38	59	—	0	48	—
Grazed, burned	—	57	—	—	—	—

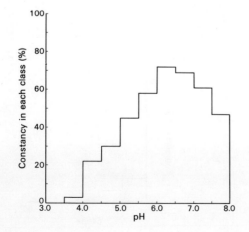
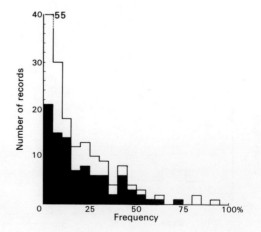

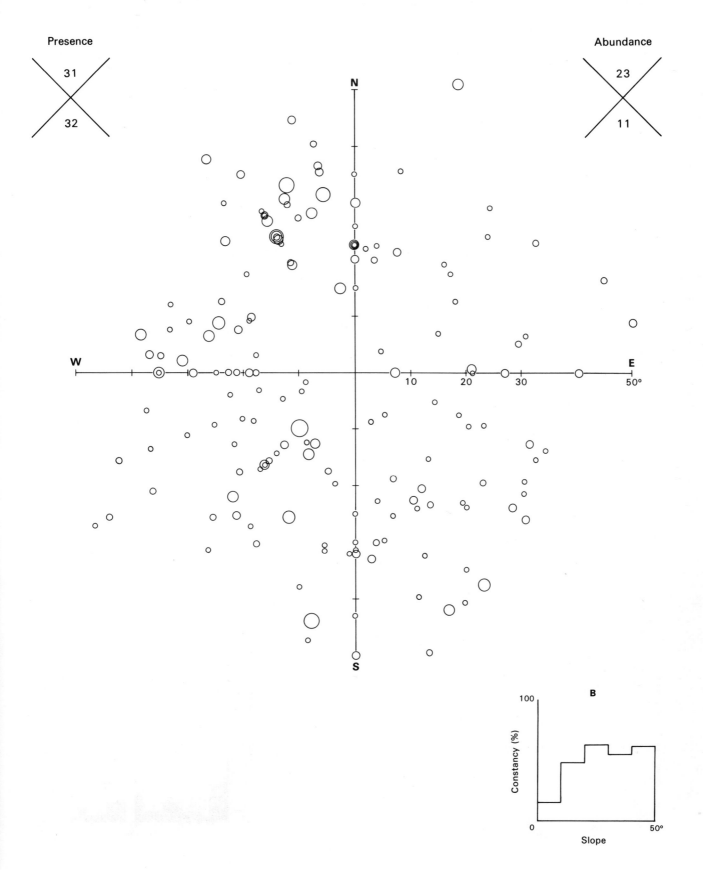

Carex caryophyllea Spring Sedge

Shortly creeping perennial sedge, 5–15(–30) cm.

Occurrence 15%

Grassland

Substratum   Virtually confined to the limestones and the Toadstone and most common on circum-neutral soils.

Slope and aspect   On all aspects in the range of slope 20–40°.

Grazing and burning   Relatively uncommon in tall ungrazed and unburned grasslands of the Carboniferous Limestone. On the Magnesian Limestone the species is mainly confined to grazed habitats.

Frequency distribution   Class 2.

B.S.B.I. Atlas   Widely distributed but predominantly on calcareous substrata.

	TS	CL	MG	CM	ML	BS
			Geological formation			
pH (0–3 cm)						
3.0–4.0	—	1	1	—	—	—
4.1–5.0	2	11	—	—	1	—
5.1–6.0	5	23	—	—	3	—
6.1–7.0	5	20	—	—	1	—
7.1–8.0	1	14	—	—	8	—
pH (9–12 cm)						
2.8–4.0	—	2	1	—	—	—
4.1–5.0	8	6	—	—	1	—
5.1–6.0	4	16	—	—	1	—
6.1–7.0	1	19	—	—	3	—
7.1–8.1	—	27	—	—	8	—
Constancy (%)	**34**	**39**	*1*	*0*	15	*0*
Ungrazed, unburned	—	19	0	0	—	0
Grazed, unburned	40	42	1	0	50	—
Ungrazed, burned	31	46	—	0	9	—
Grazed, burned	—	33	—	—	—	—

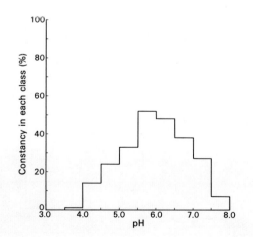

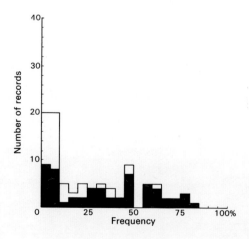

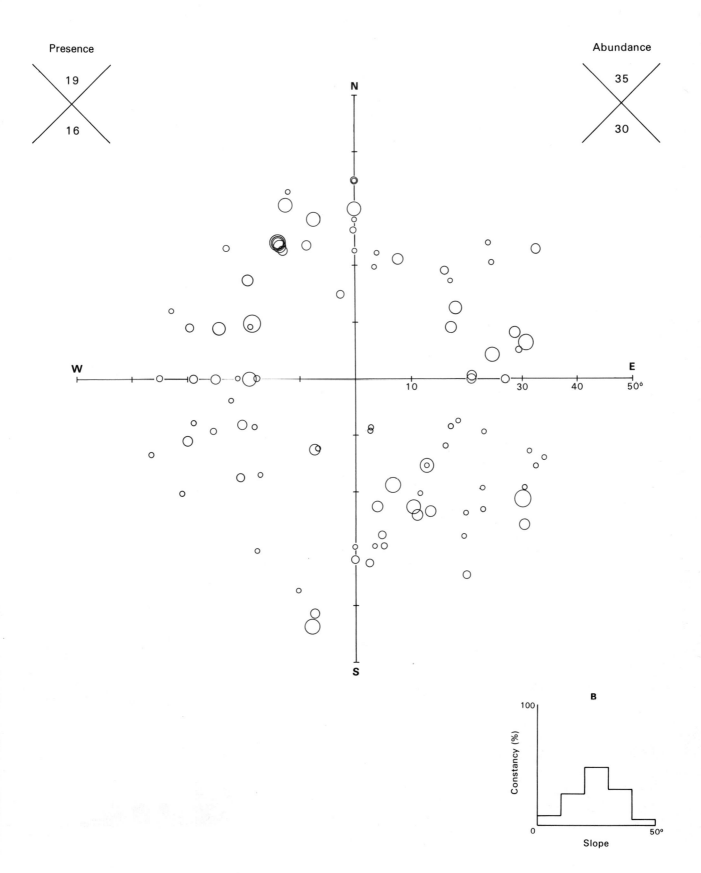

Presence

19

16

Abundance

35

30

N

W   10   20   30   40   50°   E

S

B

Constancy (%)

100

0   Slope   50°

Carex flacca Carnation-grass

Occurrence 18%

Rhizomatous perennial sedge, 10–40 cm.

Grassland, fens and marshes

Substratum Common on the limestones, rare elsewhere. More strongly calcicolous than *C. caryophyllea*.

Slope and aspect Distribution very similar to that of *C. caryophyllea* but with a northern bias in high frequency values which is of interest in relation to the known occurrence of the species in fens, marshes, dune slacks and 'flushed' grasslands (Burnett 1964). Appears to be particularly common in phosphorus-deficient habitats (Willis and Yemm 1961).

Grazing and burning Fairly persistent in the ungrazed, unburned habitats (in distinction to *C. caryophyllea*).

Frequency distribution Class 2.

B.S.B.I. Atlas Common throughout Britain, but relatively scarce in the north and west.

Biological Flora Taylor (1956).

	TS	CL	MG	CM	ML	BS
			Geological formation			
pH (0–3 cm)						
3.0–4.0	—	—	—	—	—	—
4.1–5.0	—	6	—	—	—	—
5.1–6.0	1	21	—	1	3	—
6.1–7.0	2	24	—	—	4	—
7.1–8.0	—	30	—	—	21	—
pH (9–12 cm)						
2.8–4.0	—	—	—	—	—	—
4.1–5.0	2	4	—	—	—	—
5.1–6.0	—	12	—	—	1	—
6.1–7.0	1	21	—	—	3	—
7.1–8.1	—	44	—	1	24	—
Constancy (%)	8	**46**	*0*	*1*	**33**	*0*
Ungrazed, unburned	—	52	0	2	—	0
Grazed, unburned	13	43	0	0	80	—
Ungrazed, burned	0	43	—	0	19	—
Grazed, burned	—	48	—	—	—	—

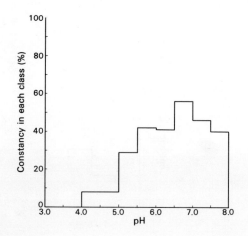

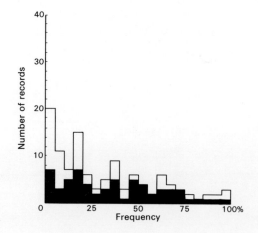

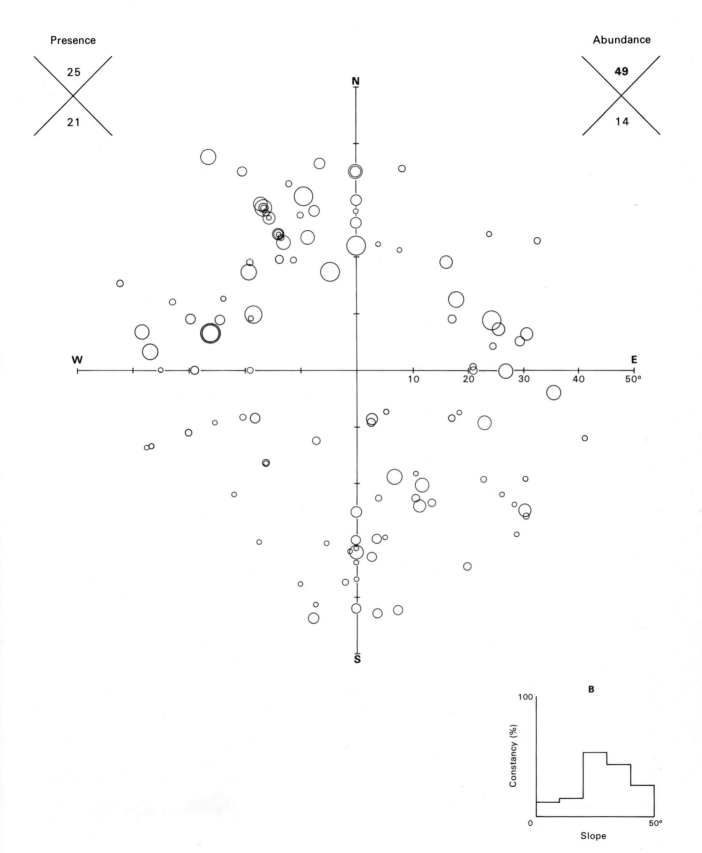

Presence

25

21

Abundance

49

14

N

W   10   20   30   40   50°   E

S

B

100

Constancy (%)

0   50°

Slope

Centaurea nigra Lesser Knapweed

Occurrence 13%

Perennial herb, 15–60(–90) cm.

Grassland and waste places

Substratum Recorded only on base-rich substrata but rather uncommon on Carboniferous Limestone. Most abundant on circum-neutral soils; absent from strongly acidic sites.

Slope and aspect Widely distributed, but less common on slopes < 10°.

Grazing and burning Encountered typically as a component of tall-herb communities at ungrazed sites, but also a constant component of cattle pasture on the Magnesian Limestone. Tolerant of annual burning (Lloyd 1968).

Frequency distribution Class 1.

B.S.B.I. Atlas Ubiquitous.

	TS	CL	MG	CM	ML	BS
			Geological formation			
pH (0–3 cm)						
3.0–4.0	—	—	—	—	—	—
4.1–5.0	3	—	—	—	1	—
5.1–6.0	5	3	—	—	7	—
6.1–7.0	3	8	—	—	8	—
7.1–8.0	1	9	—	—	36	—
pH (9–12 cm)						
2.8–4.0	—	—	—	—	—	—
4.1–5.0	4	—	—	—	2	—
5.1–6.0	6	2	—	—	1	—
6.1–7.0	1	6	—	—	9	—
7.1–8.0	1	12	—	—	41	—
Constancy (%)	**32**	11	*0*	*0*	**61**	*0*
Ungrazed, unburned	—	13	0	0	—	0
Grazed, unburned	0	13	0	0	80	—
Ungrazed, burned	62	5	—	0	58	—
Grazed, burned	—	10	—	—	—	—

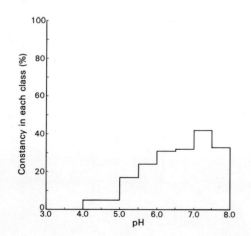

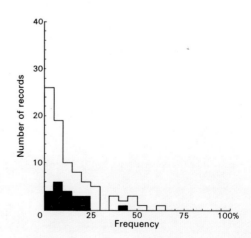

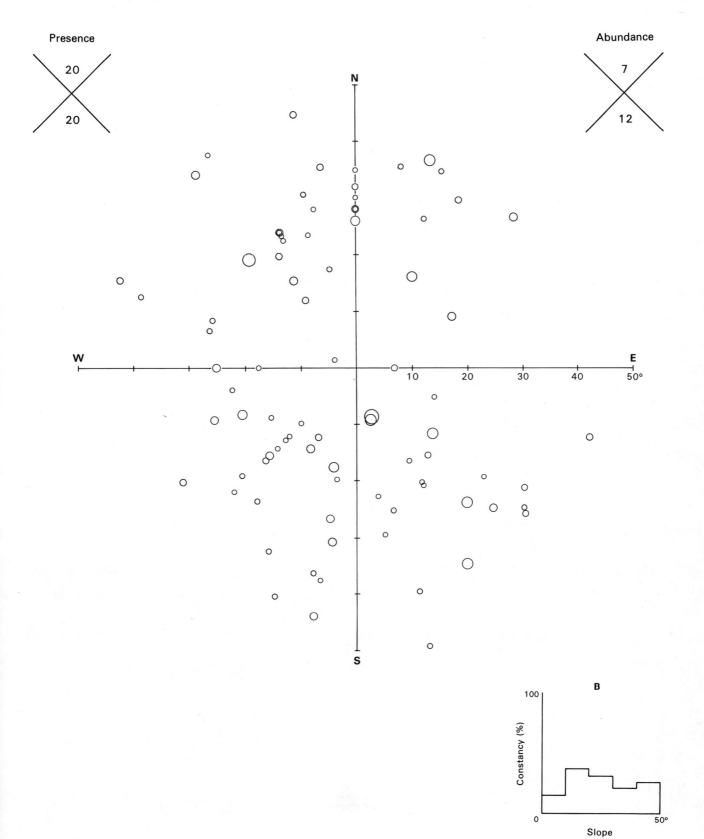

Centaurea scabiosa Greater Knapweed

Perennial herb, 30–90 cm.

Occurrence 4%

Grassland and waste places

Substratum   A calcicole, common on the Magnesian Limestone, but relatively infrequent on the Carboniferous Limestone and Toadstone.

Slope and aspect   All sites on the Carboniferous Limestone and Toadstone face south or south-west.

Grazing and burning   Despite its abundance on the Magnesian Limestone, *C. scabiosa* is absent from cattle-pasture on this substratum. Apparently tolerant of burning.

Frequency distribution   Class 1.

B.S.B.I. Atlas   Frequent only on calcareous substrata in SE England.

| | Geological formation | | | | | |
	TS	CL	MG	CM	ML	BS
pH (0–3 cm)						
3.0–4.0	—	—	—	—	—	—
4.1–5.0	—	—	—	—	1	—
5.1–6.0	—	—	—	—	3	—
6.1–7.0	3	1	—	—	5	—
7.1–8.0	—	1	—	—	14	—
pH (9–12 cm)						
2.8–4.0	—	—	—	—	—	—
4.1–5.0	—	—	—	—	—	—
5.1–6.0	—	—	—	—	—	—
6.1–7.0	2	1	—	—	1	—
7.1–8.1	1	1	—	—	21	—
Constancy (%)	8	1	0	0	27	0
Ungrazed, unburned	—	0	0	0	—	0
Grazed, unburned,	0	1	0	0	0	—
Ungrazed, burned	19	2	—	0	34	—
Grazed, burned	—	0	—	—	—	—

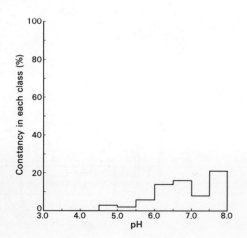

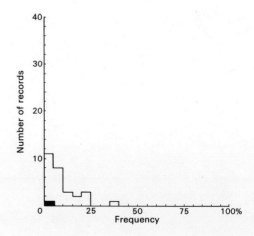

54

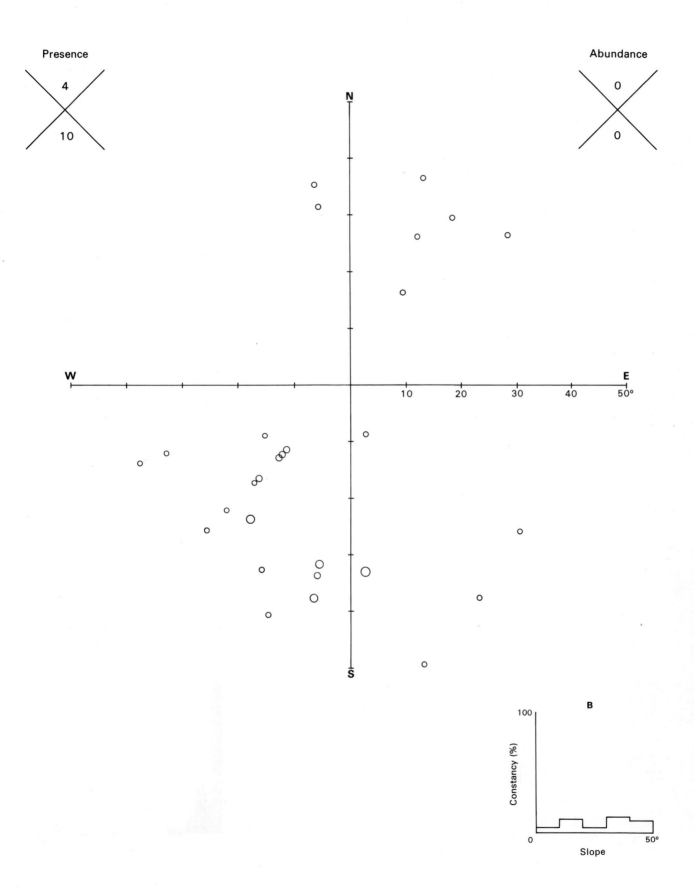

Presence
4
10

Abundance
0
0

N

W E
10 20 30 40 50°

S

B
100
Constancy (%)
0 50°
Slope

Cerastium holosteoides　Common Mouse-ear Chickweed　　　　*Occurrence* 13%

Short-lived perennial herb, 15–45 cm.　　　　　　　　Grassland, path verges and rock outcrops

Substratum　Frequent on base-rich and calcareous substrata; absent or rare elsewhere. Most common on mildly acidic soils of the Toadstone and Carboniferous Limestone.

Slope and aspect　Widely distributed.

Grazing and burning　Most common in grazed turf. *C. holosteoides* is a decumbent species which appears to be suppressed in tall and closed grassland.

Frequency distribution　Class 1.

B.S.B.I. Atlas　Ubiquitous.

			Geological formation			
	TS	CL	MG	CM	ML	BS
pH (0–3 cm)						
3.0–4.0	—	1	1	1	—	—
4.1–5.0	1	3	—	3	—	—
5.1–6.0	5	17	1	1	3	—
6.1–7.0	3	11	—	—	1	—
7.1–8.0	1	21	—	—	6	—
pH (9–12 cm)						
2.8–4.0	—	—	1	2	—	—
4.1–5.0	7	2	—	1	—	—
5.1–6.0	2	10	1	2	—	—
6.1–7.0	1	11	—	—	3	—
7.1–8.1	—	28	—	—	7	—
Constancy (%)	**26**	**30**	*1*	*4*	12	*0*
Ungrazed, unburned	—	10	0	5	—	0
Grazed, unburned	60	37	2	5	40	—
Ungrazed, burned	0	30	—	0	9	—
Grazed, burned	—	19	—	—	—	—

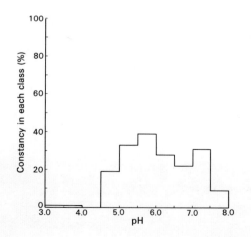

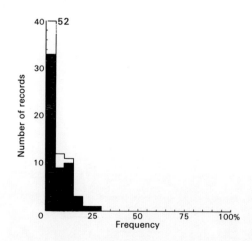

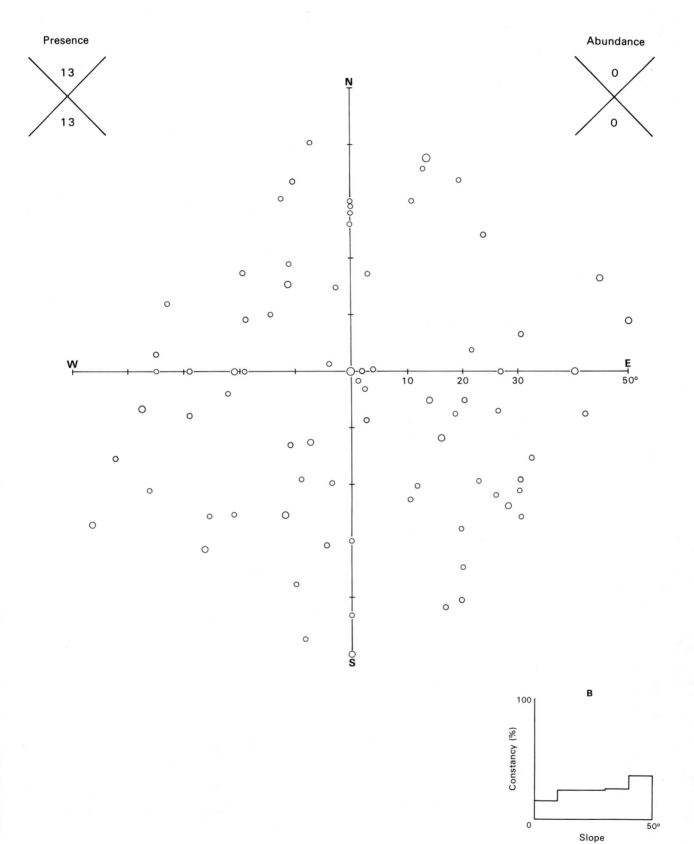

Presence

13
13

Abundance

0
0

N

W   10   20   30   50°   E

S

B

100

Constancy (%)

0   50°

Slope

Chamaenerion angustifolium Rosebay Willowherb

Occurrence 3%

Rhizomatous perennial herb, 30–150 cm.

Woodland and waste places

Substratum   *C. angustifolium* is abundant throughout the region, as a weed of derelict land, commons and roadsides in urban and rural localities. The species produces numerous wind-dispersed seeds and in consequence seedlings are not uncommon in grassland. In the present survey, the species was most often recorded on acidic soils.

    Slope and aspect   Occurrences scattered over a wide range of slope and aspect.

    Grazing and burning   More common at burned sites.

    Frequency distribution   Class 1. The majority of the records are due to isolated seedlings.

    B.S.B.I. Atlas   Throughout lowland Britain. Scarce only in NW Scotland and in Ireland.

	TS	CL	MG	CM	ML	BS
				Geological formation		
pH (0–3 cm)						
3.0–4.0	—	—	1	5	—	—
4.1–5.0	1	3	—	—	1	—
5.1–6.0	—	5	—	—	3	—
6.1–7.0	—	—	—	—	—	—
7.1–8.0	—	—	—	—	—	—
pH (9–12 cm)						
2.8–4.0	—	—	1	3	—	—
4.1–5.0	1	2	—	2	1	—
5.1–6.0	—	2	—	—	—	—
6.1–7.0	—	3	—	—	3	—
7.1–8.1	—	1	—	—	—	—
Constancy (%)	3	5	*1*	4	5	0
Ungrazed, unburned	—	0	0	3	—	0
Grazed, unburned	0	0	1	3	0	—
Ungrazed, burned	6	19	—	10	6	—
Grazed, burned	—	5	—	—	—	—

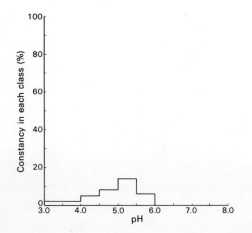

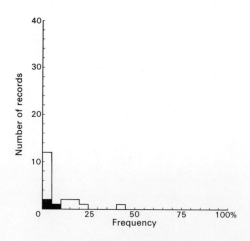

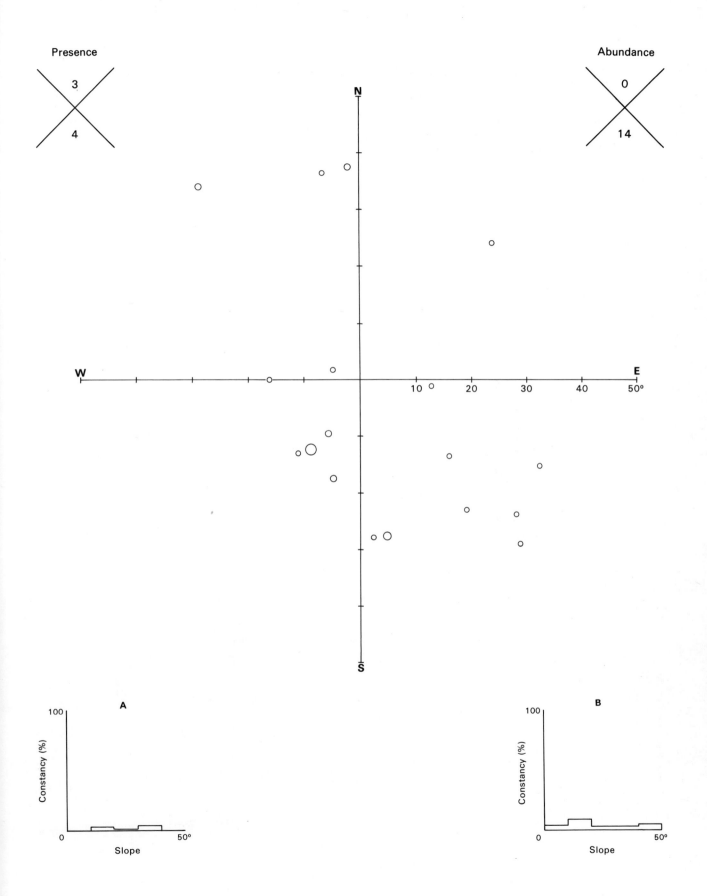

Chrysanthemum leucanthemum Ox-eye Daisy

Occurrence 5%

Perennial herb, 20–70 cm, with non-flowering rosettes.

Meadows, cliffs and waste places

Substratum   Common in grassland only on the Magnesian Limestone. Familiar throughout the region as a meadow plant. The apparently calcicolous distribution is a reflection of its abundance on the Magnesian Limestone.

Slope and aspect   The slight northern bias is interesting in view of the virtual restriction of the species to the Magnesian Limestone sites. On the Magnesian Limestone the species may be suppressed on south-facing slopes by competition from *Brachypodium pinnatum*.

Grazing and burning   Records inadequate.

Frequency distribution   Class 1–2.

B.S.B.I. Atlas   Ubiquitous.

Biological Flora   Howarth and Williams (1968).

	TS	CL	MG	CM	ML	BS
			Geological formation			
pH (0–3 cm)						
3.0–4.0	—	—	—	—	—	—
4.1–5.0	—	—	—	2	—	—
5.1–6.0	—	—	—	1	—	—
6.1–7.0	—	—	—	—	3	—
7.1–8.0	—	—	—	—	26	—
pH (9–12 cm)						
2.8–4.0	—	—	—	—	—	—
4.1–5.0	—	—	—	—	—	—
5.1–6.0	—	—	—	2	—	—
6.1–7.0	—	—	—	—	1	—
7.1–8.1	—	—	—	1	28	—
Constancy (%)	0	0	0	2	34	0
Ungrazed, unburned	—	0	0	5	—	0
Grazed, unburned	0	0	0	0	20	—
Ungrazed, burned	0	0	—	0	33	—
Grazed, burned	—	0	—	—	—	—

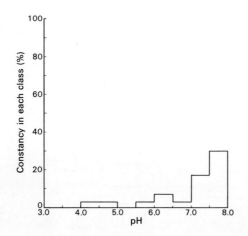

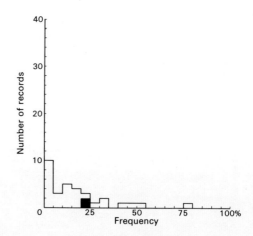

60

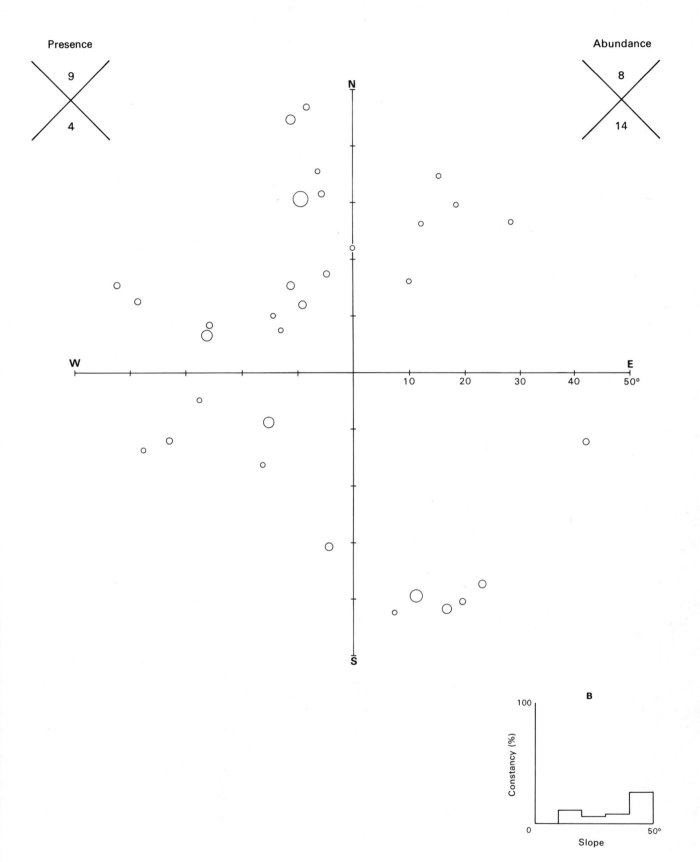

Presence

9

4

Abundance

8

14

N

W

E

10   20   30   40   50°

S

B

100

Constancy (%)

0   50°

Slope

Cirsium arvense Creeping Thistle

Rhizomatous perennial herb, 30–90(–150) cm.

Occurrence 7%

Pastures and waste places

Substratum A wind-dispersed adventive. Seedlings are often observed in grasslands with a surface pH > 4.0. The species is absent from the Millstone Grit and Bunter Sandstone. Primarily, a weed of derelict ground, field margins, and neglected pasture.

Slope and aspect Most records on slopes <30°; a bias towards slopes of southern aspect.

Grazing and burning *C. arvense* has leaf and stem spines and is avoided by grazing animals. The species is strongly rhizomatous and may be expected to be resistant to fire. However, since many of the records were of seedlings, features of the established plant should be used with caution in interpretation of the data.

Frequency distribution Class 1.

B.S.B.I. Atlas Ubiquitous.

		Geological formation				
	TS	CL	MG	CM	ML	BS
pH (0–3 cm)						
3.0–4.0	—	—	—	—	—	—
4.1–5.0	2	9	—	—	2	—
5.1–6.0	2	6	—	2	—	—
6.1–7.0	1	3	—	—	2	—
7.1–8.0	—	3	—	—	10	—
pH (9–12 cm)						
2.8–4.0	—	—	—	—	—	—
4.1–5.0	2	4	—	1	—	—
5.1–6.0	2	6	—	—	1	—
6.1–7.0	1	5	—	—	3	—
7.1–8.1	—	6	—	1	10	—
Constancy (%)	13	**12**	*0*	2	**16**	0
Ungrazed, unburned	—	3	0	3	—	0
Grazed, unburned	13	9	0	0	30	—
Ungrazed, burned	6	27	—	0	15	—
Grazed, burned	—	10	—	—	—	—

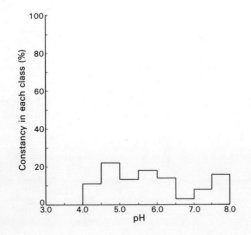

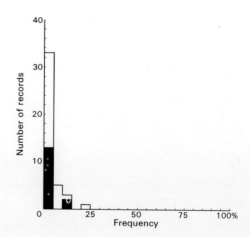

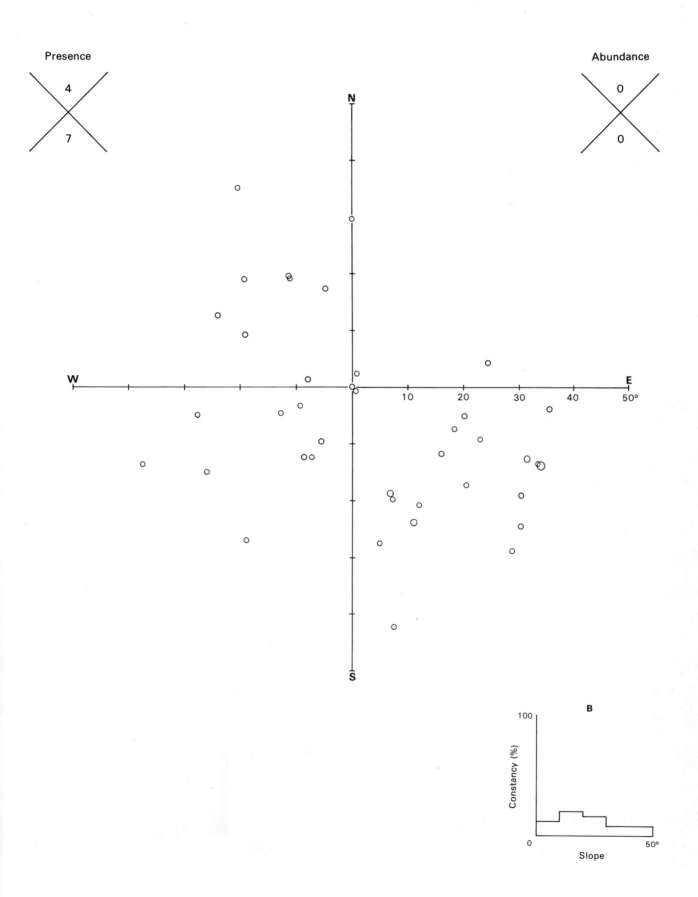

Presence

4

7

Abundance

0

0

N

W
10   20   30   40   50°
E

S

B

100

Constancy (%)

0   50°
Slope

Cirsium palustre Marsh Thistle

Biennial herb, 30–150 cm, forming a rosette.

Occurrence 5%

Marshes and wet pasture

Substratum   Common only on the Carboniferous Limestone where it is most frequent in the pH range 5.0–6.0.

Slope and aspect   Most records are on north-facing slopes. This pattern may be influenced by soil moisture; the species is a common constituent of marsh and fen.

Grazing and burning   Poorly represented in the ungrazed/unburned grasslands. In the tall, dense communities frequent in this category, it is to be expected that the reduced opportunity for seedling establishment will be selective against a biennial species.

Frequency distribution   Class 1.

B.S.B.I. Atlas   Ubiquitous.

		Geological formation				
	TS	CL	MG	CM	ML	BS
pH (0–3 cm)						
3.0–4.0	1	—	—	—	—	—
4.1–5.0	—	5	2	—	—	—
5.1–6.0	2	16	—	—	—	—
6.1–7.0	—	3	—	—	—	—
7.1–8.0	—	5	—	—	1	—
pH (9–12 cm)						
2.8–4.0	—	—	—	—	—	—
4.1–5.0	1	3	—	—	—	—
5.1–6.0	2	13	2	—	—	—
6.1–7.0	—	7	—	—	—	—
7.1–8.1	—	6	—	—	1	—
Constancy (%)	8	**16**	*1*	*0*	1	0
Ungrazed, unburned	—	3	0	0	—	0
Grazed, unburned	0	19	2	0	0	—
Ungrazed, burned	19	8	—	0	1	—
Grazed, burned	—	29	—	—	—	—

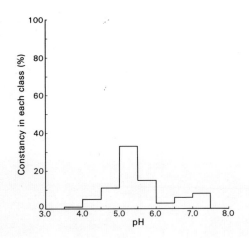

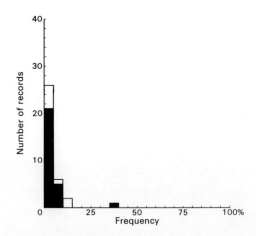

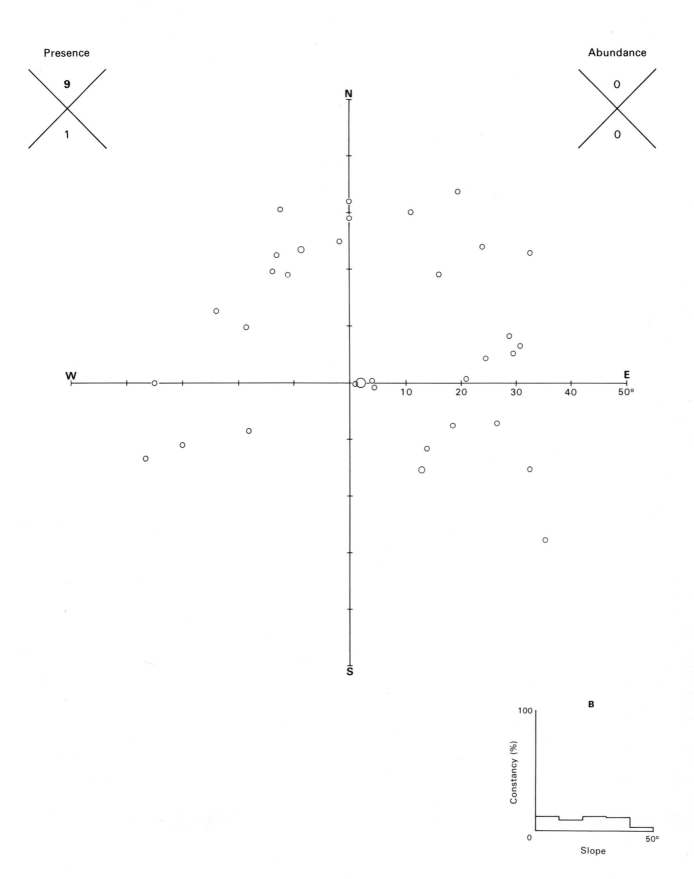

Conopodium majus Pignut

Tuberous perennial herb, 30–50(–90) cm.

Occurrence 4%

Open woods and meadows

Substratum Restricted to soils of intermediate pH and common only on the Toadstone. The single Millstone Grit locality is a formerly limed pasture.

Slope and aspect The distribution shows a slight northern bias. This is of interest in view of the frequent occurrence of the species in woods.

Grazing and burning Frequent in permanent pasture on the Carboniferous Limestone. The leaves wither early in the summer and this phenology may cause the species to be sensitive to spring burning. *C. majus* is in fact almost unrecorded in burned sites.

Frequency distribution Class 2.

B.S.B.I. Atlas Widespread but scarce in East Anglia and southern Ireland.

	TS	CL	MG	CM	ML	BS
			Geological formation			
pH (0–3 cm)						
3.0–4.0	—	—	—	—	—	—
4.1–5.0	2	4	1	—	—	—
5.1–6.0	5	3	—	—	1	—
6.1–7.0	4	1	—	—	—	—
7.1–8.0	2	1	—	—	2	—
pH (9–12 cm)						
2.8–4.0	—	—	—	—	—	—
4.1–5.0	8	4	—	—	—	—
5.1–6.0	5	2	1	—	—	—
6.1–7.0	—	2	—	—	2	—
7.1–8.1	—	1	—	—	1	—
Constancy (%)	34	5	*1*	*0*	4	0
Ungrazed, unburned	—	0	0	0	—	0
Grazed, unburned	60	7	1	0	10	—
Ungrazed, burned	0	0	—	0	3	—
Grazed, burned	—	10	—	—	—	—

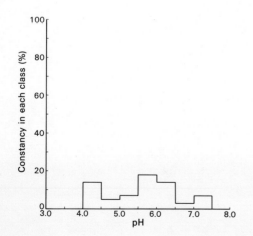

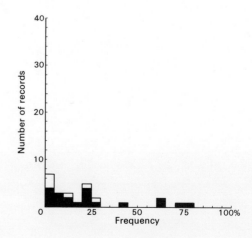

66

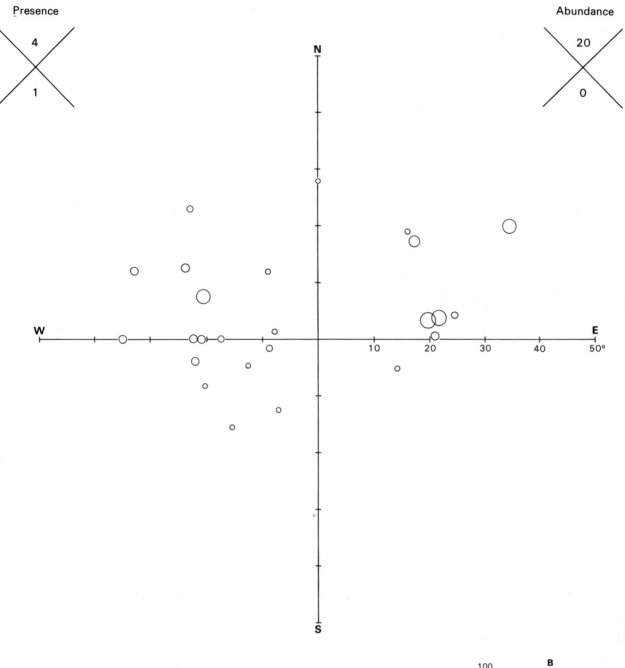

Presence

4

1

Abundance

20

0

N

W   10   20   30   40   50°   E

S

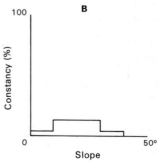

B

100

Constancy (%)

0   50°

Slope

Dactylis glomerata Cock's-foot

Tussock grass, up to 100 cm.

Occurrence 28%

Grassland and waste places

Substratum   Frequent only on limestone and toadstone; absent from the Bunter Sandstone. Of common occurrence over the pH range 4.5–8.0. *D. glomerata* shows high constancy on unleached calcareous soils on the Magnesian Limestone but is relatively scarce on rendzinas and screes of the Carboniferous Limestone. This suggests a preference for mineral soils, whether brown-earths (Toadstone) or mull-rendzinas (Magnesian Limestone).

Slope and aspect   Widely distributed, but with a bias to south-facing slopes on both limestones.

Grazing and burning   No marked effects of grazing or burning. The low representation at ungrazed, unburned sites on the Carboniferous Limestone partly reflects the absence of this species from screes.

Frequency distribution   Class 1–2. Most records in semi-natural grassland are of small plants with few tillers. However, because of the tussock growth-form the species may be recorded with low rooted frequency even where it is a more important constituent.

B.S.B.I. Atlas   Ubiquitous.

Biological Flora   Beddows (1959).

	Geological formation					
	TS	CL	MG	CM	ML	BS
pH (0–3 cm)						
3.0–4.0	—	—	—	1	—	—
4.1–5.0	5	5	1	9	3	—
5.1–6.0	14	23	—	2	12	—
6.1–7.0	6	17	—	—	11	—
7.1–8.0	—	21	—	—	45	—
pH (9–12 cm)						
2.8–4.0	—	—	—	1	—	—
4.1–5.0	7	2	1	4	1	—
5.1–6.0	11	15	—	6	2	—
6.1–7.0	6	14	—	—	14	—
7.1–8.1	1	33	—	1	54	—
Constancy (%)	**66**	**37**	*1*	*10*	**84**	*0*
Ungrazed, unburned	—	13	0	20	—	0
Grazed, unburned	60	44	0	0	70	—
Ungrazed, burned	75	41	—	0	84	—
Grazed, burned	—	33	—	—	—	—

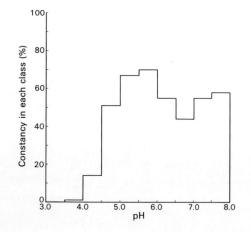

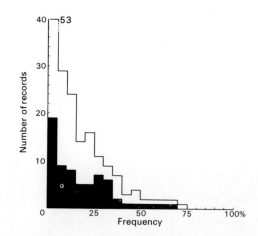

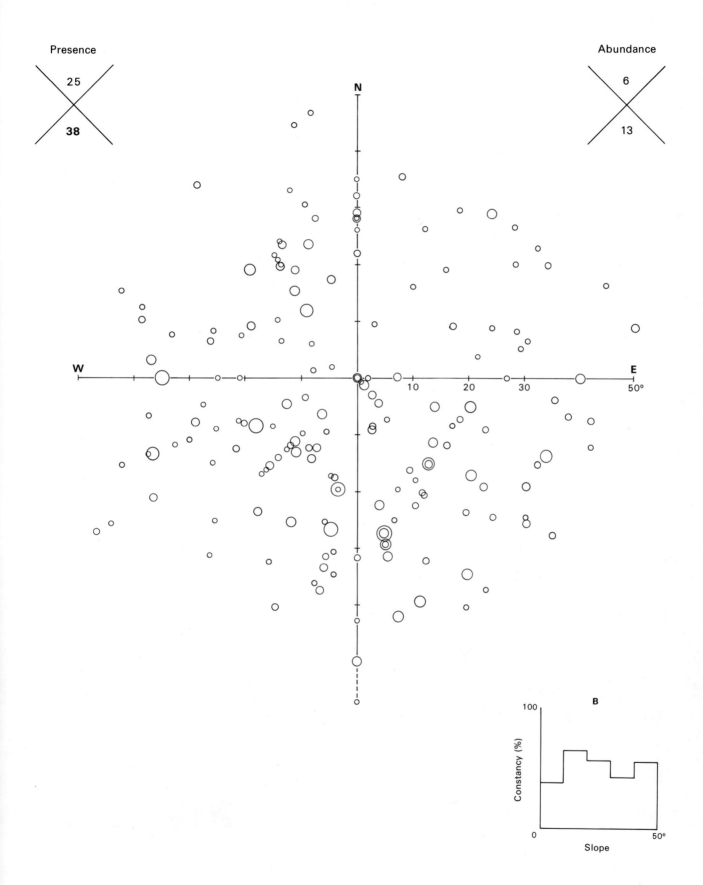

Presence

25

38

Abundance

6

13

N

W

E

10 20 30 50°

B

100

Constancy (%)

0 50°

Slope

Deschampsia cespitosa Tufted Hair-grass

Robust tussock grass, 50–200 cm.

Occurrence 6%

Woods and marshes

Substratum Frequent only on the Carboniferous Limestone and the Toadstone. Occurs over a very wide range in soil pH with an ill-defined optimum on mildly acidic soils.

Slope and aspect On the Carboniferous Limestone *D. cespitosa* is restricted to level ground and to north-facing slopes. This aspect preference is consistent with the well-known association of the species with moist shaded habitats.

Grazing and burning Resistant to fire damage, but relatively infrequent in habitats susceptible to burning.

Frequency distribution Class 2. *D. cespitosa* probably attains Class 3 status in marshland and in open woods.

B.S.B.I. Atlas Ubiquitous.

	TS	CL	MG	CM	ML	BS
			Geological formation			
pH (0–3 cm)						
3.0–4.0	1	4	—	1	—	—
4.1–5.0	2	7	3	—	—	—
5.1–6.0	1	5	2	1	—	—
6.1–7.0	2	2	—	—	—	—
7.1–8.0	—	6	—	—	1	—
pH (9–12 cm)						
2.8–4.0	—	2	—	1	—	—
4.1–5.0	4	4	2	1	—	—
5.1–6.0	1	6	3	—	—	—
6.1–7.0	1	3	—	—	—	—
7.1–8.0	—	9	—	—	1	—
Constancy (%)	**16**	**13**	3	*2*	*1*	0
Ungrazed, unburned	—	16	0	2	—	0
Grazed, unburned	20	16	4	3	0	—
Ungrazed, burned	13	0	—	0	0	—
Grazed, burned	—	19	—	—	—	—

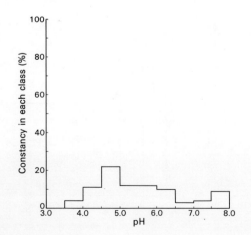

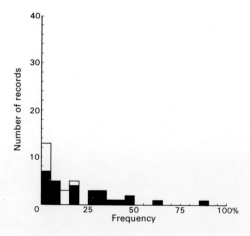

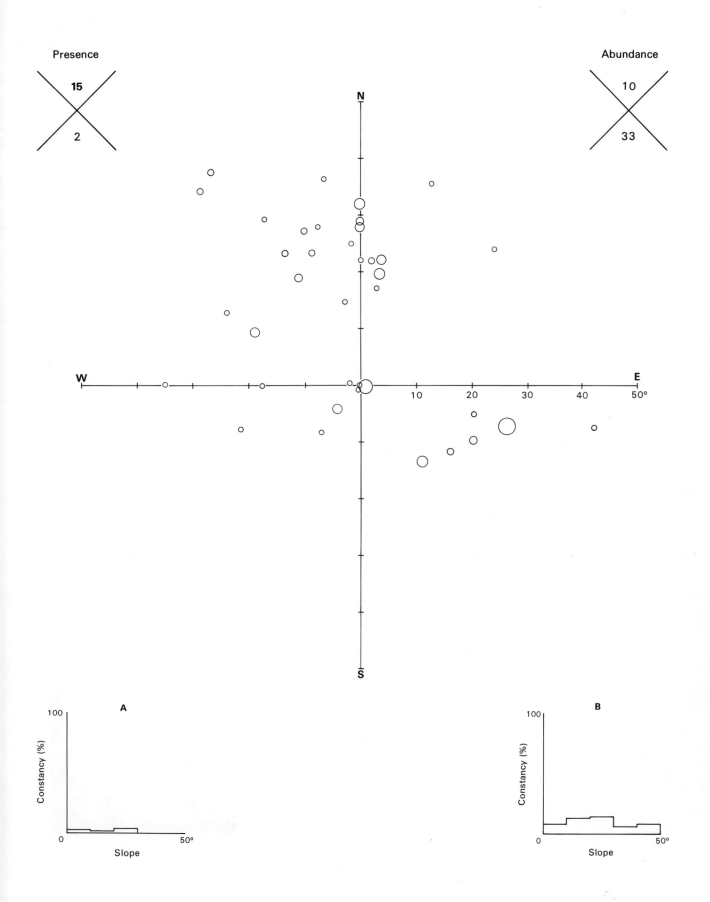

Deschampsia flexuosa Wavy Hair-grass

Tufted perennial grass, 25–40 cm.

Occurrence 51%

Woodland, moorland and waste places

Substratum   Of widespread occurrence on acidic soils on five strata. The absence of *D. flexuosa* from sites on the Magnesian Limestone is correlated with the scarcity of acidic soils on this stratum. Occurs at 95% of the sites with a surface pH < 4.0. An extraordinarily strict calcifuge, common on acidic soils in all but the wettest habitats.

Slope and aspect   Particularly on the Carboniferous Limestone most of the sites at which the species occurs are on flat ground and gentle slope. On acidic substrata however, *D. flexuosa* extends on to steep hillsides.

Grazing and burning   Present on acidic soils irrespective of grazing or burning regimes.

Frequency distribution   Class 3.

B.S.B.I. Atlas   Northern and western in England; virtually confined to acidic substrata in S England. Apparently infrequent in Ireland.

Biological flora   Scurfield (1954).

	TS	CL	MG	CM	ML	BS
			Geological formation			
pH (0–3 cm)						
3.0–4.0	1	15	150	93	—	27
4.1–5.0	1	11	4	6	—	2
5.1–6.0	2	3	2	2	—	—
6.1–7.0	2	—	—	—	—	—
7.1–8.0	1	—	—	—	—	—
pH (9–12 cm)						
2.8–4.0	—	15	151	82	—	21
4.1–5.0	6	7	4	19	—	8
5.1–6.0	1	5	—	—	—	—
6.1–7.0	—	1	—	—	—	—
7.1–8.1	—	1	—	—	—	—
Constancy (%)	*18*	*16*	**95**	**83**	*0*	**81**
Ungrazed, unburned	—	10	100	69	—	81
Grazed, unburned	27	20	93	97	0	—
Ungrazed, burned	0	8	—	90	0	—
Grazed, burned	—	14	—	—	—	—

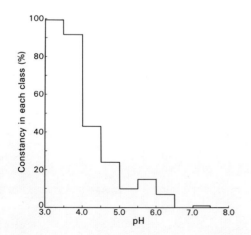

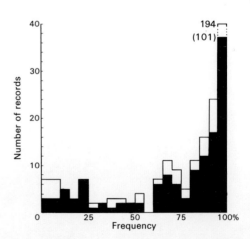

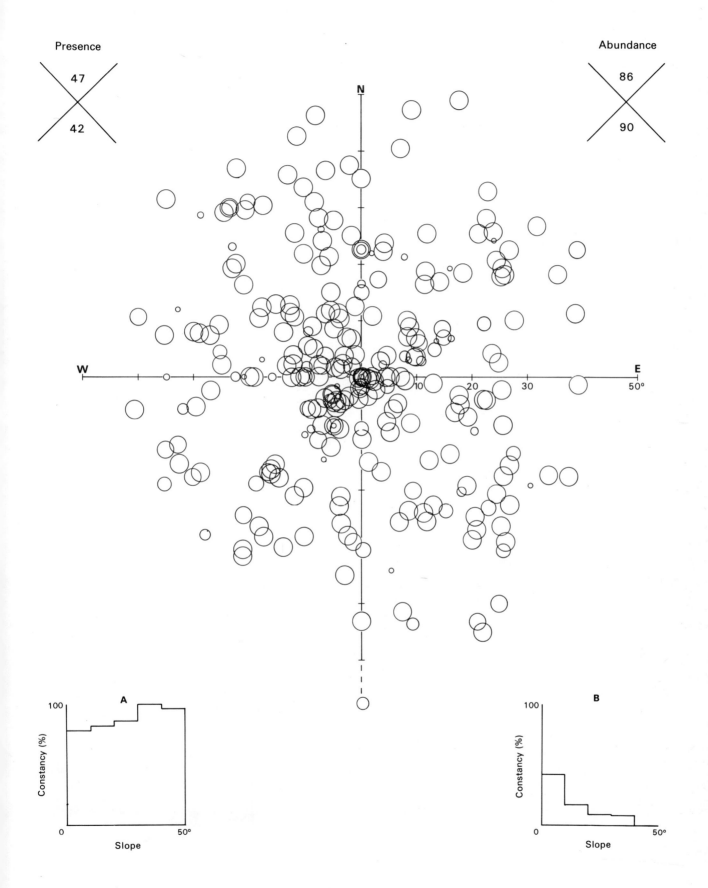

Presence
47
42

Abundance
86
90

N

W ———— E
                    10   20   30   50°

A
100
Constancy (%)
0   50°
      Slope

B
100
Constancy (%)
0   50°
      Slope

Euphrasia officinalis agg. Eyebright

Occurrence 4%

Hemi-parasitic annual herbs, 1–40 cm.   Grassland, moorland and mine waste

Microspecies have not been distinguished but the following are those most likely to have been encountered during the survey (Perring 1968): *E. nemorosa* (widespread), *E. confusa* (Carboniferous Limestone).

Euphrasia species are parasitic on a wide range of herbaceous plants (Yeo 1964).

Substratum   Virtually confined to limestone; strongly calcicolous.

Slope and aspect   Absent from flat ground; the NW–SE aspect bias is unexplained and probably due to chance.

Grazing and burning   Most frequently in short grazed turf.

Frequency distribution   Class 1–2. High frequency values are in some cases due to the presence of large numbers of seedlings.

B.S.B.I. Atlas   Widespread in northern and western Britain but confined to calcareous strata in central and eastern England. Individual species are more restricted in distribution.

		TS	CL	MG	CM	ML	BS
				Geological formation			
pH (0–3 cm)							
	3.0–4.0	—	—	—	—	—	—
	4.1–5.0	—	—	—	—	—	—
	5.1–6.0	—	4	—	—	—	—
	6.1–7.0	1	7	—	—	1	—
	7.1–8.0	—	8	—	—	7	—
pH (9–12 cm)							
	2.8–4.0	—	—	—	—	—	—
	4.1–5.0	1	—	—	—	—	—
	5.1–6.0	—	1	—	—	—	—
	6.1–7.0	—	9	—	—	—	—
	7.1–8.1	—	9	—	—	8	—
Constancy (%)		3	**11**	*0*	*0*	9	0
Ungrazed, unburned		—	0	0	0	—	0
Grazed, unburned		7	19	0	0	30	—
Ungrazed, burned		0	0	—	0	6	—
Grazed, burned		—	5	—	—	—	—

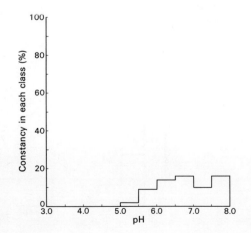

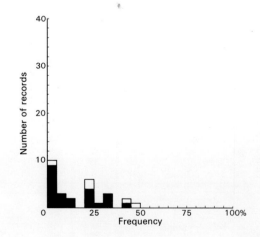

74

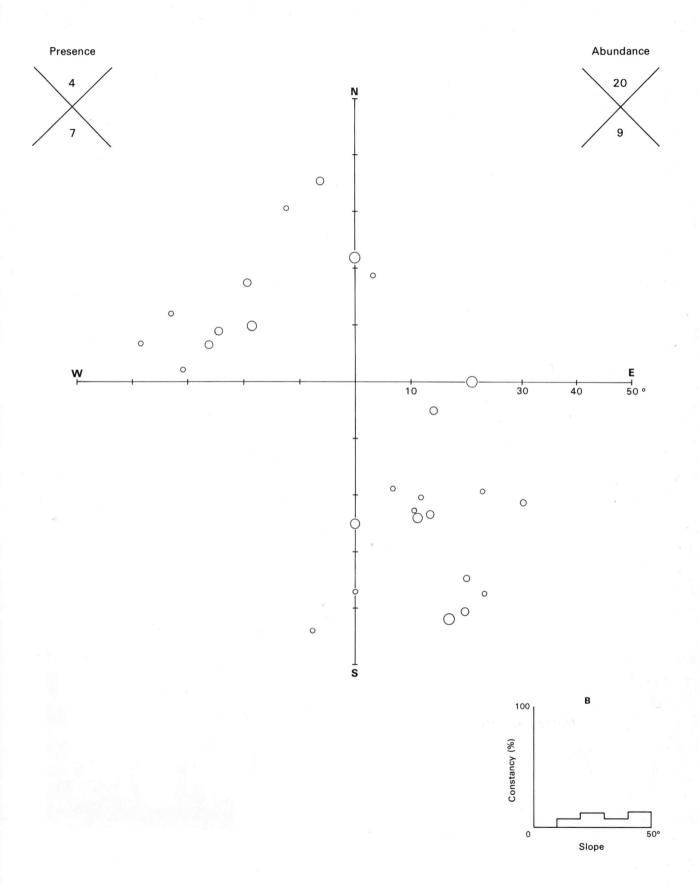

Presence

4

7

Abundance

20

9

N

W

E

10 30 40 50 °

S

100

B

Constancy (%)

0 50°

Slope

Festuca ovina Sheep's Fescue

Tufted perennial grass, 10–50 cm.

Occurrence 57%

Grassland and rock outcrops

Substratum   On all formations, but relatively scarce on the Coal Measures and Magnesian Limestone. The only species encountered which is present with high constancy over the full range of soil pH. The slightly lower values in the middle of the pH range coincide with peak values in taller, more productive grass species.

Slope and aspect   Occurs with wide variation in frequency on all slopes and aspects.

Grazing and burning   On five strata highest constancy values coincide with grazing. The low frequency of the species on the Coal Measures and Magnesian Limestone is associated with the preponderance of ungrazed often burned sites on these strata. *F. ovina* has been shown to be sensitive to burning (Lloyd 1968) and it also appears to have a limited ability to survive in competition with taller species.

Frequency distribution   Class 3.

B.S.B.I. Atlas   Ubiquitous.

	Geological formation					
	TS	CL	MG	CM	ML	BS
pH (0–3 cm)						
3.0–4.0	1	9	92	32	—	29
4.1–5.0	7	24	8	7	1	4
5.1–6.0	10	28	2	1	1	—
6.1–7.0	7	30	—	—	3	—
7.1–8.0	2	45	—	—	13	—
pH (9–12 cm)						
2.8–4.0	—	9	92	28	—	23
4.1–5.0	15	13	7	12	1	10
5.1–6.0	7	21	3	—	1	—
6.1–7.0	5	29	—	—	—	—
7.1–8.1	—	66	—	—	15	—
Constancy (%)	71	**76**	62	*33*	*21*	**92**
Ungrazed, unburned	—	65	21	25	—	92
Grazed, unburned	93	80	70	65	50	—
Ungrazed, burned	38	73	—	5	16	—
Grazed, burned	—	81	—	—	—	—

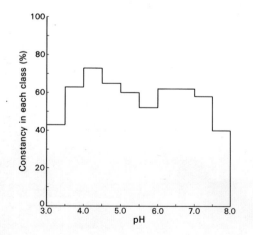

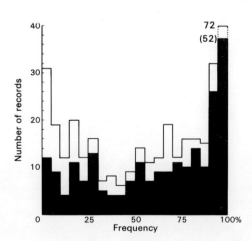

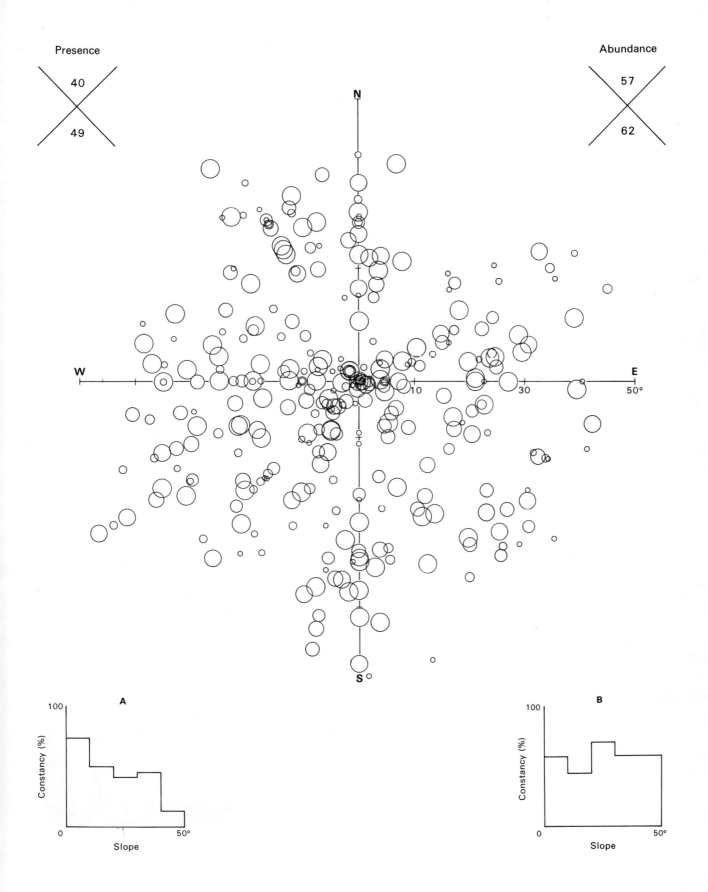

Presence

40

49

Abundance

57

62

N

W   10   30   50°   E

S

A

100

Constancy (%)

0   50°

Slope

B

100

Constancy (%)

0   50°

Slope

Festuca rubra   Creeping Fescue

Rhizomatous perennial grass, 10–70 cm.

All records are considered to be of ssp. *rubra*.

Occurrence 41%

Grassland and wasteland

Substratum   On all formations, but rare on the Millstone Grit and Bunter Sandstone. Absent only from the most acidic soils.

Slope and aspect   Present with high frequency values on all slopes and aspects, but showing a higher density of occurrences on slopes of northern aspect.

Grazing and burning   F. rubra is relatively insensitive to burning or grazing regime (cf. *F. ovina*). This may be attributed to the rhizomatous habit and rather plastic growth form.

Frequency distribution   Class 2–3. Often a subsidiary component in both open and closed turf.

B.S.B.I. Atlas   Ubiquitous.

		Geological formation				
	TS	CL	MG	CM	ML	BS
pH (0–3 cm)						
3.0–4.0	—	2	—	8	—	—
4.1–5.0	4	19	6	11	1	2
5.1–6.0	15	34	1	2	7	—
6.1–7.0	6	32	—	—	11	—
7.1–8.0	1	44	—	—	47	—
pH (9–12 cm)						
2.8–4.0	—	2	—	1	—	—
4.1–5.0	6	9	2	12	1	2
5.1–6.0	14	21	5	7	1	—
6.1–7.0	5	30	—	—	9	—
7.1–8.1	1	67	—	1	54	—
Constancy (%)	**68**	**74**	*4*	*17*	**78**	*6*
Ungrazed, unburned	—	61	0	33	—	6
Grazed, unburned	73	79	5	0	80	—
Ungrazed, burned	69	54	—	5	75	—
Grazed, burned	—	100	—	—	—	—

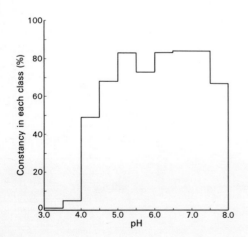

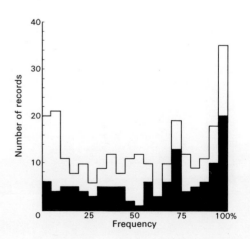

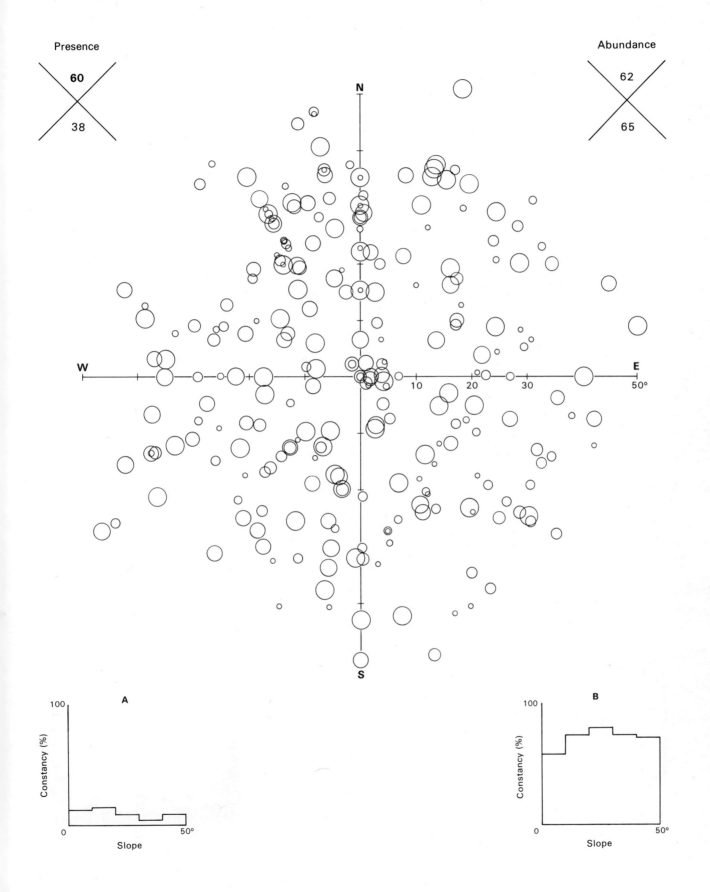

Galium saxatile Heath Bedstraw

Prostrate perennial herb, up to 20 cm.

Occurrence 25%

Grassland and heathland

Substratum Present on acidic soils from each stratum except the Magnesian Limestone. A strict calcifuge.

Slope and aspect On the Carboniferous Limestone *G. saxatile* is confined to flat ground and gentler slopes. On those strata which provide acidic soils over the full range in slope the species extends over 0–40°. Abundant on north-facing slopes; almost completely absent from those facing due south.

Grazing and burning On those strata for which an adequate comparison is possible *G. saxatile* occurs more frequently at grazed sites than at ungrazed (± burning). The species is, however, extremely common on the ungrazed grasslands of the Bunter Sandstone.

Frequency distribution Class 2.

B.S.B.I. Atlas Widespread in Britain but scarce in areas of SE England and central Ireland.

| | Geological formation | | | | | |
	TS	CL	MG	CM	ML	BS
pH (0–3 cm)						
3.0–4.0	1	9	58	25	—	18
4.1–5.0	3	19	6	7	—	3
5.1–6.0	2	6	2	—	—	—
6.1–7.0	1	—	—	—	—	—
7.1–8.0	—	—	—	—	—	—
pH (9–12 cm)						
2.8–4.0	—	9	56	17	—	15
4.1–5.0	16	11	7	13	—	6
5.1–6.0		6	3	2	—	—
6.1–7.0	—	5	—	—	—	—
7.1–8.1	—	3	—	—	—	—
Constancy (%)	18	*19*	**40**	26	*0*	**58**
Ungrazed, unburned	—	13	25	23	—	58
Grazed, unburned	13	24	43	46	0	—
Ungrazed, burned	19	5	—	0	0	—
Grazed, burned	—	24	—	—	—	—

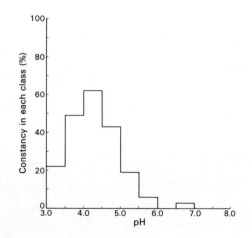

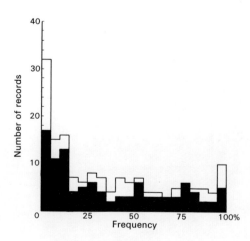

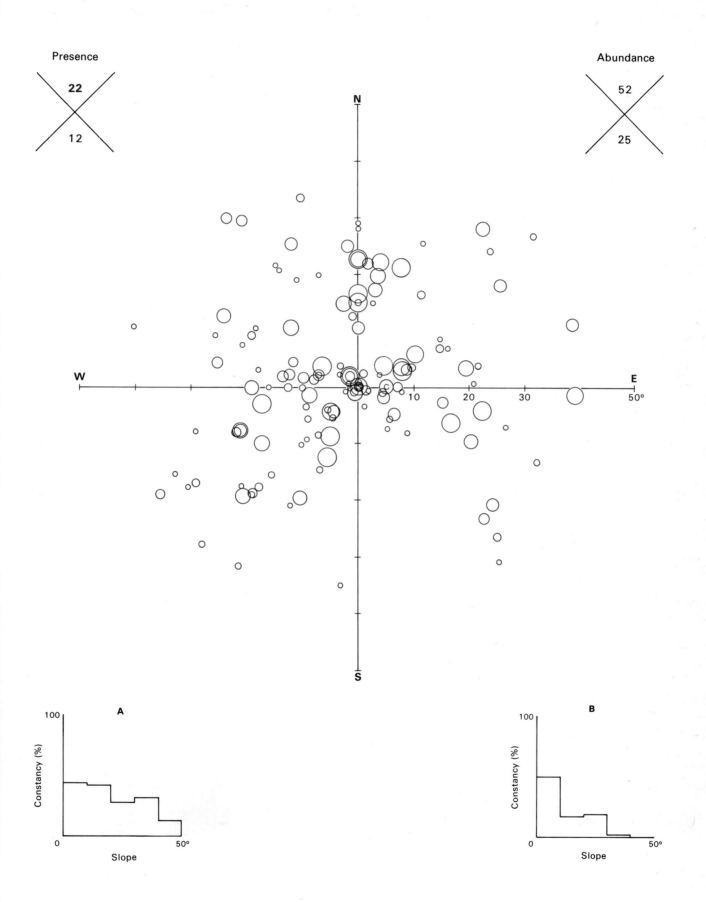

Presence

22

12

Abundance

52

25

N

W
10   20   30   50°
E

S

100
Constancy (%)

A

0
Slope
50°

100
Constancy (%)

B

0
Slope
50°

Galium sterneri Slender Bedstraw

Prostrate perennial herb, up to 20 cm.

Occurrence 13%

Grassland

Substratum   Confined to Carboniferous Limestone. A calcicole with a maximum frequency of occurrence at pH 7.0.

Slope and aspect   The species was not recorded from sites at which the slope is less than 20°. This reflects the fact that the species (which is considerably less robust than *G. verum*) is most common in open sites (broken turf, scree margins or rock outcrops) on the dale sides.

Grazing and burning   The relatively low frequency recorded for ungrazed, unburned habitats confirms the association of *G. sterneri* with open sites.

Frequency distribution   Class 1–2.

B.S.B.I. Atlas   Confined to the limestones of north and west Britain.

| | | Geological formation | | | | |
	TS	CL	MG	CM	ML	BS
pH (0–3 cm)						
3.0–4.0	—	—	—	—	—	—
4.1–5.0	1	1	—	—	—	—
5.1–6.0	—	16	—	—	—	—
6.1–7.0	—	25	—	—	—	—
7.1–8.0	—	39	—	—	—	—
pH (9–12 cm)						
2.8–4.0	—	—	—	—	—	—
4.1–5.0	1	—	—	—	—	—
5.1–6.0	—	8	—	—	—	—
6.1–7.0	—	21	—	—	—	—
7.1–8.1	—	52	—	—	—	—
Constancy (%)	3	**45**	*0*	*0*	*0*	*0*
Ungrazed, unburned	—	29	0	0	—	0
Grazed, unburned	7	46	0	0	0	—
Ungrazed, burned	0	54	—	0	0	—
Grazed, burned	—	52	—	—	—	—

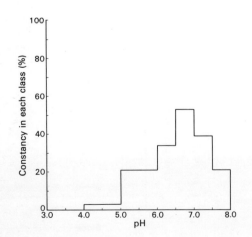

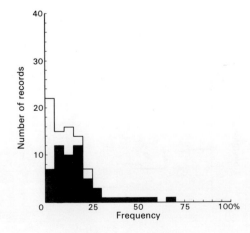

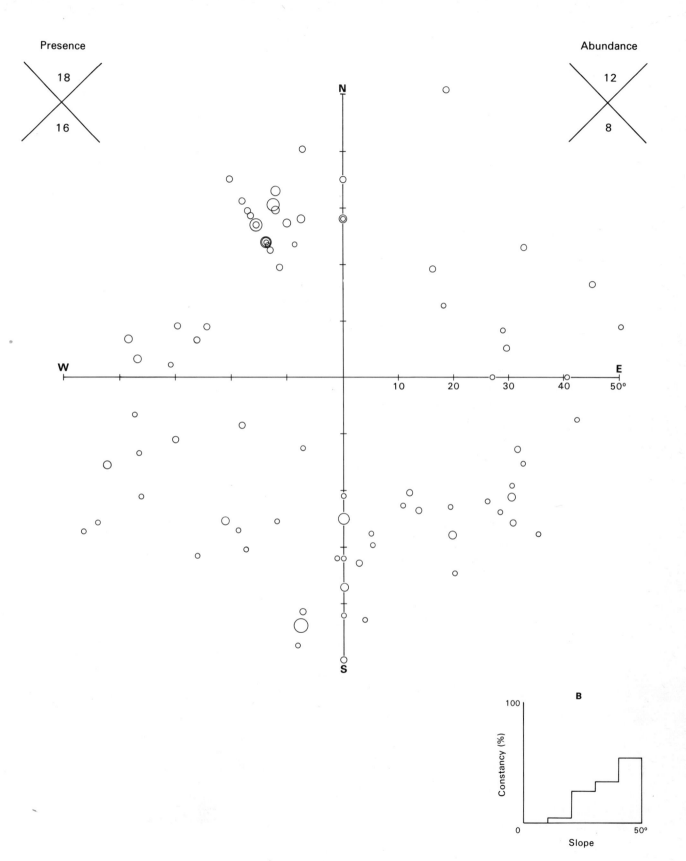

Presence

18

16

Abundance

12

8

N

W   E

10   20   30   40   50°

S

Constancy (%)

100

B

0   50°

Slope

Galium verum Lady's Bedstraw

Perennial herb, 15–100 cm, with decumbent or ascending shoots.

Occurrence 7%

Grassland and scrub

Substratum Present on the two limestones; relatively frequent in occurrence on the Toadstone. With respect to pH at the soil surface, *G. verum* shows a clear optimum at pH 6.0. Many of the soils on which the species occurs have stratified profiles, being either surface leached mineral soils on plateau edges over the Carboniferous Limestone (acidic above, calcareous below) or Toadstone soils subject to dust blown from a limestone quarry (calcareous above, acidic below).

Slope and aspect The majority of the sites fall in the range of slope 10–30°.

Grazing and burning No consistent pattern apparent.

Frequency distribution Class 2. The high frequencies coincide with the development of extensive mats.

B.S.B.I. Atlas Widespread.

	TS	CL	MG	CM	ML	BS
			Geological formation			
pH (0–3 cm)						
3.0–4.0	—	1	—	—	—	—
4.1–5.0	2	5	—	—	—	—
5.1–6.0	9	8	—	—	1	—
6.1–7.0	2	6	—	—	3	—
7.1–8.0	2	3	—	—	3	—
pH (9–12 cm)						
2.8–4.0	—	1	—	—	—	—
4.1–5.0	7	2	—	—	1	—
5.1–6.0	6	5	—	—	—	—
6.1–7.0	2	9	—	—	2	—
7.1–8.1	—	5	—	—	4	—
Constancy (%)	**40**	**13**	*0*	*0*	**8**	*0*
Ungrazed, unburned	—	16	0	0	—	0
Grazed, unburned	40	11	0	0	0	—
Ungrazed, burned	25	11	—	0	9	—
Grazed, burned	—	19	—	—	—	—

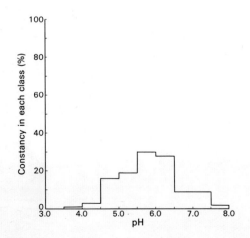

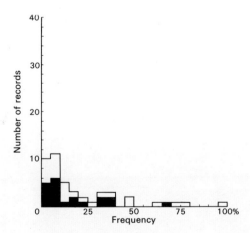

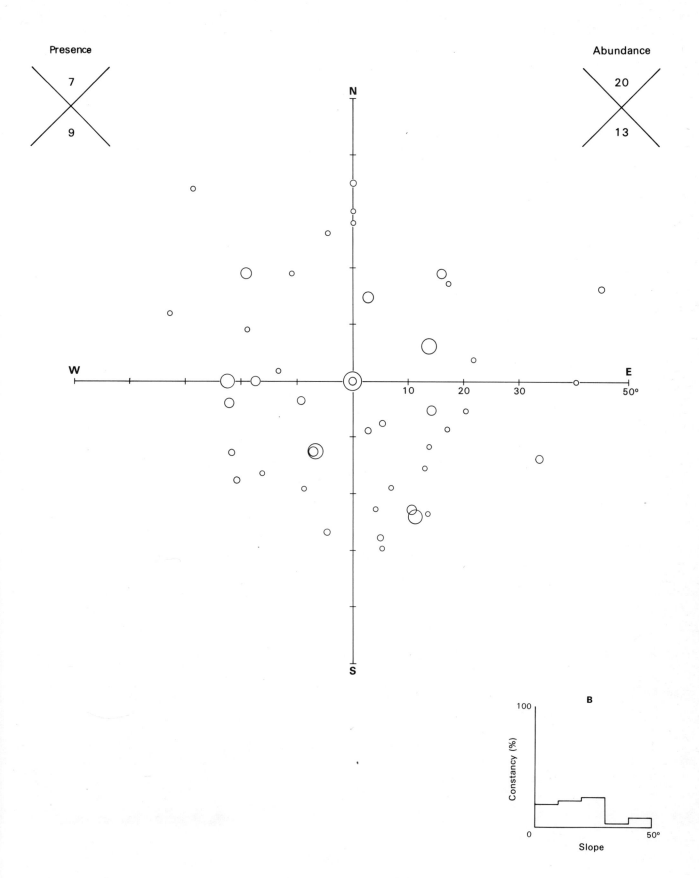

Helianthemum chamaecistus Common Rockrose

Woody undershrub, 5–30 cm, with procumbent or ascending shoots.

Occurrence 10%

Grassland and scrub

Substratum   Frequent on the Carboniferous Limestone. A calcicole.

Slope and aspect   Confined to areas of sloping ground.

Grazing and burning   On the Carboniferous Limestone *H. chamaecistus* is commoner in burned sites, although it is unlikely to be tolerant of frequent or intense fires. Associated with grazing on the Magnesian Limestone.

Frequency distribution   Class 2.

B.S.B.I. Atlas   Virtually confined to calcareous substrata in England, Scotland and Wales.

Biological Flora   Proctor (1956).

	TS	CL	MG	CM	ML	BS
			Geological formation			
pH (0–3 cm)						
3.0–4.0	—	—	—	—	—	—
4.1–5.0	1	2	—	—	—	—
5.1–6.0	—	9	—	—	2	—
6.1–7.0	—	17	—	—	2	—
7.1–8.0	—	23	—	—	6	—
pH (9–12 cm)						
2.8–4.0	—	—	—	—	—	—
4.1–5.0	1	2	—	—	—	—
5.1–6.0	—	5	—	—	—	—
6.1–7.0	—	13	—	—	3	—
7.1–8.1	—	31	—	—	7	—
Constancy (%)	3	**29**	*0*	*0*	12	*0*
Ungrazed, unburned	—	19	0	0	—	0
Grazed, unburned	0	22	0	0	40	—
Ungrazed, burned	6	35	—	0	6	—
Grazed, burned	—	52	—	—	—	—

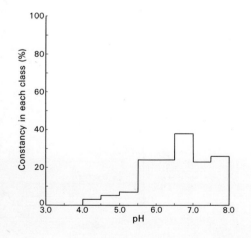

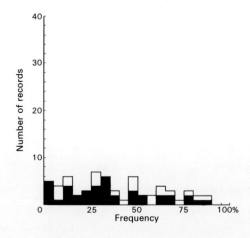

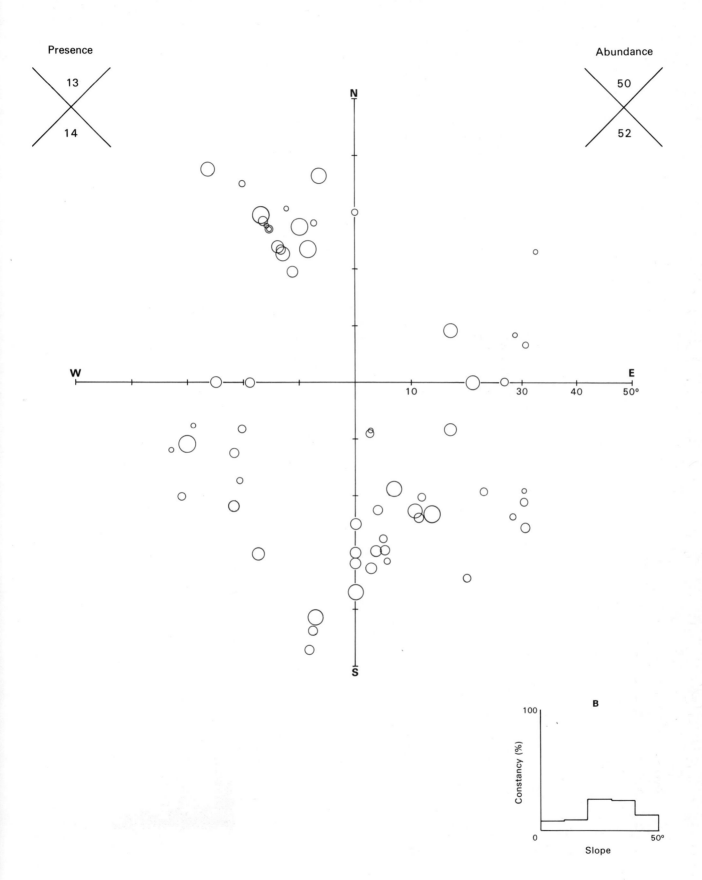

Helictotrichon pratense Meadow Oat

Tufted perennial grass, 30–60 cm.

Occurrence 16%

Grassland

Substratum Abundant on Carboniferous Limestone. Frequent on Toadstone and Magnesian Limestone. Common only on soils of high base-status.

Slope and aspect Concentrated on slopes between 10° and 40°. No statistically significant differences associated with aspect, although the highest frequencies occur on south-facing slopes.

Grazing and burning Apparently favoured by grazing on Toadstone and Magnesian Limestone. Frequent in each category on the Carboniferous Limestone. Known to be tolerant of periodic burning (Lloyd 1968).

Frequency distribution Class 2.

B.S.B.I. Atlas Confined to calcareous substrata. Absent from Ireland.

		Geological formation				
	TS	CL	MG	CM	ML	BS
pH (0–3 cm)						
3.0–4.0	—	2	—	—	—	—
4.1–5.0	3	9	—	—	—	—
5.1–6.0	5	20	—	—	4	—
6.1–7.0	2	23	—	—	2	—
7.1–8.0	—	22	—	—	10	—
pH (9–12 cm)						
2.8–4.0	—	—	—	—	—	—
4.1–5.0	6	5	—	—	—	—
5.1–6.0	3	14	—	—	1	—
6.1–7.0	1	20	—	—	5	—
7.1–8.1	—	37	—	—	10	—
Constancy (%)	26	**42**	*0*	*0*	19	*0*
Ungrazed, unburned	—	29	0	0	—	0
Grazed, unburned	53	45	0	0	50	—
Ungrazed, burned	6	49	—	0	13	—
Grazed, burned	—	33	—	—	—	—

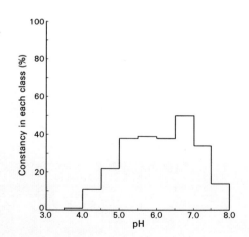

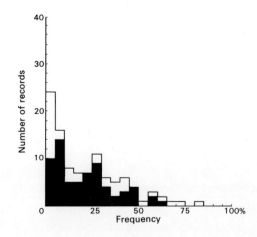

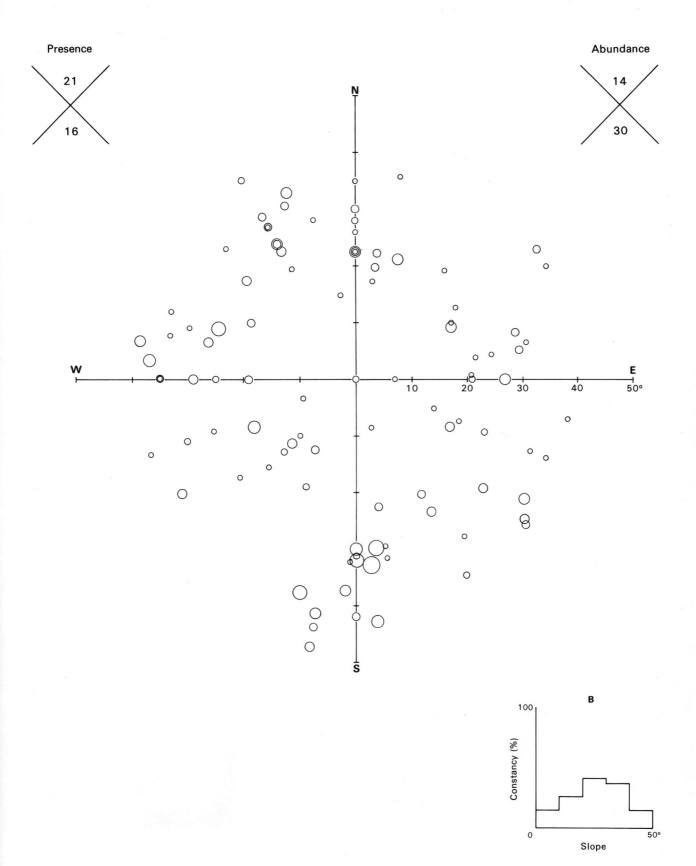

Presence
21
16

Abundance
14
30

N

W   E
10   20   30   40   50°

S

B

100

Constancy (%)

0   50°
Slope

Helictotrichon pubescens Hairy Oat

Erect perennial grass, 30–70 cm.

Occurrence 12%

Grassland and scrub

Substratum Except for four occurrences on the Toadstone, confined to limestone. Restricted to base-rich and calcareous soils.

Slope and aspect Most common on sloping ground in the range 20–40°. No obvious influence of aspect.

Grazing and burning No marked effects.

Frequency distribution Class 2.

B.S.B.I. Atlas Virtually confined to calcareous substrata. Frequent in Ireland.

	TS	CL	MG	CM	ML	BS
			Geological formation			
pH (0–3 cm)						
3.0–4.0	—	—	—	—	—	—
4.1–5.0	—	2	—	—	1	—
5.1–6.0	1	18	—	—	4	—
6.1–7.0	2	17	—	—	3	—
7.1–8.0	1	18	—	—	8	—
pH (9–12 cm)						
2.8–4.0	—	—	—	—	—	—
4.1–5.0	1	1	—	—	—	—
5.1–6.0	1	7	—	—	1	—
6.1–7.0	1	17	—	—	7	—
7.1–8.1	1	29	—	—	8	—
Constancy (%)	11	**31**	*0*	*0*	**19**	*0*
Ungrazed, unburned	—	19	0	0	—	0
Grazed, unburned	0	30	0	0	30	—
Ungrazed, burned	19	27	—	0	19	—
Grazed, burned	—	52	—	—	—	—

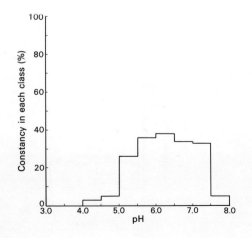

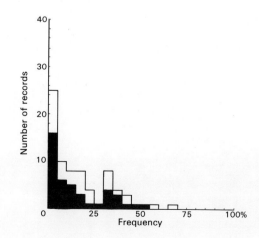

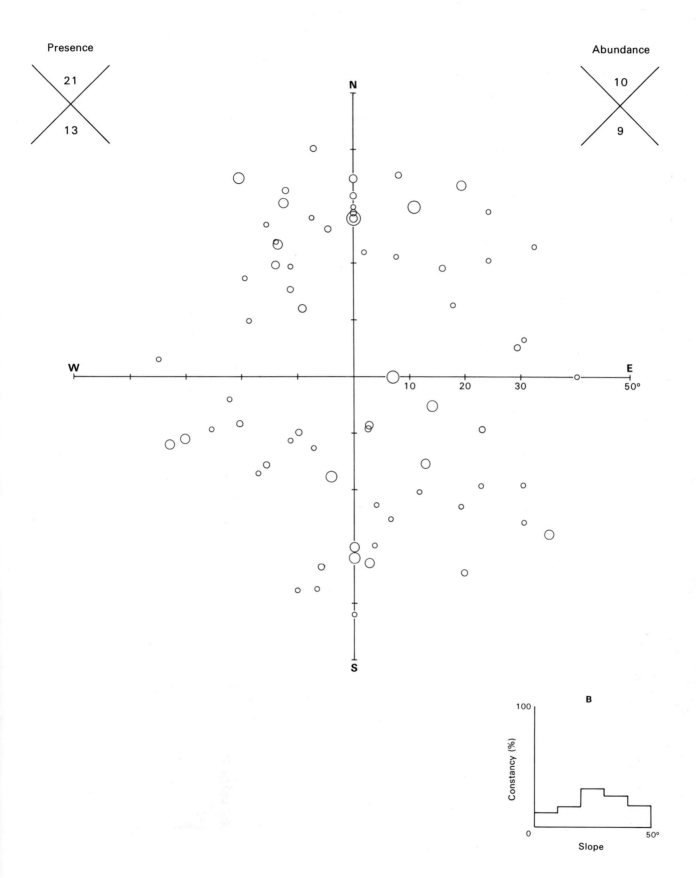

Presence

21

13

Abundance

10

9

N

W   E

10   20   30   50°

S

Constancy (%)

100

B

0   50°

Slope

Heracleum sphondylium Cow Parsnip

Erect biennial herb, 50–200 cm.

Occurrence 10%

Meadows and waste places

Substratum Abundant on the Magnesian Limestone and of common occurrence on the Carboniferous Limestone and Toadstone. Restricted to soils of high base-status.

Slope and aspect Absent only from the steepest slopes. Rather more frequent on southern aspects.

Grazing and burning On the Toadstone the species is confined to ungrazed sites.

Frequency distribution Class 1. A high proportion of the records were due to isolated seedlings.

B.S.B.I. Atlas Ubiquitous.

		Geological formation				
	TS	CL	MG	CM	ML	BS
pH (0–3 cm)						
3.0–4.0	—	—	—	—	—	—
4.1–5.0	—	—	—	3	3	—
5.1–6.0	6	4	—	—	6	—
6.1–7.0	1	8	—	—	6	—
7.1–8.0	1	5	—	—	20	—
pH (9–12 cm)						
2.8–4.0	—	—	—	—	—	—
4.1–5.0	1	—	—	1	2	—
5.1–6.0	6	2	—	2	1	—
6.1–7.0	1	4	—	—	9	—
7.1–8.1	—	12	—	—	23	—
Constancy (%)	**21**	10	*0*	2	**41**	*0*
Ungrazed, unburned	—	10	0	5	—	0
Grazed, unburned	0	11	0	0	30	—
Ungrazed, burned	44	14	—	0	40	—
Grazed, burned	—	0	—	—	—	—

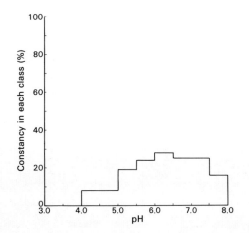

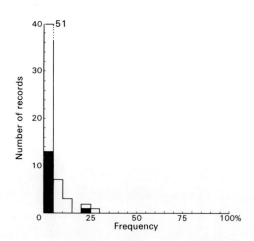

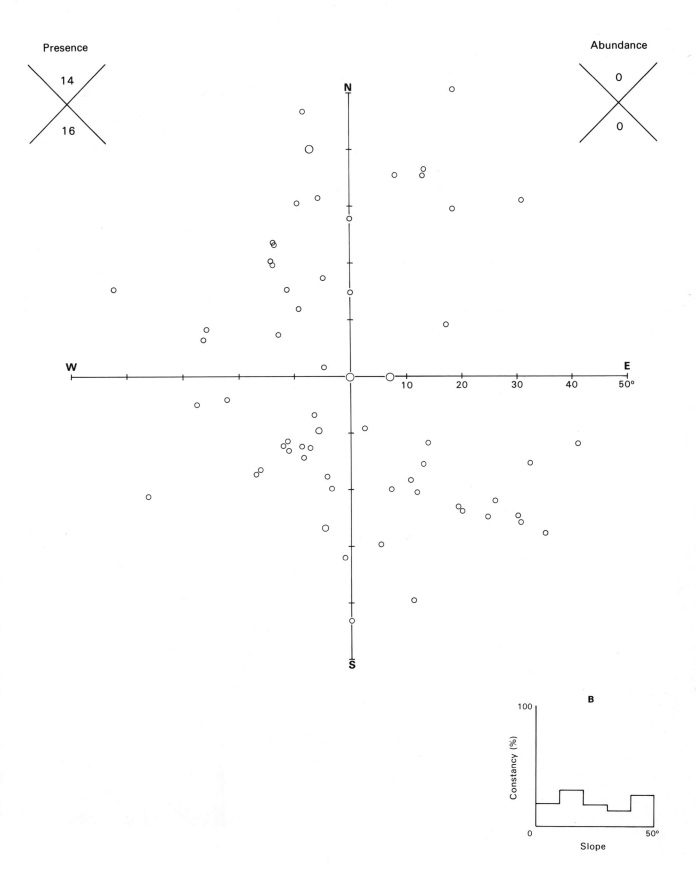

Presence

14

16

Abundance

0

0

N

W

E

10 20 30 40 50°

S

B

Constancy (%)

100

0

0 50°

Slope

Hieracium pilosella   Mouse-ear Hawkweed   *Occurrence* 16%
Perennial herb, 5–15 cm, with prostrate leafy stolons.   Pastures, mine waste and rock outcrops

Substratum   The species is virtually confined to the limestones and the Toadstone. The one record from the Millstone Grit is from a formerly limed pasture. A rather broad calcicolous distribution.

Slope and aspect   Absent from level ground and most frequently recorded on slopes of southern aspect.

Grazing and burning   Consistently commoner in grazed turf than in taller ungrazed or burned vegetation.

Frequency distribution   Class 1–2. High frequency values were recorded in samples situated at the margins of screes.

B.S.B.I. Atlas   Ubiquitous.

		Geological formation				
	TS	CL	MG	CM	ML	BS
pH (0–3 cm)						
3.0–4.0	—	—	—	—	—	—
4.1–5.0	3	4	1	—	1	—
5.1–6.0	5	16	—	1	3	—
6.1–7.0	4	11	—	—	5	—
7.1–8.0	—	12	—	—	29	—
pH (9–12 cm)						
2.8–4.0	—	—	—	—	—	—
4.1–5.0	6	3	1	—	—	—
5.1–6.0	3	11	—	—	1	—
6.1–7.0	3	15	—	—	3	—
7.1–8.1	—	14	—	1	33	—
Constancy (%)	**32**	**24**	*1*	*1*	**45**	*0*
Ungrazed, unburned	—	23	0	2	—	0
Grazed, unburned	47	33	1	0	60	—
Ungrazed, burned	19	19	—	0	45	—
Grazed, burned	—	5	—	—	—	—

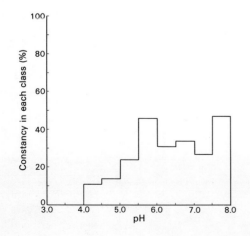

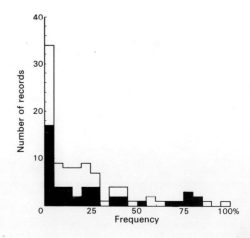

94

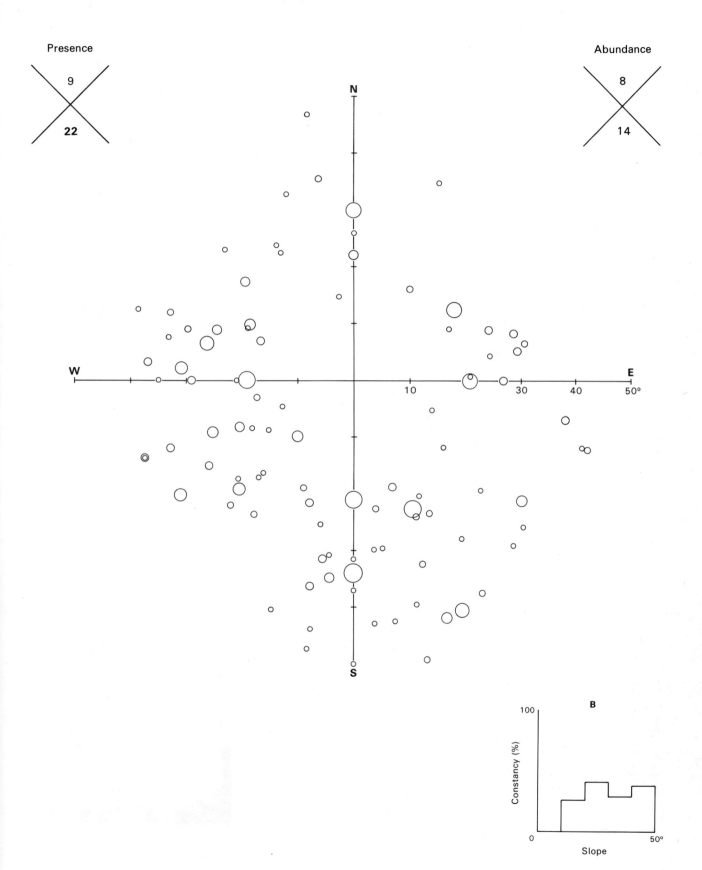

Holcus lanatus Yorkshire Fog

Perennial grass, 20–60 cm.

Occurrence 21%

Grassland (especially meadows) and waste places

Substratum   A common species but scarce on the Millstone Grit and not recorded on the Bunter Sandstone. With increasing soil acidity the species becomes more constant in occurrence but suffers a marked decline below pH 4.0.

Slope and aspect   Widely distributed, but rather more records on north-facing slopes. The eastern bias in higher frequency values deserves an explanation!

Grazing and burning   On the Toadstone and Magnesian Limestone burning appears to have a deleterious effect on the species.

Frequency distribution   Class 1–2.

B.S.B.I. Atlas   Ubiquitous.

Biological Flora   Beddows (1961).

	Geological formation					
	TS	CL	MG	CM	ML	BS
pH (0–3 cm)						
3.0–4.0	—	1	2	2	—	—
4.1–5.0	3	19	5	12	3	—
5.1–6.0	9	28	1	2	2	—
6.1–7.0	1	16	—	—	2	—
7.1–8.0	1	12	—	—	10	—
pH (9–12 cm)						
2.8–4.0	—	2	2	—	—	—
4.1–5.0	6	11	1	8	1	—
5.1–6.0	6	19	5	7	2	—
6.1–7.0	2	19	—	—	3	—
7.1–8.1	—	22	—	1	11	—
Constancy (%)	**37**	**43**	*5*	*13*	20	*0*
Ungrazed, unburned	—	26	0	23	—	0
Grazed, unburned	47	45	6	5	50	—
Ungrazed, burned	19	49	—	0	15	—
Grazed, burned	—	43	—	—	—	—

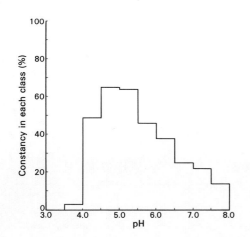

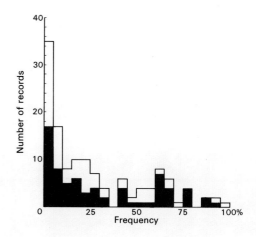

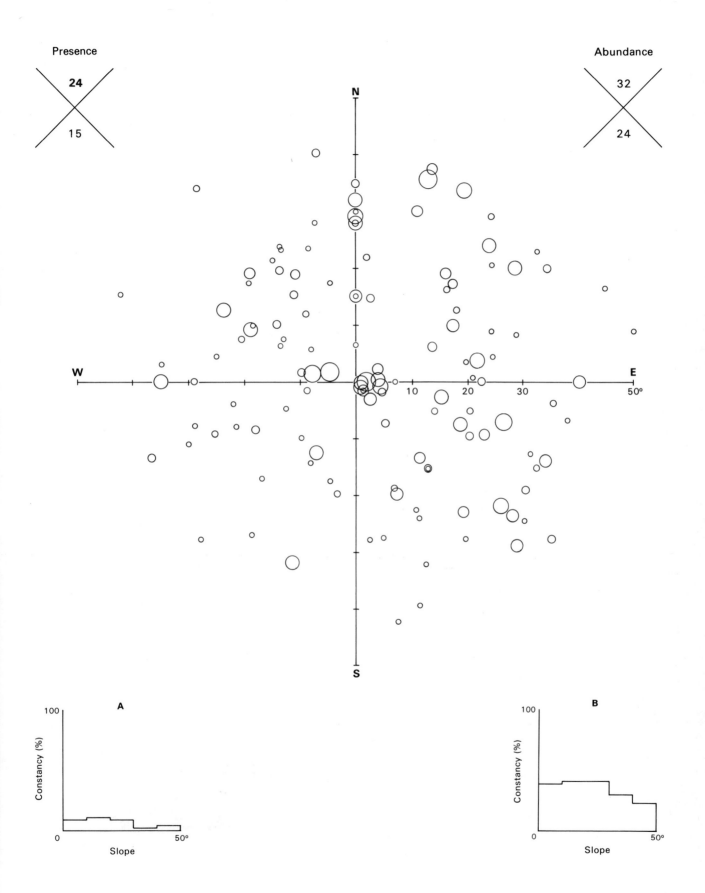

Presence

24

15

Abundance

32

24

N

W   10   20   30   E   50°

S

A

100

Constancy (%)

0   50°

Slope

B

100

Constancy (%)

0   50°

Slope

Holcus mollis Creeping Soft-grass

Rhizomatous perennial grass, 20–60 cm.

Occurrence 8%

Woodland and scrub

Substratum Common only on the Bunter Sandstone, but frequent on the Coal Measures. Very few sites on other strata. A calcifuge species, more familiar as a plant of acidic woodland soils.

Slope and aspect The concentration of the species on flat or gently sloping ground coincides with the distribution of samples from the Bunter Sandstone. On other strata the species does not show a distinct pattern with respect to slope or aspect.

Grazing and burning The species is particularly abundant on the Bunter Sandstone where only ungrazed and unburned sites were available. On the Coal Measures, there are no clear differences with respect to grazing or burning regime.

Frequency distribution Class 2–3.

B.S.B.I. Atlas Ubiquitous except in the SE Midlands.

Biological Flora Ovington and Scurfield (1956).

	TS	CL	MG	CM	ML	BS
			Geological formation			
pH (0–3 cm)						
3.0–4.0	—	—	6	21	—	16
4.1–5.0	1	—	—	4	—	1
5.1–6.0	—	1	—	—	—	—
6.1–7.0	1	—	—	—	—	—
7.1–8.0	—	—	—	—	1	—
pH (9–12 cm)						
2.8–4.0	—	—	6	14	—	13
4.1–5.0	1	—	—	8	—	4
5.1–6.0	—	—	—	3	—	—
6.1–7.0	1	—	—	—	1	—
7.1–8.1	—	1	—	—	—	—
Constancy (%)	5	*1*	*4*	**20**	*1*	**47**
Ungrazed, unburned	—	0	0	16	—	47
Grazed, unburned	13	1	4	22	0	—
Ungrazed, burned	0	0	—	33	1	—
Grazed, burned	—	0	—	—	—	—

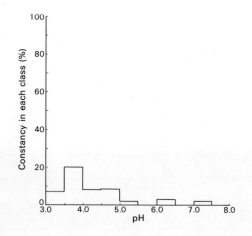

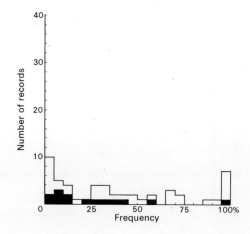

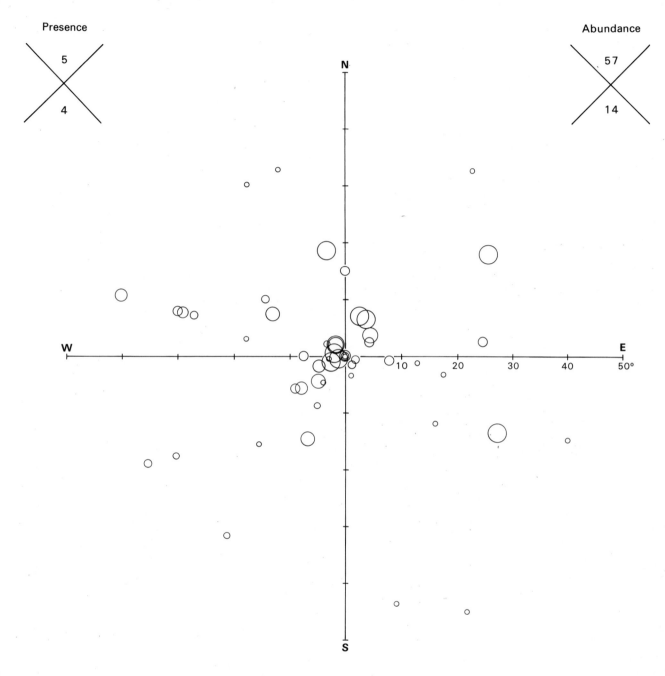

Presence

5
4

Abundance

57
14

N

W   E
                                    10   20   30   40   50°

S

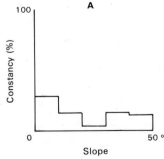

A

100

Constancy (%)

0   50°

Slope

Hypochoeris radicata Cat's Ear   *Occurrence* 6%

Perennial herb, 7–25 cm, with prostrate rosettes.   Pastures, lawns and waste places

Substratum   Frequent on the Magnesian Limestone; scattered occurrences elsewhere. Confined to base rich or calcareous soils.

Slope and aspect   Occurrences over the range in slope 0–50°. The concentration of sites containing the species on slopes of SW aspect reflects a bias in sampling from the Magnesian Limestone.

Grazing and burning   No clear relationships apparent.

Frequency distribution   Class 1.

B.S.B.I. Atlas   Ubiquitous.

		Geological formation				
	TS	CL	MG	CM	ML	BS
pH (0–3 cm)						
3.0–4.0	—	—	—	2	—	—
4.1–5.0	—	1	—	3	1	—
5.1–6.0	3	3	—	—	4	—
6.1–7.0	—	—	—	—	5	—
7.1–8.0	1	—	—	—	16	—
pH (9–12 cm)						
2.8–4.0	—	—	—	—	—	—
4.1–5.0	2	1	—	3	—	—
5.1–6.0	2	2	—	2	1	—
6.1–7.0	—	1	—	—	4	—
7.1–8.1	—	—	—	—	20	—
Constancy (%)	11	2	0	4	31	0
Ungrazed, unburned	—	0	0	8	—	0
Grazed, unburned	7	4	0	0	20	—
Ungrazed, burned	13	0	—	0	36	—
Grazed, burned	—	0	—	—	—	—

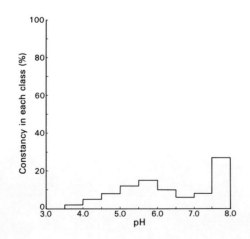

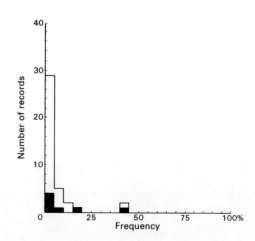

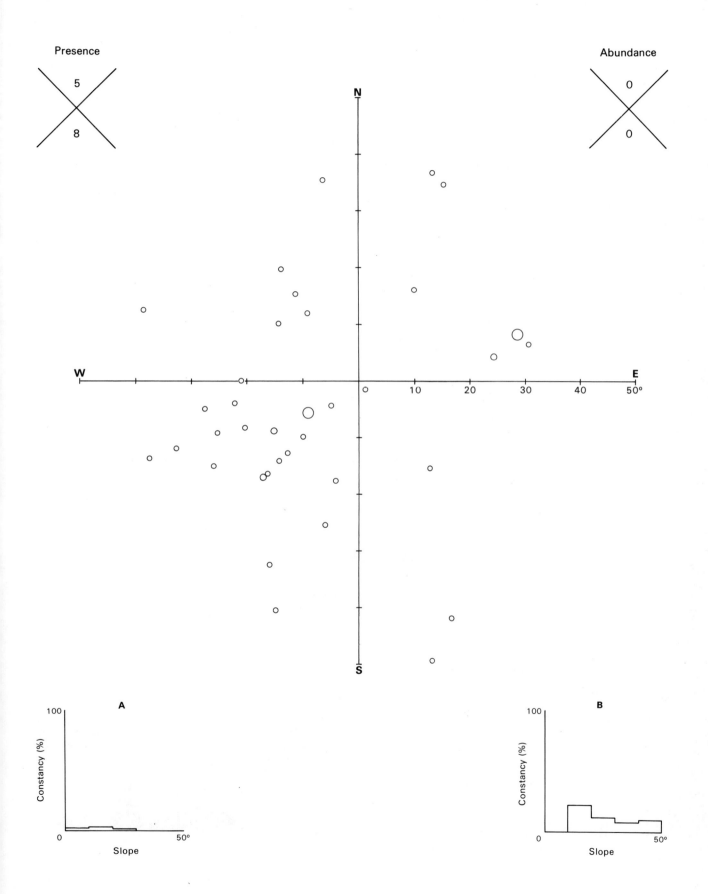

Presence

5
8

Abundance

0
0

N

W

E

S

0   10   20   30   40   50°

A

Constancy (%)

100

0   50°

Slope

B

Constancy (%)

100

0   50°

Slope

Koeleria cristata Crested Hair-grass
Tufted perennial grass, 10–40 cm.

Occurrence 22%

Grassland and stable sand dunes

Substratum Abundant on the Carboniferous Limestone and on grazed sites on the Toadstone and Magnesian Limestone. Frequent on base-rich and calcareous soils and showing a fairly abrupt decline in frequency of occurrence below pH 4.5.

Slope and aspect The species is of common occurrence on slopes over the range 20–50°. There are no apparent differences in occurrence or frequency associated with aspect.

Grazing and burning A marked association with grazing on the Toadstone and Magnesian Limestone. The apparent lack of a similar relationship on the Carboniferous Limestone may reflect the changing practices of management on this stratum, one result of which is the inclusion of recently abandoned pastures in the ungrazed categories.

Frequency distribution Class 2.

B.S.B.I. Atlas Virtually confined to calcareous substrata (including coastal dunes).

| | Geological formation | | | | | |
	TS	CL	MG	CM	ML	BS
pH (0–3 cm)						
3.0–4.0	—	1	—	—	—	—
4.1–5.0	2	15	—	—	—	—
5.1–6.0	4	30	—	—	1	—
6.1–7.0	6	28	—	—	1	—
7.1–8.0	2	36	—	—	7	—
pH (9–12 cm)						
2.8–4.0	—	—	—	—	—	—
4.1–5.0	9	9	—	—	—	—
5.1–6.0	2	19	—	—	—	—
6.1–7.0	3	28	—	—	2	—
7.1–8.1	—	52	—	—	7	—
Constancy (%)	**37**	**60**	*0*	*0*	*11*	*0*
Ungrazed, unburned	—	39	0	0	—	0
Grazed, unburned	53	69	0	0	50	—
Ungrazed, burned	6	65	—	0	3	—
Grazed, burned	—	43	—	—	—	—

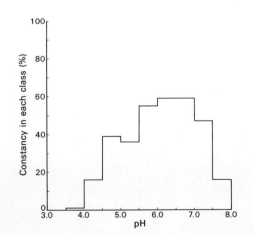

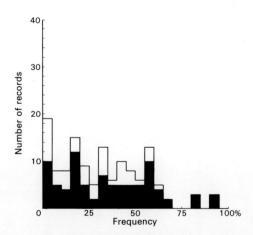

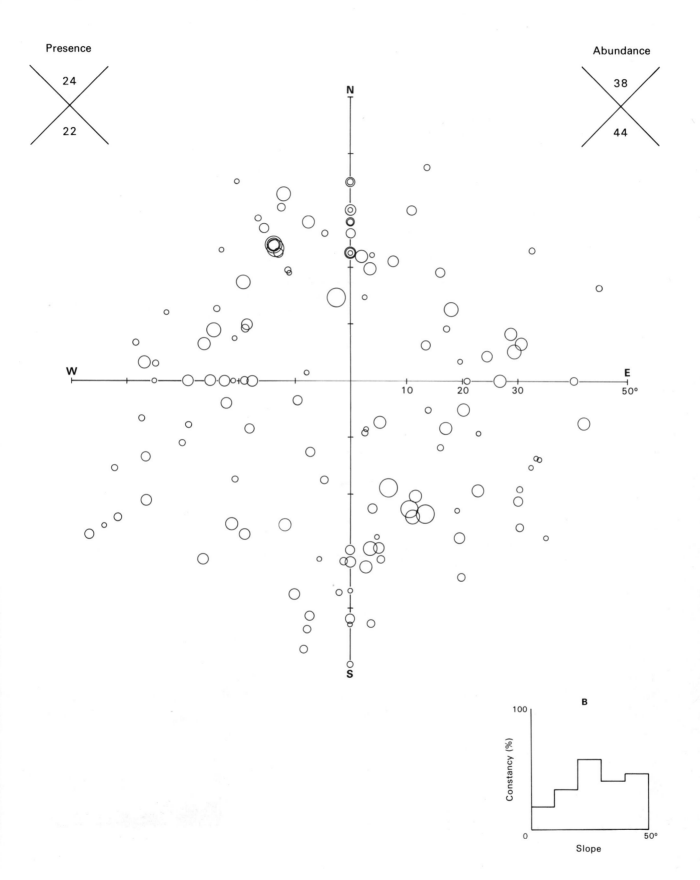

Presence

24

22

Abundance

38

44

N

W ⊢————————————————————————————————————— E
10   20   30   50°

S

B

100

Constancy (%)

0   50°
Slope

Leontodon hispidus Rough Hawkbit

Occurrence 13%

Perennial herb, 10–20 cm, with rosette of ascending leaves.

Grassland and waste places

Substratum A calcicole, particularly abundant on the Magnesian Limestone where the constancy is twice that attained on the Carboniferous Limestone.

Slope and aspect Confined to sloping ground (10–40°). Rather more abundant on north-facing slopes. The scarcity of *Leontodon hispidus* from south-facing grassland on the Magnesian Limestone may be due to competition from *Brachypodium pinnatum* (cf. *Chrysanthemum leucanthemum*).

Grazing and burning The species is most common in grazed sites.

Frequency distribution Class 2.

B.S.B.I. Atlas Widespread in England, Wales and central Ireland. Infrequent elsewhere.

	TS	CL	MG	CM	ML	BS
			Geological formation			
pH (0–3 cm)						
3.0–4.0	—	—	—	—	—	—
4.1–5.0	—	2	—	—	—	—
5.1–6.0	1	10	—	—	3	—
6.1–7.0	1	11	—	—	8	—
7.1–8.0	—	18	—	—	29	—
pH (9–12 cm)						
2.8–4.0	—	—	—	—	—	—
4.1–5.0	—	1	—	—	—	—
5.1–6.0	1	7	—	—	1	—
6.1–7.0	1	12	—	—	6	—
7.1–8.1	—	23	—	—	32	—
Constancy (%)	5	**23**	*0*	*0*	**47**	*0*
Ungrazed, unburned	—	26	0	0	—	0
Grazed, unburned	7	35	0	0	100	—
Ungrazed, burned	0	0	—	0	36	—
Grazed, burned	—	10	—	—	—	—

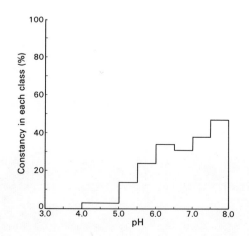

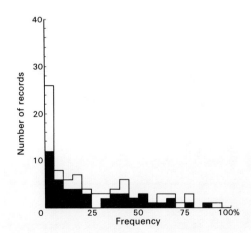

Presence

17

12

Abundance

38

20

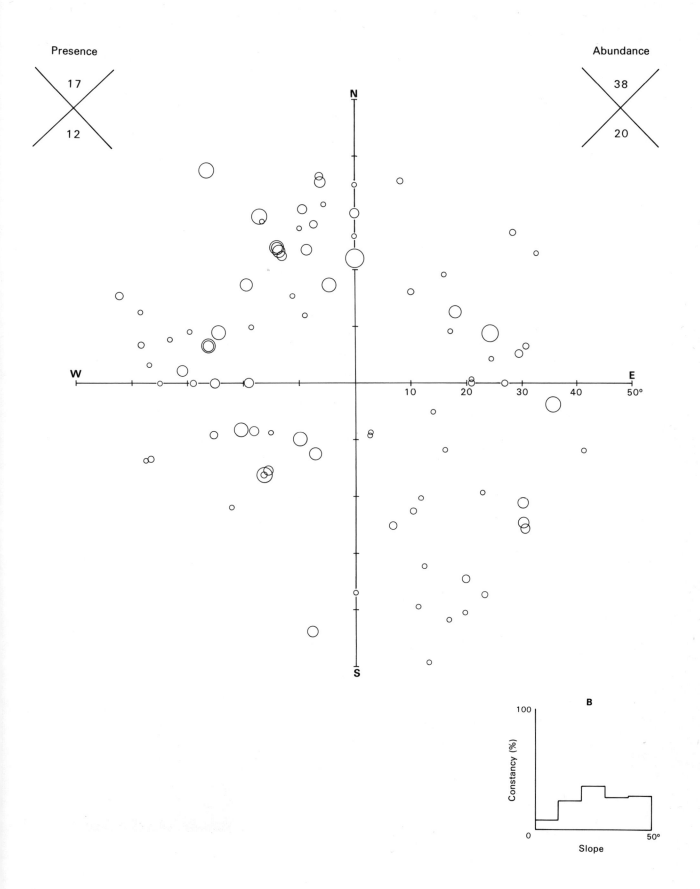

N

W   E

10   20   30   40   50°

S

B

100

Constancy (%)

0   50°

Slope

Linum catharticum Purging Flax

Annual or biennial herb, 5–25 cm.

Occurrence 16%

Grassland, rock outcrops and calcareous flushes

Substratum   Virtually confined to limestone. Known to occur locally on roadsides and other base-rich areas of the Millstone Grit. Elsewhere *L. catharticum* also occurs in meso- and eutrophic mire (Ratcliffe 1964). Calcicole with an optimum about pH 7.0.

Slope and aspect   Occurs most commonly in slope range 20–45°. The species shows a tendency to occur with increased frequencies on north-facing slopes.

Grazing and burning   On the Magnesian Limestone, most common on grazed sites.

Frequency distribution   Class 2.

B.S.B.I. Atlas   A fairly common plant throughout the British Isles.

	TS	CL	MG	CM	ML	BS
			Geological formation			
pH (0–3 cm)						
3.0–4.0	—	—	—	—	—	—
4.1–5.0	1	1	—	—	—	—
5.1–6.0	—	13	—	—	2	—
6.1–7.0	—	25	—	—	5	—
7.1–8.0	—	29	—	—	26	—
pH (9–12 cm)						
2.8–4.0	—	—	—	—	—	—
4.1–5.0	1	—	—	—	—	—
5.1–6.0	—	7	—	—	1	—
6.1–7.0	—	23	—	—	3	—
7.1–8.1	—	36	—	—	29	—
Constancy (%)	*3*	**38**	*0*	*0*	**39**	*0*
Ungrazed, unburned	—	19	0	0	—	0
Grazed, unburned	7	44	0	0	70	—
Ungrazed, burned	0	41	—	0	31	—
Grazed, burned	—	29	—	—	—	—

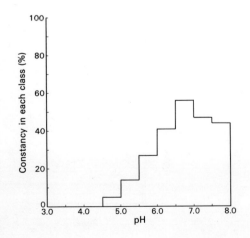

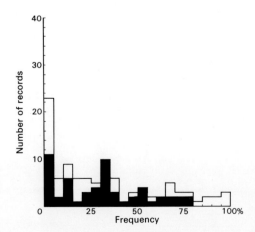

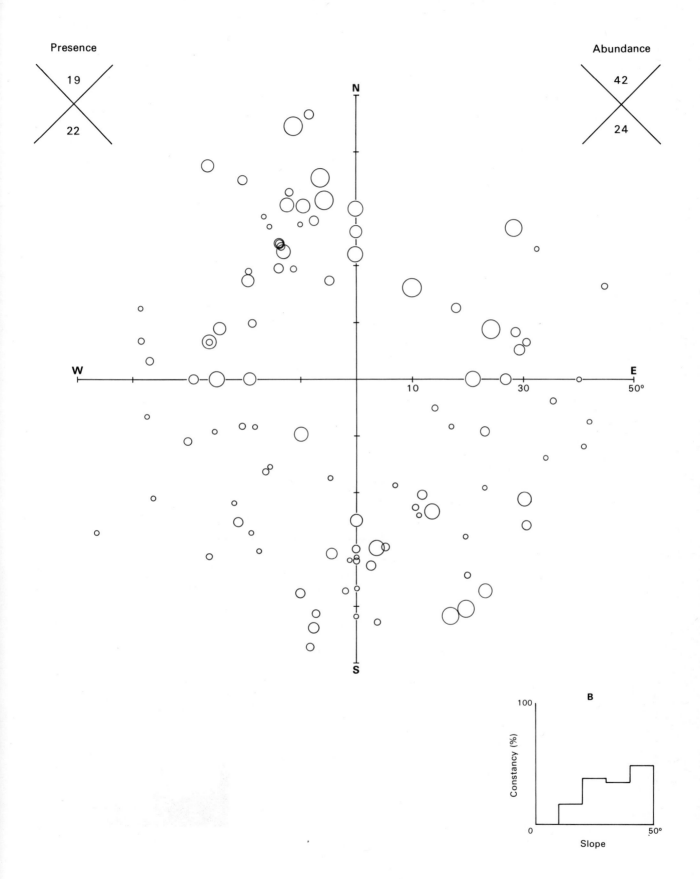

Lotus corniculatus Birdsfoot-trefoil

Occurrence 25%

Perennial herb, 10–40 cm, with prostrate or ascending shoots.

Grassland and waste places

Substratum *L. corniculatus* is the most commonly occurring legume in the semi-natural grasslands examined. It is abundant on limestone and Toadstone and shows a peak in occurrence in the pH range 6.0–6.5.

Slope and aspect Records are concentrated in the slope range 15–40° and are more numerous where the aspect is southern. High frequencies are particularly common on steep south-facing slopes.

Grazing and burning *L. corniculatus* is equally common in grazed and burned grassland.

Frequency distribution Class 2.

B.S.B.I. Atlas Ubiquitous.

	TS	CL	MG	CM	ML	BS
			Geological formation			
pH (0–3 cm)						
3.0–4.0	—	—	—	—	—	—
4.1–5.0	2	12	—	4	1	—
5.1–6.0	8	28	—	1	10	—
6.1–7.0	7	26	—	—	8	—
7.1–8.0	2	18	—	—	32	—
pH (9–12 cm)						
2.8–4.0	—	—	—	—	—	—
4.1–5.0	7	5	—	2	1	—
5.1–6.0	7	18	—	2	1	—
6.1–7.0	4	25	—	—	11	—
7.1–8.1	1	36	—	1	38	—
Constancy (%)	**50**	**47**	*0*	*4*	**60**	*0*
Ungrazed, unburned	—	32	0	5	—	0
Grazed, unburned	53	42	0	5	60	—
Ungrazed, burned	25	65	—	0	58	—
Grazed, burned	—	52	—	—	—	—

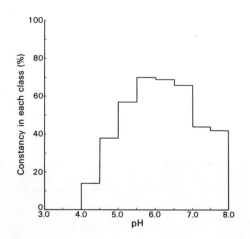

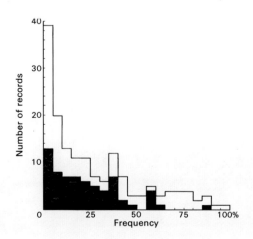

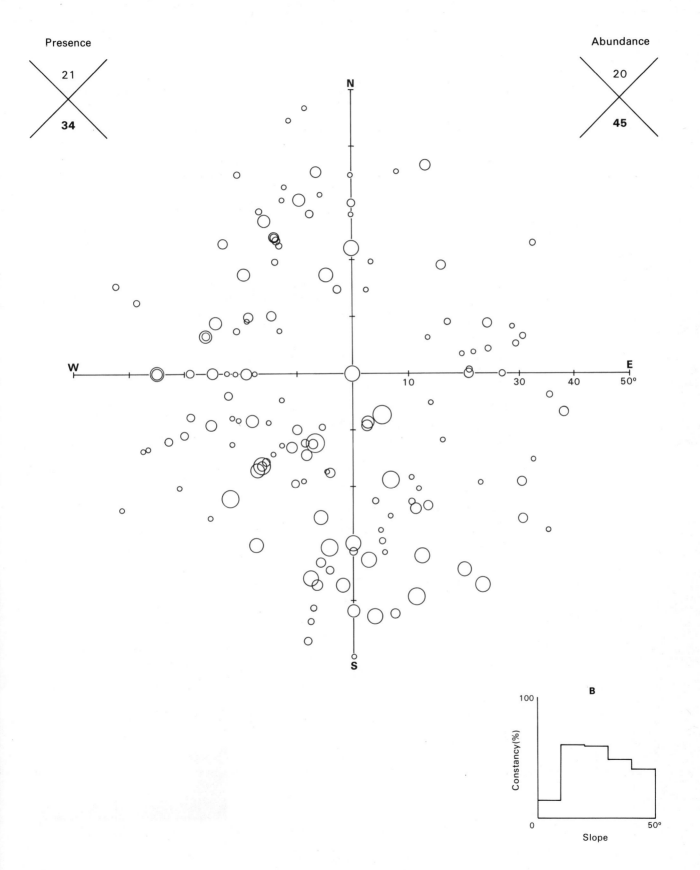

Presence
21
34

Abundance
20
45

N

W
10   30   40   50°
E

S

B

100

Constancy (%)

0   50°
Slope

Luzula campestris Field Woodrush

Tufted perennial rush, up to 15 cm.
A few of the records on very acidic soils may be of *L. multiflora*.

Occurrence 29%
Grassland and heathland

Substratum   Present in grassland on all strata; very abundant on the Toadstone. Very wide-ranging with respect to soil type, but most common on soils of intermediate base-status.

Slope and aspect   Most common on flat ground and gentle slopes but present on slopes of all aspects up to 45° with a bias towards those of northern aspect. On the Carboniferous Limestone, *L. campestris* shows the highest frequency values on north-facing slopes.

Grazing and burning   Consistently more abundant at grazed rather than burned sites.
Frequency distribution   Class 2.
B.S.B.I. Atlas   Widespread.

	Geological formation					
	TS	CL	MG	CM	ML	BS
pH (0–3 cm)						
3.0–4.0	1	5	16	10	—	7
4.1–5.0	7	19	4	5	—	3
5.1–6.0	12	24	2	1	3	—
6.1–7.0	5	18	—	—	3	—
7.1–8.0	2	8	—	—	4	—
pH (9–12 cm)						
2.8–4.0	—	4	15	7	—	6
4.1–5.0	15	11	4	8	1	4
5.1–6.0	9	22	3	1	1	—
6.1–7.0	3	16	—	—	3	—
7.1–8.1	—	22	—	—	5	—
Constancy (%)	**71**	**40**	*13*	*15*	*12*	28
Ungrazed, unburned	—	16	0	18	—	28
Grazed, unburned	93	53	16	14	20	—
Ungrazed, burned	38	38	—	9	12	—
Grazed, burned	—	24	—	—	—	—

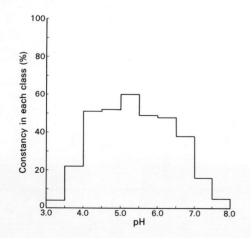

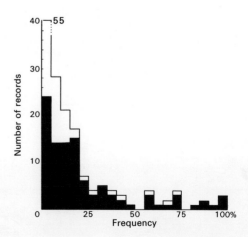

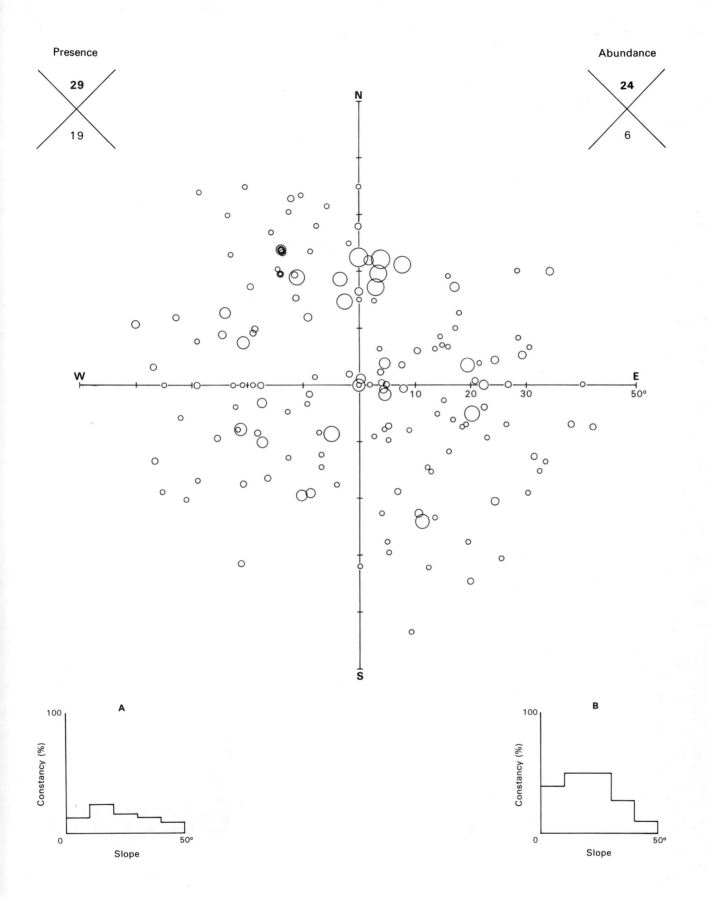

Medicago lupulina Black Medick

Annual or short-lived perennial herb, 5–50 cm.

Occurrence 6%

Open grassland, rock outcrops, waste places

Substratum A calcicole, frequent over the pH range 6.0–8.0. Virtually restricted to limestone.

Slope and aspect Confined rather strictly to slopes of southern aspect.

Grazing and burning On the Carboniferous Limestone locally frequent in burned, ungrazed habitats in which fire has created an open turf (Lloyd 1968).

Frequency distribution Class 2. *M. lupulina* occurred with highest rooted frequency at a burned site on the Carboniferous Limestone.

B.S.B.I. Atlas Ubiquitous in SE Britain, less common elsewhere.

		Geological formation				
	TS	CL	MG	CM	ML	BS
pH (0–3 cm)						
3.0–4.0	—	—	—	—	—	—
4.1–5.0	—	1	—	—	—	—
5.1–6.0	2	5	—	—	—	—
6.1–7.0	—	8	—	—	—	—
7.1–8.0	—	14	—	—	11	—
pH (9–12 cm)						
2.8–4.0	—	—	—	—	—	—
4.1–5.0	—	1	—	—	—	—
5.1–6.0	—	1	—	—	—	—
6.1–7.0	1	7	—	—	—	—
7.1–8.1	1	20	—	—	11	—
Constancy (%)	5	**16**	*0*	*0*	**13**	0
Ungrazed, unburned	—	13	0	0	—	0
Grazed, unburned	0	7	0	0	20	—
Ungrazed, burned	13	46	—	0	12	—
Grazed, burned	—	0	—	—	—	—

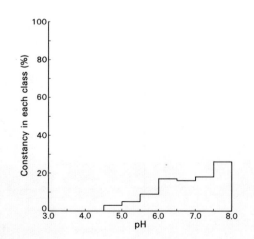

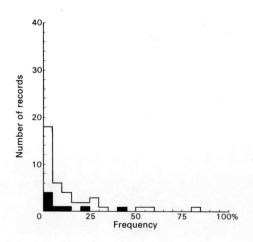

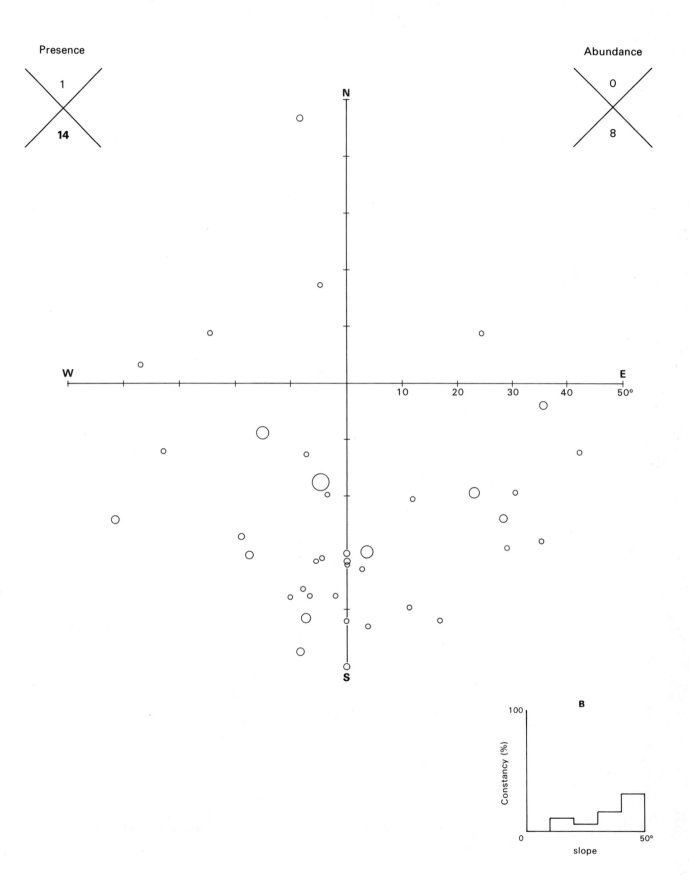

Presence

1

14

Abundance

0

8

N

W

10   20   30   40   50°

E

S

B

100

Constancy (%)

0   50°

slope

Mercurialis perennis Dog's Mercury

Rhizomatous perennial herb, 15–40 cm.

Occurrence 4%

Woodland, scrub and hedgerows

Substratum   Found only at sites over limestone. The distribution is that of a strict calcicole. A similar conclusion was reached by De Silva (1934) who examined woodland habitats of *M. perennis* in southern England.

Slope and aspect   With few exceptions the species is restricted to steep slopes of northern aspect. *M. perennis* is a very common woodland plant on the Carboniferous Limestone and the excursion of the species into grassland may be related to the similarity in climate between steep north-facing grassland and woodland. At certain of the sites *M. perennis* may be a relic of former woodland, but it was recorded with highest frequencies at a site which shows no evidence of tree cover in the recent past.

Grazing and burning   Proportionately, the species is most common in sites which are ungrazed and unburned.

Frequency distribution   Class 2.

B.S.B.I. Atlas   Ubiquitous except in north Scotland.

			Geological formation			
	TS	CL	MG	CM	ML	BS
pH (0–3 cm)						
3.0–4.0	—	—	—	—	—	—
4.1–5.0	—	—	—	—	—	—
5.1–6.0	—	3	—	—	—	—
6.1–7.0	—	7	—	—	—	—
7.1–8.0	—	15	—	—	1	—
pH (9–12 cm)						
2.8–4.0	—	—	—	—	—	—
4.1–5.0	—	—	—	—	—	—
5.1–6.0	—	—	—	—	—	—
6.1–7.0	—	5	—	—	—	—
7.1–8.1	—	19	—	—	1	—
Constancy (%)	0	**14**	*0*	*0*	1	0
Ungrazed, unburned	—	29	0	0	—	0
Grazed, unburned	0	12	0	0	0	—
Ungrazed, burned	0	14	—	0	0	—
Grazed, burned	—	0	—	—	—	—

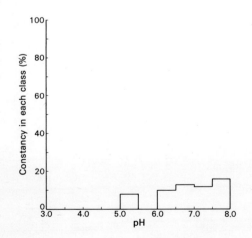

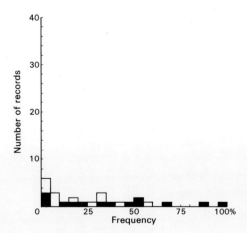

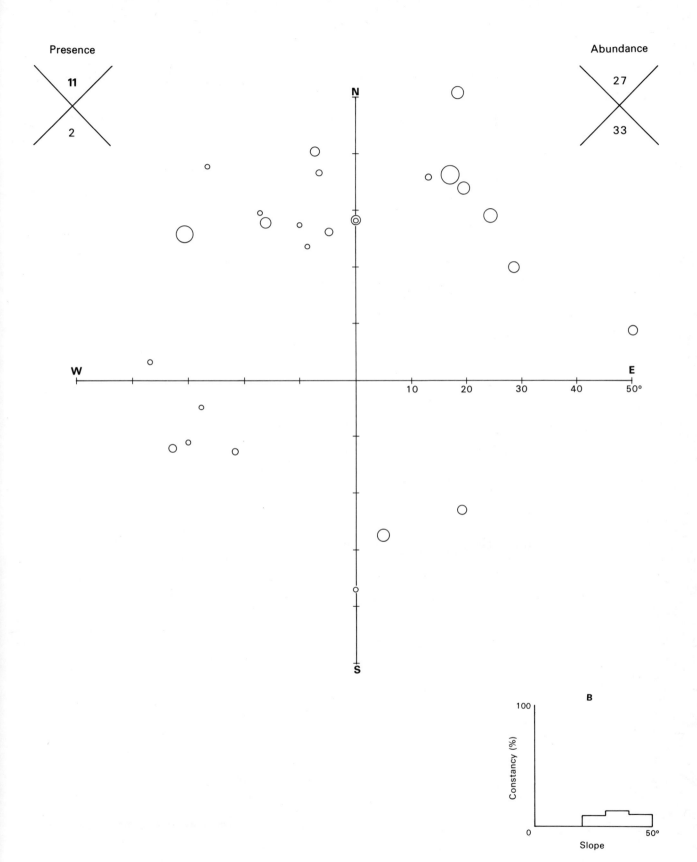

Presence

11

2

Abundance

27

33

N

W   E

10   20   30   40   50°

S

B

100

Constancy (%)

0   50°

Slope

Molinia caerulea Purple Moor-grass

Perennial grass, 30–130 cm, often forming tussocks.

Occurrence 3%

Moorland, fens and grassland

Substratum Recorded locally on Millstone Grit and Coal Measures. Although the distribution pattern obtained is that of a strong calcifuge, the species is known to occur occasionally on base-rich or even calcareous soils in the region.

Slope and aspect The few records show a distinct tendency for the species to occur on flat ground or on gentle slopes of northern aspect.

Grazing and burning Insufficient records.

Frequency distribution Class 2.

B.S.B.I. Atlas Widespread in Britain, but commoner in the north and west.

	TS	CL	MG	CM	ML	BS
				Geological formation		
pH (0–3 cm)						
3.0–4.0	—	—	12	7	—	—
4.1–5.0	—	—	—	1	—	—
5.1–6.0	—	—	—	—	—	—
6.1–7.0	—	—	—	—	—	—
7.1–8.0	—	—	—	—	—	—
pH (9–12 cm)						
2.8–4.0	—	—	12	5	—	—
4.1–5.0	—	—	—	3	—	—
5.1–6.0	—	—	—	—	—	—
6.1–7.0	—	—	—	—	—	—
7.1–8.1	—	—	—	—	—	—
Constancy (%)	0	0	7	7	0	0
Ungrazed, unburned	—	0	32	5	—	0
Grazed, unburned	0	0	2	0	0	—
Ungrazed, burned	0	0	—	5	0	—
Grazed, burned	—	0	—	—	—	—

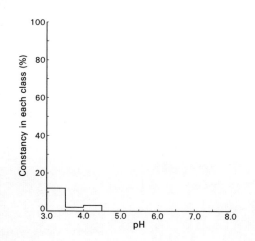

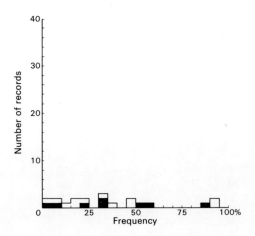

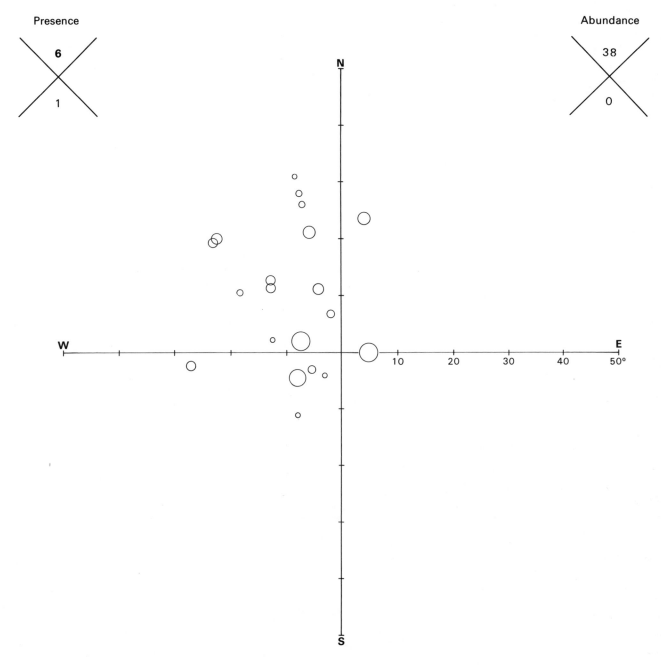

Presence

6

1

Abundance

38

0

N

W

E

10 20 30 40 50°

S

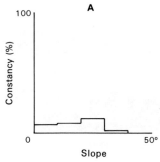

A

100

0

Constancy (%)

Slope

0 50°

Nardus stricta Mat-grass

Tufted perennial grass, 10–30 cm.

Occurrence 21%

Grassland and heathland

Substratum On acidic soils irrespective of geological formation, but frequent only on the Millstone Grit. A strict calcifuge.

Slope and aspect Very common on level ground. On steeper slopes, number of occurrences and frequency values tend to be greater where the aspect is south.

Grazing and burning More frequent in grazed than in ungrazed habitats.

Frequency distribution Class 2.

B.S.B.I. Atlas Predominantly northern and western.

Biological Flora Chadwick (1960).

		TS	CL	MG	CM	ML	BS
				Geological formation			
pH (0–3 cm)							
3.0–4.0		1	5	89	22	—	3
4.1–5.0		1	3	1	1	—	1
5.1–6.0		—	—	2	1	—	—
6.1–7.0		—	—	—	—	—	—
7.1–8.0		—	—	—	—	—	—
pH (9–12 cm)							
2.8–4.0		1	6	90	20	—	4
4.1–5.0		1	2	2	4	—	—
5.1–6.0		—	—	—	—	—	—
6.1–7.0		—	—	—	—	—	—
7.1–8.1		—	—	—	—	—	—
Constancy (%)		5	5	**56**	19	*0*	11
Ungrazed, unburned		—	3	32	10	—	11
Grazed, unburned		0	5	61	35	0	—
Ungrazed, burned		13	5	—	10	0	—
Grazed, burned		—	0	—	—	—	—

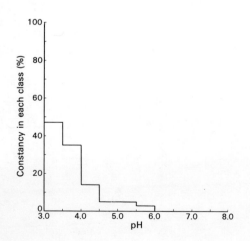

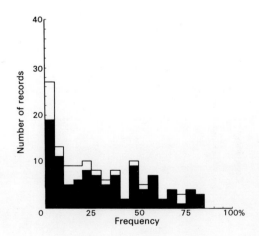

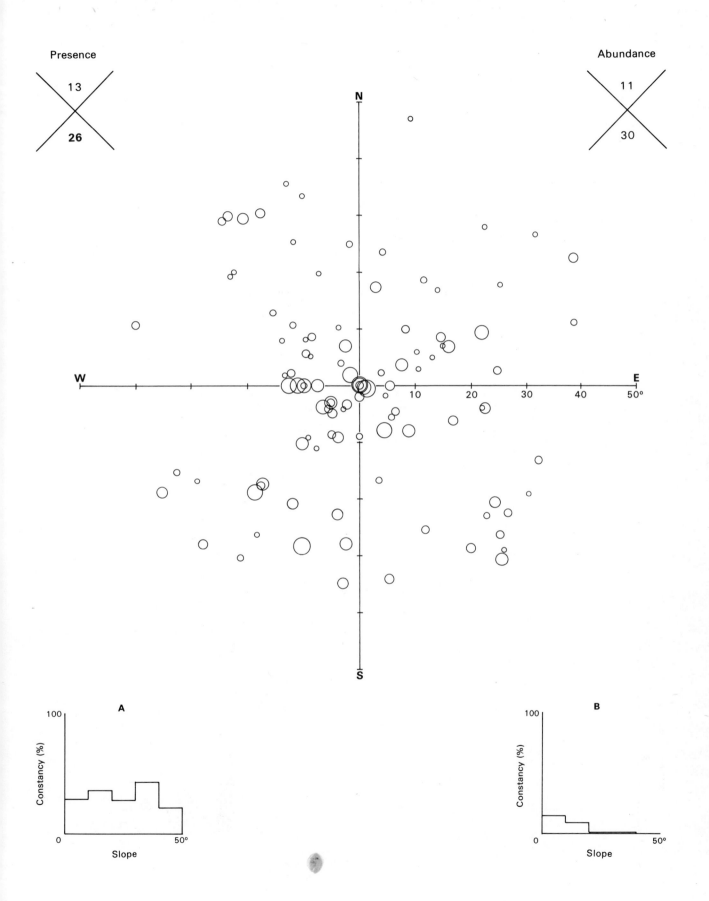

Origanum vulgare Marjoram

Rhizomatous perennial herb, 30–80 cm.

Substratum Encountered only on the Toadstone and the limestones and restricted to soils of high base status. The distribution shown in the pH histogram is due to the varying contribution of burned habitats from two strata (see below) to the different pH classes.

Slope and aspect A strong bias towards southern aspects.

Grazing and burning Strongly represented in communities subject to frequent burning. On the Toadstone these are tall-herb communities on deep soils of intermediate acidity. On the Magnesian Limestone, burned sites are again colonised but here they coincide with shallow, highly calcareous soils.

Frequency distribution Class 1–2. Highest values attained at the Toadstone sites.

B.S.B.I. Atlas Widespread, but concentrated in the south and mainly on calcareous formations.

			Geological formation			
	TS	CL	MG	CM	ML	BS
pH (0–3 cm)						
3.0–4.0	—	—	—	—	—	—
4.1–5.0	—	—	—	—	—	—
5.1–6.0	7	—	—	—	3	—
6.1–7.0	4	1	—	—	5	—
7.1–8.0	—	4	—	—	10	—
pH (9–12 cm)						
2.8–4.0	—	—	—	—	—	—
4.1–5.0	—	—	—	—	—	—
5.1–6.0	7	—	—	—	—	—
6.1–7.0	3	—	—	—	2	—
7.1–8.1	1	5	—	—	16	—
Constancy (%)	**29**	3	*0*	*0*	**21**	0
Ungrazed, unburned	—	7	0	0	—	0
Grazed, unburned	0	2	0	0	0	—
Ungrazed, burned	69	0	—	0	27	—
Grazed, burned	—	5	—	—	—	—

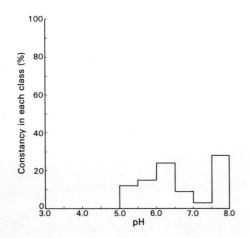

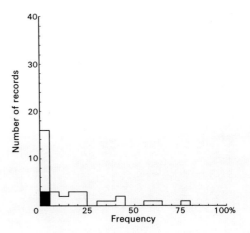

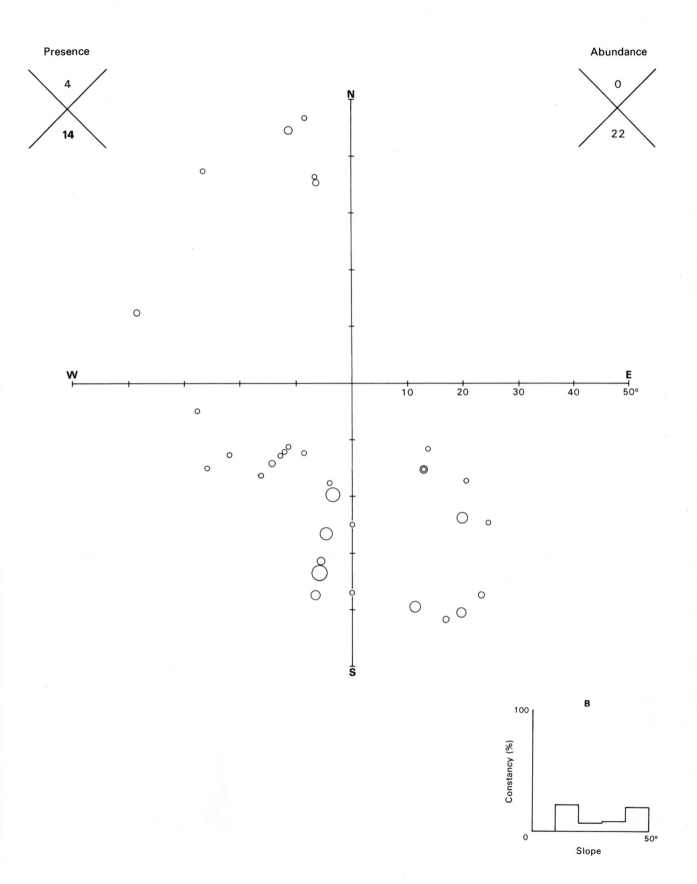

Presence

4

14

Abundance

0

22

N

W   10   20   30   40   50°   E

S

B

100

Constancy (%)

0   50°

Slope

Pimpinella saxifraga Burnet Saxifrage

Perennial herb, 30–100 cm.

Substratum   Frequent on Toadstone and limestone. Restricted to base-rich and calcareous soils.
Slope and aspect   Most abundant on steeply sloping ground. No marked differences associated with aspect.
Grazing and burning   On the Carboniferous Limestone and Toadstone, the species occurs most often in grazed, unburned sites.
Frequency distribution   Class 1–2.
B.S.B.I. Atlas   Widespread in Britain, but concentrated in SE England.

| | Geological formation | | | | | |
	TS	CL	MG	CM	ML	BS
pH (0–3 cm)						
3.0–4.0	—	—	—	—	—	—
4.1–5.0	1	1	—	—	1	—
5.1–6.0	2	8	—	—	5	—
6.1–7.0	5	14	—	—	6	—
7.1–8.0	1	18	—	—	13	—
pH (9–12 cm)						
2.8–4.0	—	—	—	—	—	—
4.1–5.0	6	1	—	—	—	—
5.1–6.0	—	2	—	—	—	—
6.1–7.0	2	13	—	—	4	—
7.1–8.1	1	25	—	—	21	—
Constancy (%)	**24**	**23**	*0*	*0*	**29**	*0*
Ungrazed, unburned	—	10	0	0	—	0
Grazed, unburned	33	33	0	0	20	—
Ungrazed, burned	19	16	—	0	31	—
Grazed, burned	—	5	—	—	—	—

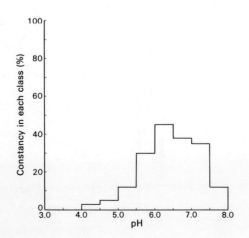

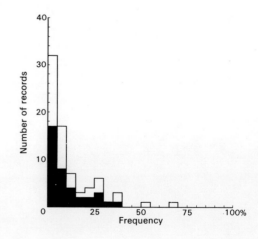

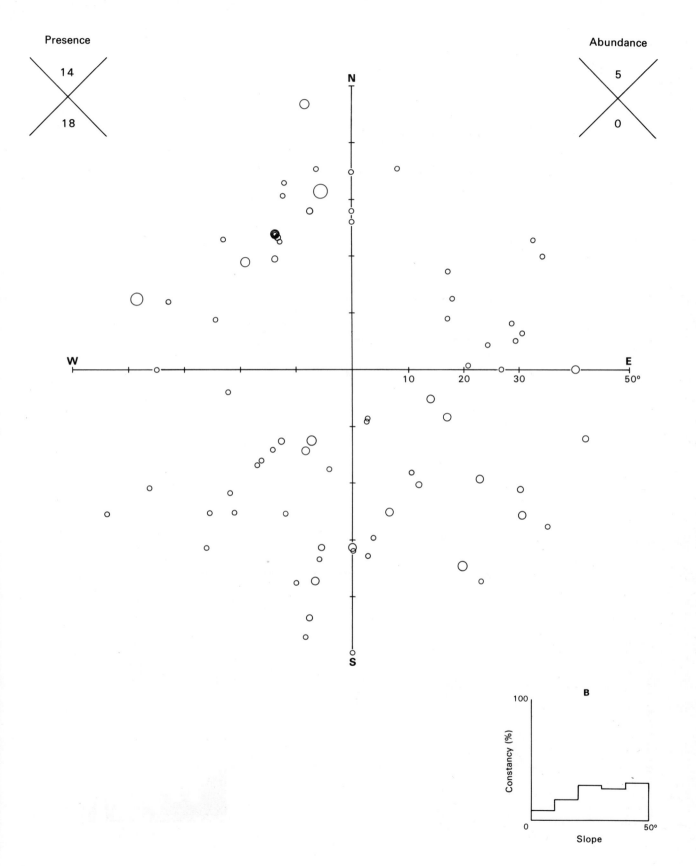

Presence
14
18

Abundance
5
0

N

W   E
                    10   20   30   50°

S

100

Constancy (%)

B

0   50°
              Slope

Plantago lanceolata Ribwort

Perennial rosette herb, (2–)10–15(–30) cm.

Occurrence 22%

Grassland and waste places

Substratum Common only on the limestones and the Toadstone. Scarce on soils with pH < 4.5. Virtually all records in pH class 7.5–8.0 are from the Magnesian Limestone.

Slope and aspect Mainly confined to slopes of 15–40° with a distinct bias towards southern aspects.

Grazing and burning On calcareous substrata *P. lanceolata* is common both in closely cropped swards and in dense ungrazed communities. The phenotype is extremely plastic (Grime and Jeffrey 1965), forming a compact rosette in broken or short turf and developing long ascending leaves when associated with taller vegetation.

Frequency distribution Class 1–2.

B.S.B.I. Atlas Ubiquitous.

Biological Flora Sagar and Harper (1964).

			Geological formation			
	TS	CL	MG	CM	ML	BS
pH (0–3 cm)						
3.0–4.0	—	—	—	—	—	—
4.1–5.0	3	6	—	4	1	—
5.1–6.0	9	28	—	1	5	—
6.1–7.0	6	18	—	—	9	—
7.1–8.0	2	14	—	—	31	—
pH (9–12 cm)						
2.8–4.0	—	—	—	—	—	—
4.1–5.0	9	3	—	1	1	—
5.1–6.0	6	17	—	3	1	—
6.1–7.0	4	25	—	—	8	—
7.1–8.1	1	22	—	1	35	—
Constancy (%)	**53**	**38**	*0*	*4*	**54**	*0*
Ungrazed, unburned	—	6	0	7	—	0
Grazed, unburned	60	42	0	3	100	—
Ungrazed, burned	44	57	—	0	48	—
Grazed, burned	—	24	—	—	—	—

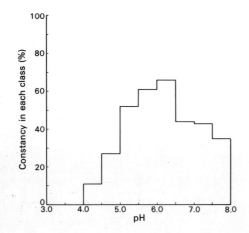

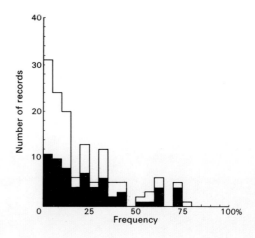

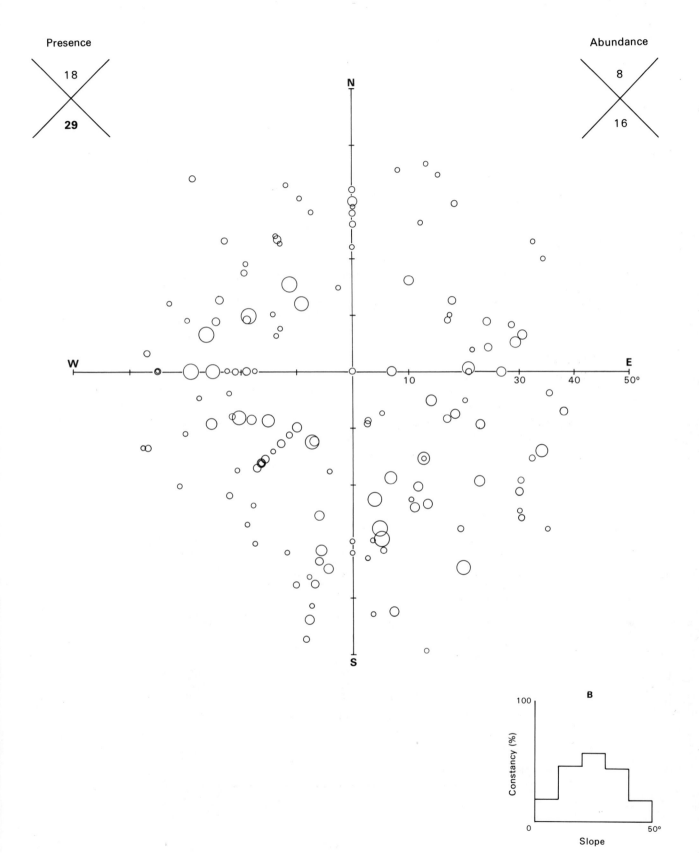

Presence

18

29

Abundance

8

16

N

W   E

10   30   40   50°

S

B

100

Constancy (%)

0   50°

Slope

Poa pratensis Meadow-grass

Tufted perennial grass, 15–80 cm. Grassland, walls and waste places

Records of ssp. *angustifolia* (see below) are given in brackets (tables), as dotted lines (histograms) and as squares (polargraph). All other records refer to ssp. *pratensis*, but there may have been incomplete separation of the two sspp. on the Magnesian Limestone.

1 ssp. *pratensis* Occurrence 27%

Substratum Most abundant on the Toadstone, frequent over limestone, and with scattered occurrences elsewhere. Occurs over a wide range in base status, with an optimum on mildly acidic soils.

Slope and aspect Most common on flat ground, but records extend over the full range of slope and aspect. Higher frequencies attained on south-facing slopes.

Grazing and burning Persistent at both grazed and burned sites; rather more common at the latter.

Frequency distribution Class 2.

B.S.B.I. Atlas Probably ubiquitous (see Perring 1968).

2 ssp. *angustifolia* Occurrence 6%

Substratum Recorded only on the Magnesian Limestone.

Slope and aspect Calcicolous and confined to sloping ground (10–40°). The subspecies is more common on south-facing slopes where it is associated with *Brachypodium pinnatum*.

Grazing and burning Very common in grassland subject to burning, but is absent from grazed sites.

Frequency distribution Distribution essentially similar to that of ssp. *pratensis*.

B.S.B.I. Atlas South-east England (Perring 1968).

			Geological formation			
	TS	CL	MG	CM	ML	BS
pH (0–3 cm)						
3.0–4.0	—	3	1	5	—	3
4.1–5.0	4	13	5	9	1(2)	2
5.1–6.0	13	19	1	2	7(5)	—
6.1–7.0	6	16	—	—	8(5)	—
7.1–8.0	2	23	—	—	13(23)	—
pH (9–12 cm)						
2.8–4.0	—	4	1	4	—	2
4.1–5.0	8	6	2	7	2	3
5.1–6.0	11	15	4	5	1(2)	—
6.1–7.0	5	13	—	—	9(6)	—
7.1–8.1	1	36	—	—	16(27)	—
Constancy (%)	66	42	4	13	34(41)	14
Ungrazed, unburned	—	16	0	21	—	14
Grazed, unburned	40	39	5	8	30(0)	—
Ungrazed, burned	75	68	—	0	31(51)	—
Grazed, burned	—	38	—	—	—	—

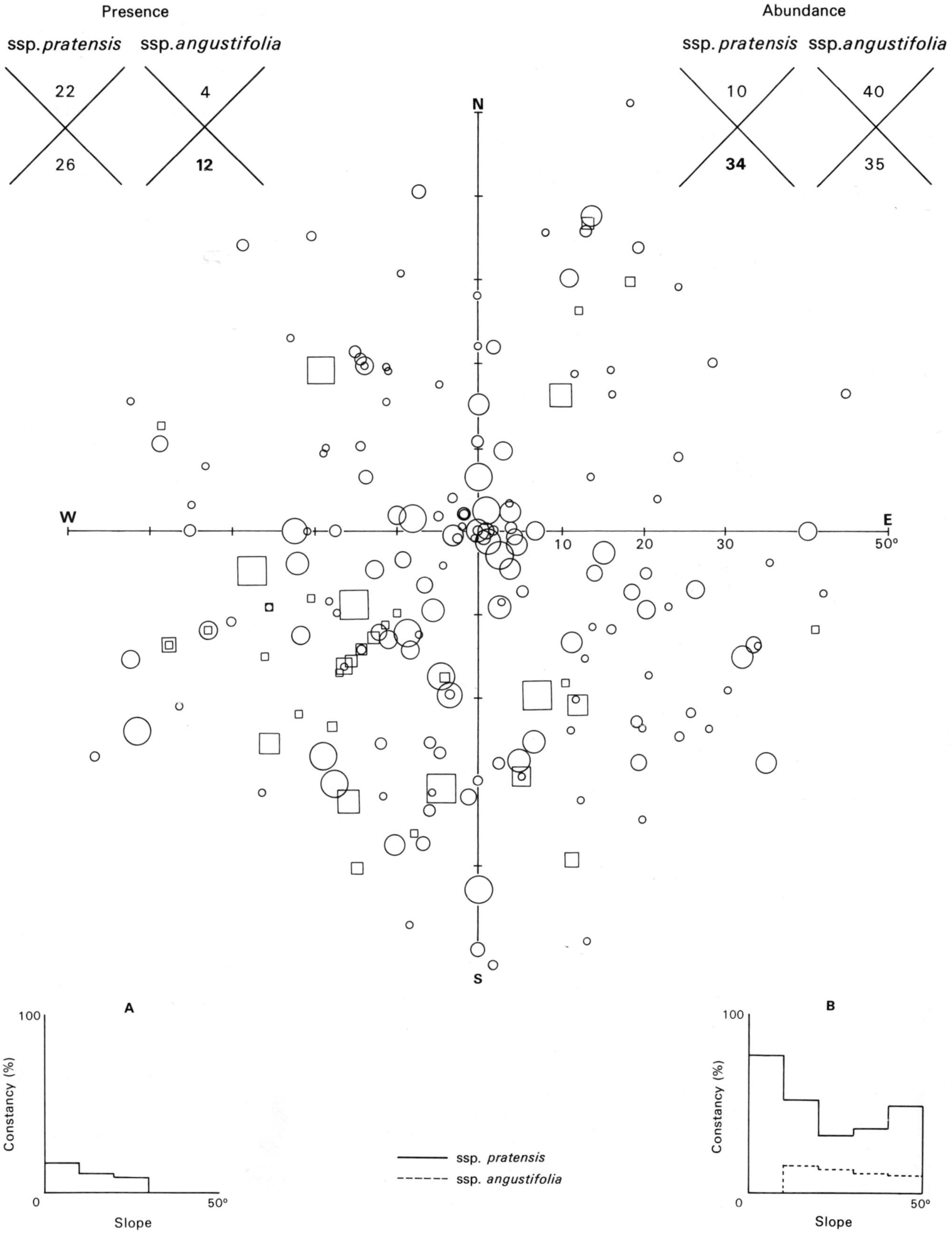

Presence

ssp. *pratensis*   ssp. *angustifolia*

22 / 26   4 / **12**

Abundance

ssp. *pratensis*   ssp. *angustifolia*

10 / **34**   40 / 35

N

W ——————————— E
10   20   30   50°

S

A

Constancy (%)
100
0
Slope
0   50°

B

Constancy (%)
100
0
Slope
0   50°

——— ssp. *pratensis*
- - - ssp. *angustifolia*

Polygala vulgaris Common Milkwort

Prostrate perennial herb, 5–30 cm.
The data may include a small number of records of *P. serpyllifolia*.

Occurrence 6%
Grassland and heathland

Substratum   Not encountered on formations giving rise to acidic soils. Distribution calcicolous but with an optimum at about pH 6.0.

Slope and aspect   Virtually confined to slopes of 15–40°. No evidence of aspect preference.

Grazing and burning   Commonest in the short turf of grazed communities.

Frequency distribution   Class 1. Highest frequencies are attained at the stabilized margins of limestone screes.

B.S.B.I. Atlas   Widely distributed, but most common on the limestones of southern England.

	Geological formation					
	TS	CL	MG	CM	ML	BS
pH (0–3 cm)						
3.0–4.0	—	—	—	—	—	—
4.1–5.0	—	—	—	—	—	—
5.1–6.0	2	8	—	1	3	—
6.1–7.0	1	7	—	—	2	—
7.1–8.0	—	12	—	—	3	—
pH (9–12 cm)						
2.8–4.0	—	—	—	—	—	—
4.1–5.0	3	—	—	—	—	—
5.1–6.0	—	2	—	—	1	—
6.1–7.0	—	9	—	—	3	—
7.1–8.1	—	15	—	1	4	—
Constancy (%)	8	**15**	*0*	*1*	9	0
Ungrazed, unburned	—	10	0	2	—	0
Grazed, unburned	20	22	0	0	10	—
Ungrazed, burned	0	5	—	0	9	—
Grazed, burned	—	5	—	—	—	—

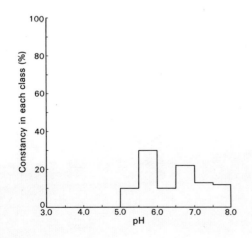

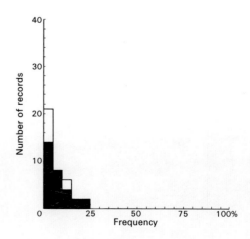

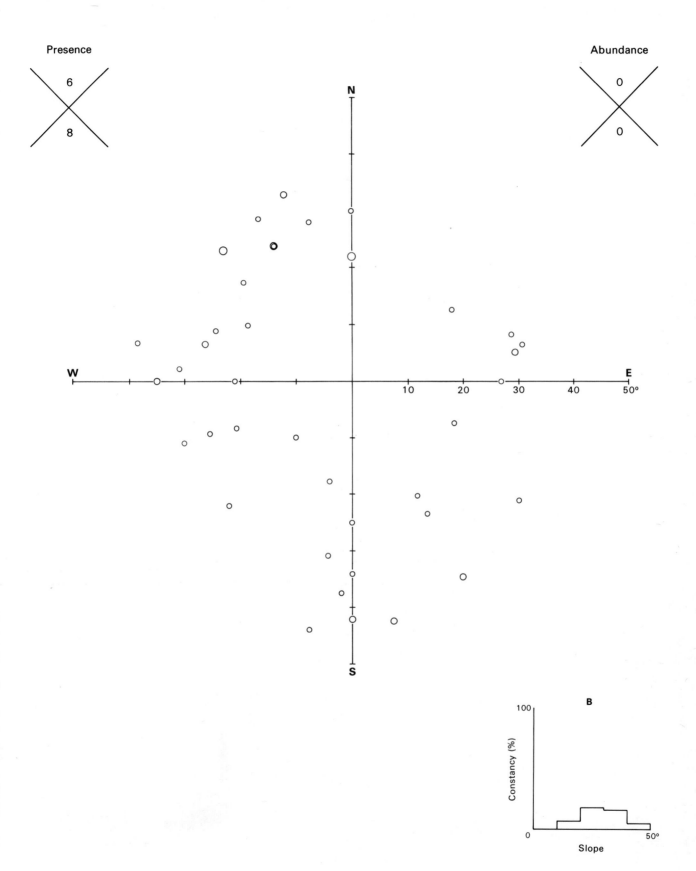

Presence

6

8

Abundance

0

0

N

W   E

10   20   30   40   50°

S

100

Constancy (%)

B

0   50°

Slope

Potentilla erecta   Common Tormentil

Decumbent perennial herb, (5–)10–30(–50) cm.

Occurrence 13%

Grassland and heathland

Substratum   On all strata, but common only on the Toadstone. A characteristic species of leached soils, occurring infrequently on both extremely acidic and highly calcareous soils.

Slope and aspect   The association with the range in slope 20–30° and the pronounced northern bias reflect the distribution of leached soils on the dalesides of the Carboniferous Limestone.

Grazing and burning   Uncommon in communities subject to burning.

Frequency distribution   Class 1–2. High frequency values are associated with high values of *Agrostis tenuis* and with the presence of one or more of the following species: *Galium verum, Lathyrus montanus, Sieglingia decumbens.*

B.S.B.I. Atlas   Ubiquitous.

			Geological formation			
	TS	CL	MG	CM	ML	BS
pH (0–3 cm)						
3.0–4.0	1	5	8	6	—	1
4.1–5.0	5	12	4	3	—	1
5.1–6.0	6	15	1	1	—	—
6.1–7.0	3	7	—	—	—	—
7.1–8.0	2	3	—	—	1	—
pH (9–12 cm)						
2.8–4.0	—	5	6	8	—	2
4.1–5.0	12	6	6	2	—	—
5.1–6.0	4	9	1	—	—	—
6.1–7.0	1	11	—	—	—	—
7.1–8.1	—	11	—	—	1	—
Constancy (%)	**45**	**24**	*9*	7	*1*	6
Ungrazed, unburned	—	29	0	5	—	6
Grazed, unburned	53	30	10	11	10	—
Ungrazed, burned	31	5	—	14	0	—
Grazed, burned	—	14	—	—	—	—

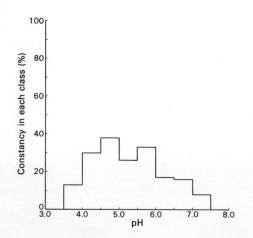
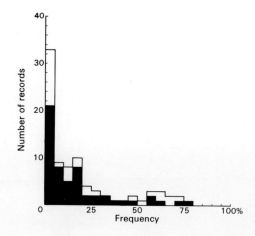

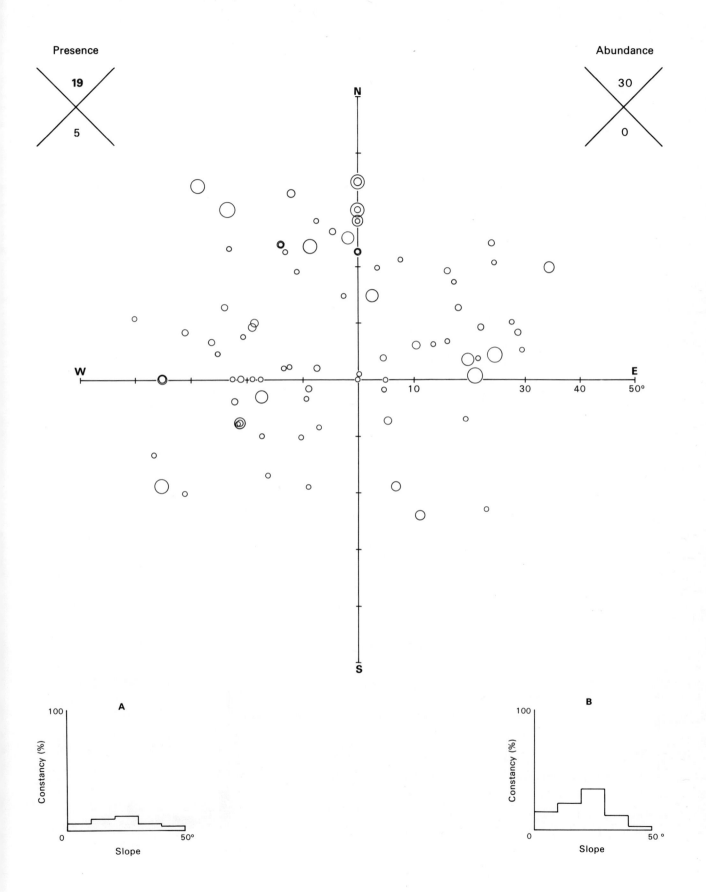

Poterium sanguisorba   Salad Burnet

Perennial rosette herb, 15–40(–60) cm.

Occurrence 12%

Grassland and rock outcrops

Substratum   A calcicole virtually confined to the limestones. Where calcareous soil has become surface leached and invaded by mor-forming species, e.g. *Deschampsia flexuosa*, established plants will survive long after seedling establishment is precluded (Grime 1963b).

Slope and aspect   Frequent only on slopes of 20–40°, with no aspect preference.

Grazing and burning   No marked response to grazing or burning on the Carboniferous Limestone, but virtually confined to grazed sites on the Magnesian Limestone.

Frequency distribution   Class 2.

B.S.B.I. Atlas   Predominantly southern and eastern in the British Isles and concentrated on calcareous substrata.

		Geological formation				
	TS	CL	MG	CM	ML	BS
pH (0–3 cm)						
3.0–4.0	—	—	—	—	—	—
4.1–5.0	1	4	—	—	1	—
5.1–6.0	1	22	—	—	1	—
6.1–7.0	1	20	—	—	2	—
7.1–8.0	—	17	—	—	7	—
pH (9–12 cm)						
2.8–4.0	—	—	—	—	—	—
4.1–5.0	2	2	—	—	—	—
5.1–6.0	—	14	—	—	—	—
6.1–7.0	1	17	—	—	2	—
7.1–8.1	—	30	—	—	9	—
Constancy (%)	8	**35**	*0*	*0*	13	*0*
Ungrazed, unburned	—	31	0	0	—	0
Grazed, unburned	7	37	0	0	50	—
Ungrazed, burned	6	32	—	0	6	—
Grazed, burned	—	29	—	—	—	—

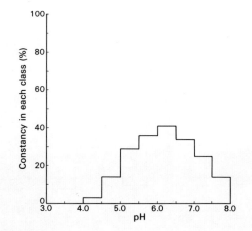

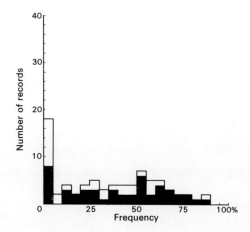

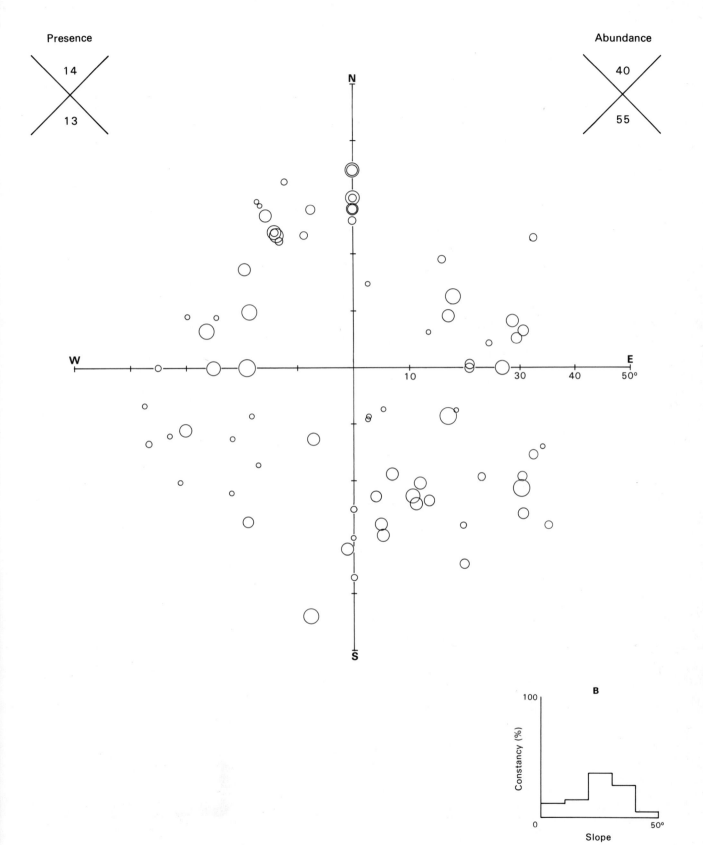

Primula veris Cowslip

Occurrence 5%

Perennial herb, 5–15(–20) cm, with prostrate rosettes.

Grassland and scrub

Substratum   A fairly strict calcicole recorded only on the limestones.
Slope and aspect   Occurrences scattered but rather more frequent on gentle slopes.
Grazing and burning   Most records are from grazed sites.
Frequency distribution   Class 1.
B.S.B.I. Atlas   Throughout England but scarce elsewhere.

	TS	CL	MG	CM	ML	BS
			Geological formation			
pH (0–3 cm)						
3.0–4.0	—	—	—	—	—	—
4.1–5.0	—	—	—	—	—	—
5.1–6.0	—	4	—	—	2	—
6.1–7.0	—	9	—	—	3	—
7.1–8.0	—	7	—	—	4	—
pH (9–12 cm)						
2.8–4.0	—	—	—	—	—	—
4.1–5.0	—	—	—	—	—	—
5.1–6.0	—	1	—	—	—	—
6.1–7.0	—	9	—	—	2	—
7.1–8.1	—	9	—	—	7	—
Constancy (%)	0	11	0	0	11	0
Ungrazed, unburned	—	3	0	0	—	0
Grazed, unburned	0	18	0	0	20	—
Ungrazed, burned	0	3	—	0	9	—
Grazed, burned	—	5	—	—	—	—

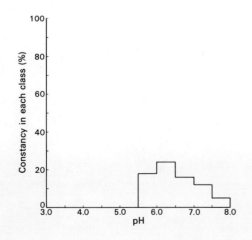

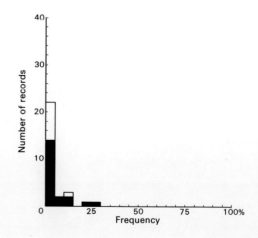

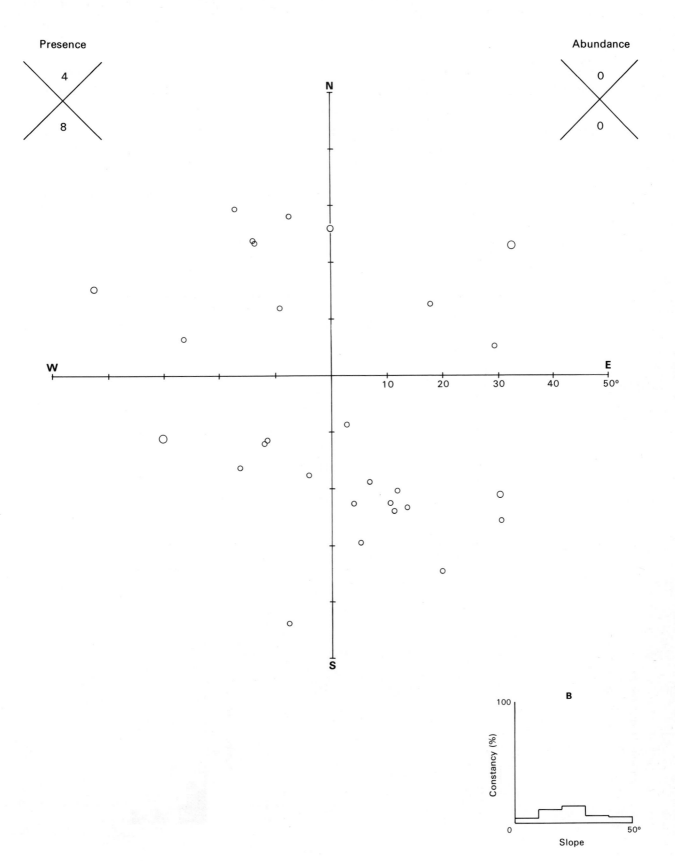

Presence

4

8

Abundance

0

0

N

W   E

10   20   30   40   50°

S

B

Constancy (%)

100

0   50°

Slope

Prunella vulgaris Self-heal

Occurrence 7%

Decumbent perennial herb, 5–30 cm.

Grasslands and grassy paths

Substratum Virtually confined to base-rich and calcareous soils on the limestones. The two peaks of the pH histogram are associated with records of the species on the Carboniferous Limestone (pH 5.5–6.0) and Magnesian Limestone (pH > 7.0) (cf. *Dactylis glomerata*).

Slope and aspect Scarce outside the range of slopes 20–30°. The data indicate a bias towards north-facing sites, particularly on the Magnesian Limestone.

Grazing and burning Most frequent in grazed communities. In addition to its role as a grassland species, *P. vulgaris* is of widespread occurrence in a variety of open (often heavily trampled) habitats in which it shows a good deal of morphological variation.

Frequency distribution Class 1.

B.S.B.I. Atlas Ubiquitous.

| | Geological formation | | | | | |
	TS	CL	MG	CM	ML	BS
pH (0–3 cm)						
3.0–4.0	—	—	—	—	—	—
4.1–5.0	—	2	—	—	—	—
5.1–6.0	2	12	—	1	—	—
6.1–7.0	—	7	—	—	—	—
7.1–8.0	—	6	—	—	12	—
pH (9–12 cm)						
2.8–4.0	—	—	—	—	—	—
4.1–5.0	2	2	—	—	—	—
5.1–6.0	—	5	—	—	—	—
6.1–7.0	—	11	—	—	—	—
7.1–8.1	—	9	—	1	12	—
Constancy (%)	5	*15*	*0*	*1*	14	0
Ungrazed, unburned	—	7	0	2	—	0
Grazed, unburned	13	23	0	0	50	—
Ungrazed, burned	0	8	—	0	3	—
Grazed, burned	—	5	—	—	—	—

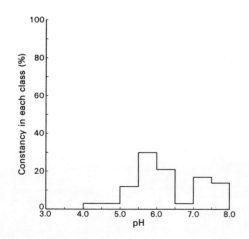

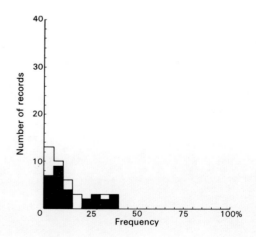

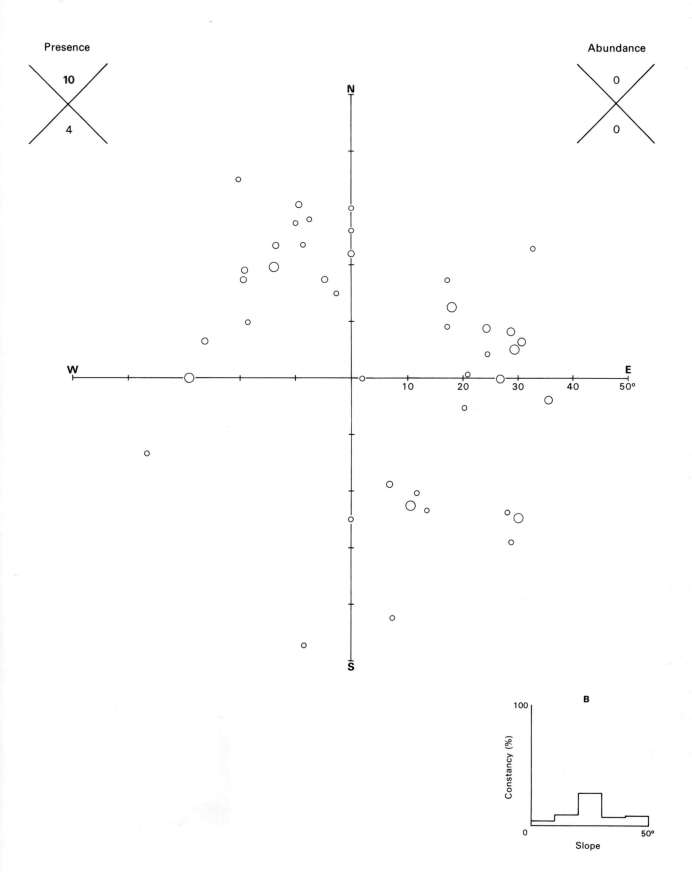

Presence

10

4

Abundance

0

0

N

W
E

10 20 30 40 50°

S

100

Constancy (%)

B

0   50°

Slope

Pteridium aquilinum Bracken

Occurrence 10%

Rhizomatous perennial fern, (15–)30–180(–400) cm.   Open woods, derelict pasture and waste ground

Substratum A calcifuge common only on the Millstone Grit. The one record at a site with pH > 6.0 is a railway cutting on the Magnesian Limestone on to which the species has extended from the more acidic soil of the adjacent plateau.

Slope and aspect High frequency values are recorded only on slopes greater than 20° and are mainly in the NE and SW quadrants. *P. aquilinum* is sensitive to frost (Watt 1950) and is more common on south-facing slopes at high altitudes in the area.

Grazing and burning Commonest at grazed sites. *P. aquilinum* is poisonous and is avoided by grazing animals.

Frequency distribution Class 1–2.

B.S.B.I. Atlas Ubiquitous.

	TS	CL	MG	CM	ML	BS
			Geological formation			
pH (0–3 cm)						
3.0–4.0	—	—	38	6	—	5
4.1–5.0	—	2	1	1	—	—
5.1–6.0	—	—	—	—	3	—
6.1–7.0	—	—	—	—	—	—
7.1–8.0	—	—	—	—	1	—
pH (9–12 cm)						
2.8–4.0	—	—	37	5	—	5
4.1–5.0	—	2	2	1	—	—
5.1–6.0	—	—	—	1	—	—
6.1–7.0	—	—	—	—	3	—
7.1–8.1	—	—	—	—	1	—
Constancy (%)	*0*	*1*	**24**	6	5	14
Ungrazed, unburned	—	0	11	5	—	14
Grazed, unburned	0	0	26	22	0	—
Ungrazed, burned	0	5	—	0	6	—
Grazed, burned	—	0	—	—	—	—

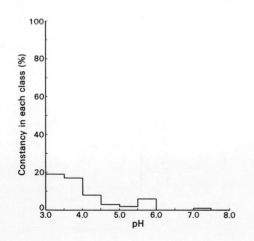

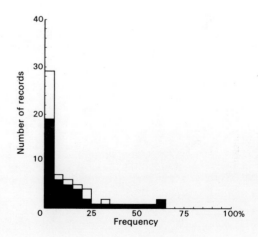

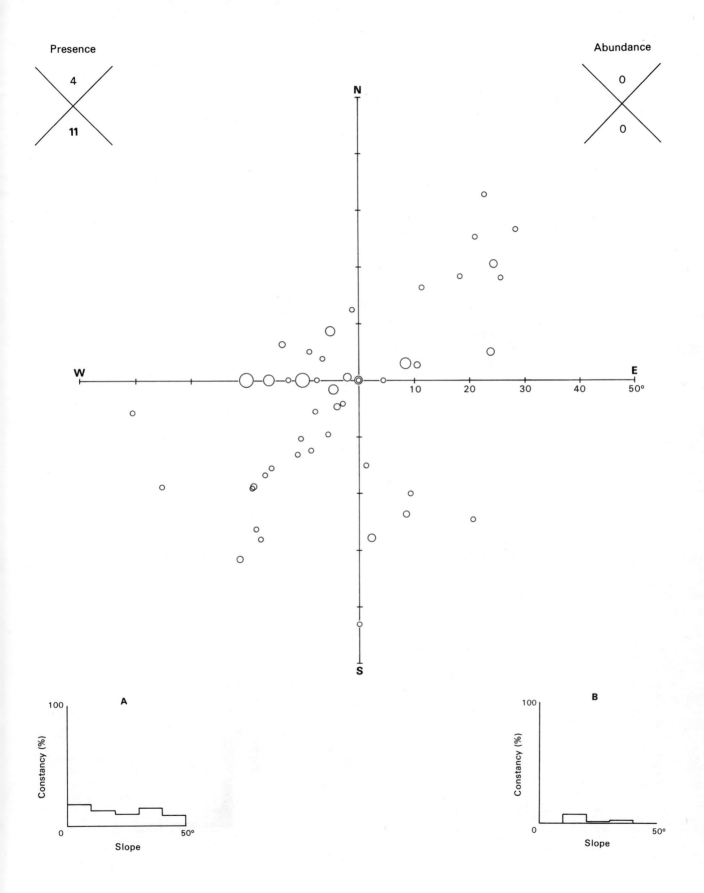

Presence

4

11

Abundance

0

0

N

W · · · · · · · · · · E
10 20 30 40 50°

S

A
100
Constancy (%)
0   50°
Slope

B
100
Constancy (%)
0   50°
Slope

Ranunculus acris Meadow Buttercup

Perennial herb, 15–100 cm.

Substratum The species is generally infrequent in the grasslands examined and was not recorded on the Millstone Grit or the Bunter Sandstone. *R. acris* is primarily a plant of meadows and over-grazed cattle pasture. The records cover a wide range of soils but there are no occurrences below pH 4.0.

Slope and aspect Most records occur on gentle slopes. No evidence of aspect preference.

Grazing and burning Consistently associated with grazed sites. The species is avoided by herbivores.

Frequency distribution Class 1–2.

B.S.B.I. Atlas Ubiquitous.

Biological Flora Harper (1957).

		Geological formation				
	TS	CL	MG	CM	ML	BS
pH (0–3 cm)						
3.0–4.0	—	—	—	—	—	—
4.1–5.0	—	6	—	1	—	—
5.1–6.0	1	4	—	—	—	—
6.1–7.0	—	5	—	—	1	—
7.1–8.0	1	3	—	—	1	—
pH (9–12 cm)						
2.8–4.0	—	—	—	—	—	—
4.1–5.0	1	4	—	—	—	—
5.1–6.0	1	3	—	1	—	—
6.1–7.0	—	7	—	—	1	—
7.1–8.1	—	4	—	—	1	—
Constancy (%)	5	**10**	*0*	1	2	0
Ungrazed, unburned	—	0	0	2	—	0
Grazed, unburned	7	18	0	0	20	—
Ungrazed, burned	0	3	—	0	0	—
Grazed, burned	—	0	—	—	—	—

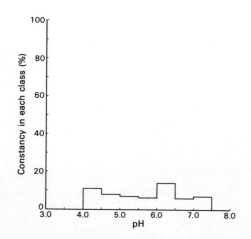

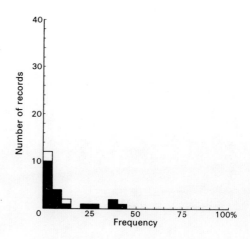

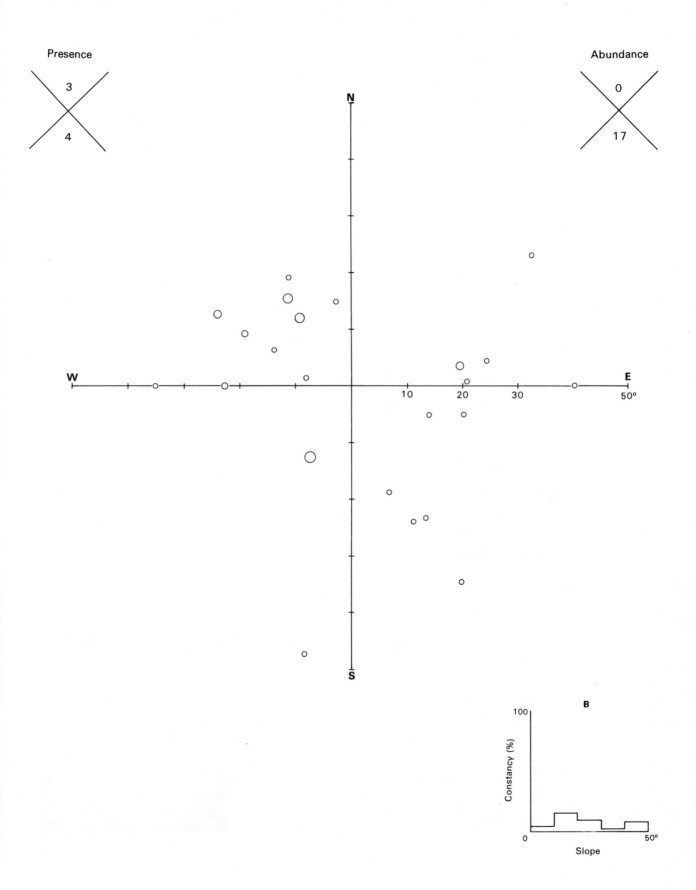

Presence
3
4

Abundance
0
17

N

W   E

10   20   30   50°

S

Constancy (%)

100

B

0   50°

Slope

Ranunculus bulbosus Bulbous Buttercup

Bulbous perennial herb, 15–40 cm.

Substratum   Present only on the Toadstone and the limestones. A majority of the sites lie within the pH range 5.0–6.5 but the species extends on to highly calcareous soils on the Magnesian Limestone.

Slope and aspect   Most common on slopes of 20–30°. The E–W bias is unusual and may reflect the distribution of closely grazed calcareous pasture.

Grazing and burning   The data show clearly that the plant is common only in grazed turf. The species is avoided by grazing animals.

Frequency distribution   Class 1.

B.S.B.I. Atlas   Throughout England, but becoming uncommon in the north and west.

Biological Flora   Harper (1957).

			Geological formation			
	TS	CL	MG	CM	ML	BS
pH (0–3 cm)						
3.0–4.0	—	—	—	—	—	—
4.1–5.0	—	3	—	—	—	—
5.1–6.0	4	10	—	—	2	—
6.1–7.0	2	4	—	—	2	—
7.1–8.0	1	5	—	—	11	—
pH (9–12 cm)						
2.8–4.0	—	—	—	—	—	—
4.1–5.0	4	2	—	—	—	—
5.1–6.0	3	5	—	—	1	—
6.1–7.0	—	10	—	—	1	—
7.1–8.1	—	5	—	—	13	—
Constancy (%)	**18**	**12**	*0*	*0*	**18**	0
Ungrazed, unburned	—	0	0	0	—	0
Grazed, unburned	33	23	0	0	80	—
Ungrazed, burned	0	0	—	0	7	—
Grazed, burned	—	0	—	—	—	—

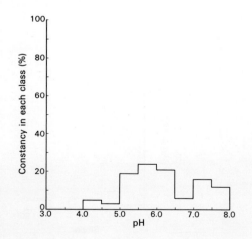

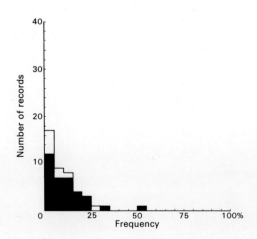

Presence

4

2

Abundance

0

0

N

W

E

10   20   30   50°

S

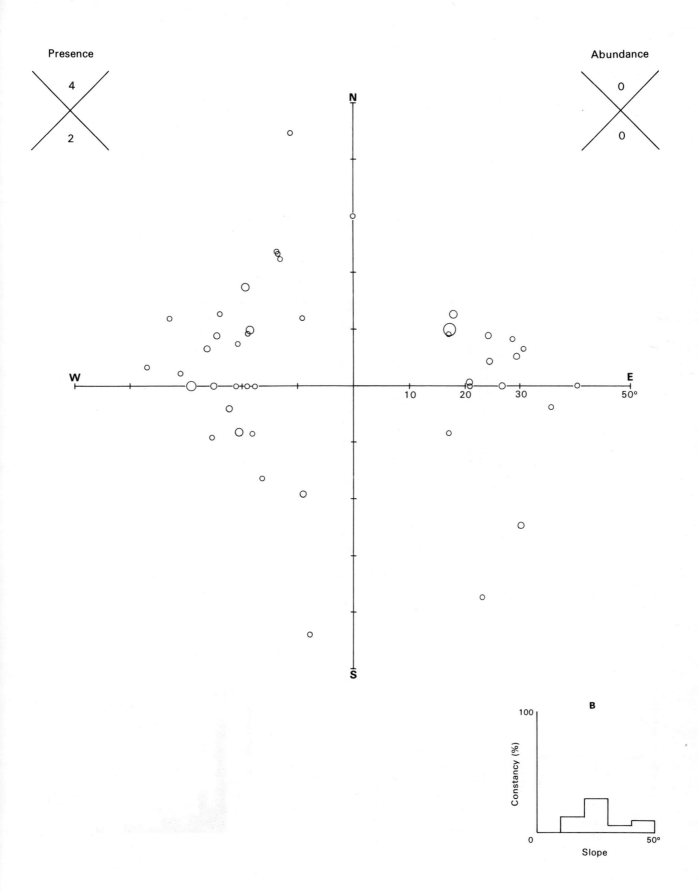

B

100

Constancy (%)

0   50°

Slope

Rumex acetosa Sorrel

Occurrence 18%

Perennial herb, up to 20 cm, with a rosette of ascending leaves. Meadows, marshes and waste places

Substratum Absent only from the Bunter Sandstone but scarce on the Millstone Grit. The pH distribution has a strong resemblance to that shown by *Holcus lanatus*. The species is of common occurrence on soils over the pH range 4.0–7.5. There is, however, an optimum below pH 5.0, followed by a catastrophic decline at pH 4.0.

Slope and aspect R. acetosa is common over the range in slope 0–40° but is rather scarce on south to south-west facing slopes.

Grazing and burning No clear evidence of a reaction to burning or grazing regime.

Frequency distribution Class 1–2. Highest frequency values are attained on NE slopes which is perhaps to be expected in view of the mesomorphic shoot.

B.S.B.I. Atlas Ubiquitous.

		Geological formation				
	TS	CL	MG	CM	ML	BS
pH (0–3 cm)						
3.0–4.0	—	2	1	4	—	—
4.1–5.0	4	13	6	11	1	—
5.1–6.0	12	11	1	1	3	—
6.1–7.0	5	11	—	—	4	—
7.1–8.0	2	15	—	—	4	—
pH (9–12 cm)						
2.8–4.0	—	3	1	—	—	—
4.1–5.0	11	5	3	8	2	—
5.1–6.0	11	11	4	7	—	—
6.1–7.0	1	9	—	—	4	—
7.1–8.1	—	20	—	1	6	—
Constancy (%)	**61**	**29**	*5*	13	14	*0*
Ungrazed, unburned	—	23	0	26	—	0
Grazed, unburned	73	33	6	0	20	—
Ungrazed, burned	50	27	—	0	13	—
Grazed, burned	—	19	—	—	—	—

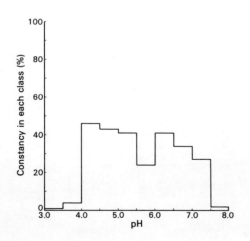

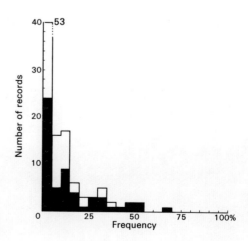

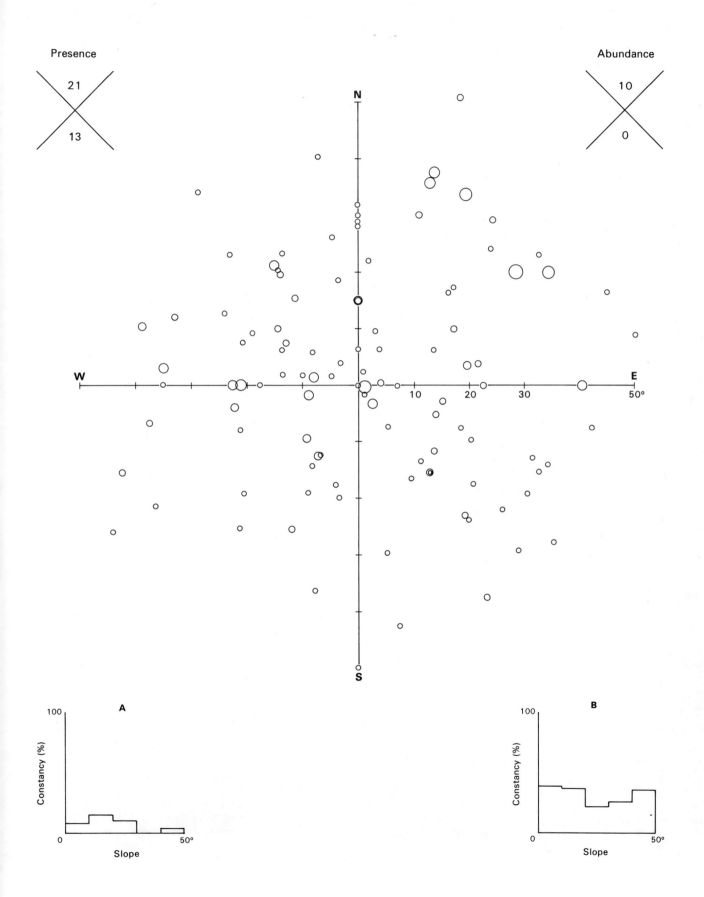

Rumex acetosella Sheep's Sorrel

Creeping perennial herb, up to 30 cm.

Occurrence 6%

Heathland, arable land and waste places

Substratum   High incidence only on the Coal Measures and the Bunter Sandstone. A calcifuge, which in its grassland habitats appears to be excluded from soils with a thick accumulation of mor humus. At the southern extremity of the Millstone Grit the species is locally abundant on shallow sandy soils. Of the two rather anomalous sites at which the pH of the surface soil is > 7.0, one has pH 4.7 at 9–12 cm depth.

Slope and aspect   The species is most often found on flat or gently sloping ground.

Grazing and burning   A plant of open sites, irrespective of grazing or burning.

Frequency distribution   Class 2.

B.S.B.I. Atlas   Ubiquitous.

	Geological formation					
	TS	CL	MG	CM	ML	BS
pH (0–3 cm)						
3.0–4.0	—	—	7	11	—	8
4.1–5.0	—	—	—	8	—	2
5.1–6.0	2	—	—	—	—	—
6.1–7.0	—	—	—	—	—	—
7.1–8.0	—	—	—	—	2	—
pH (9–12 cm)						
2.8–4.0	—	—	7	10	—	7
4.1–5.0	1	—	—	7	1	3
5.1–6.0	1	—	—	2	—	—
6.1–7.0	—	—	—	—	—	—
7.1–8.1	—	—	—	—	1	—
Constancy (%)	5	*0*	4	**15**	2	**28**
Ungrazed, unburned	—	0	0	18	—	28
Grazed, unburned	13	0	5	16	0	—
Ungrazed, burned	0	0	—	10	3	—
Grazed, burned	—	0	—	—	—	—

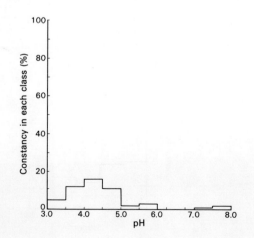

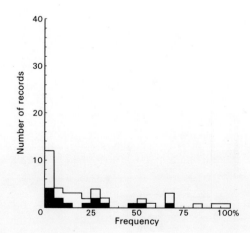

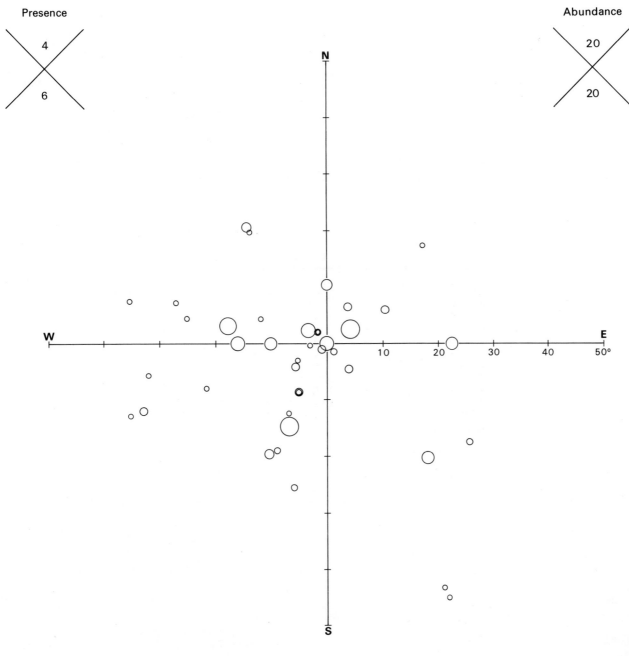

Presence

4

6

Abundance

20

20

N

W   10   20   30   40   50°   E

S

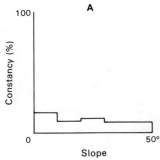

A

100

Constancy (%)

0   50°

Slope

Scabiosa columbaria Small Scabious

Perennial herb, 15–70 cm, forming a rosette.

Occurrence 8%

Grassland and rock outcrops

Substratum A calcicole confined to limestone.

Slope and aspect Scattered occurrence but with a distinct tendency to occur most frequently on steep slopes particularly those of southern aspect.

Grazing and burning A majority of the habitats on Carboniferous Limestone are grazed; on the Magnesian Limestone a majority are ungrazed and burned. On either substratum the occurrence of the species appears to coincide with that of open vegetation on shallow soils.

Frequency distribution Class 2.

B.S.B.I. Atlas On calcareous formations in SE Britain.

	TS	CL	MG	CM	ML	BS
			Geological formation			
pH (0–3 cm)						
3.0–4.0	—	—	—	—	—	—
4.1–5.0	—	—	—	—	1	—
5.1–6.0	—	7	—	—	1	—
6.1–7.0	—	9	—	—	6	—
7.1–8.0	—	14	—	—	11	—
pH (9–12 cm)						
2.8–4.0	—	—	—	—	—	—
4.1–5.0	—	—	—	—	—	—
5.1–6.0	—	5	—	—	—	—
6.1–7.0	—	8	—	—	2	—
7.1–8.1	—	17	—	—	15	—
Constancy (%)	0	17	0	0	21	0
Ungrazed, unburned	—	3	0	0	—	0
Grazed, unburned	0	28	0	0	10	—
Ungrazed, burned	0	11	—	0	24	—
Grazed, burned	—	0	—	—	—	—

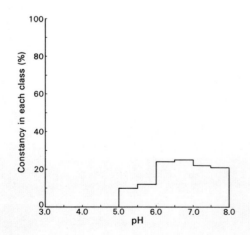

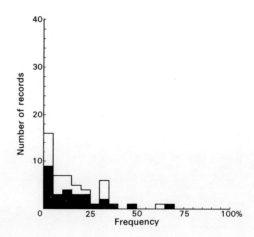

148

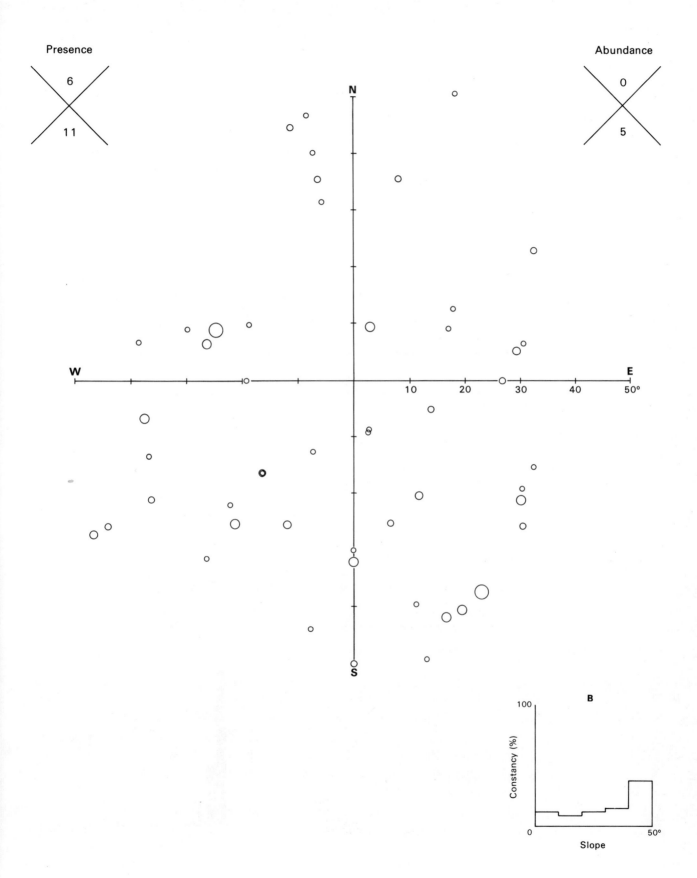

Presence

6
11

Abundance

0
5

N

W   10   20   30   40   50°   E

S

B

Constancy (%)

100

0   50°

Slope

Senecio jacobaea Ragwort

Occurrence 15%

Biennial or perennial herb, 30–150 cm, forming a rosette.

Pasture and waste ground

Substratum   Abundant on the Carboniferous Limestone, frequent on the Toadstone and Magnesian Limestone. Absent from base-poor substrata and showing a bimodal pH distribution. The peak at pH 6.0 possibly corresponds with the maximum frequency of cattle pastures on the Carboniferous Limestone (see below). The second peak, at pH 7.5–8.0, is due to the widespread occurrence of *S. jacobaea* on the Magnesian Limestone and in screes on the Carboniferous Limestone.

Slope and aspect   Rather strictly confined to slopes in the range 15–40°. No aspect preference apparent.

Grazing and burning   *S. jacobaea* is both poisonous and unpalatable and is known to be encouraged by overgrazing (Cameron 1935). On the Magnesian Limestone and on the Toadstone, two strata on which grazing is by cattle, the species does appear to be favoured by grazing. However, on the Carboniferous Limestone *S. jacobaea* is most common in burned sites.

Frequency distribution   Class 1. *S. jacobaea* is a short-lived, wind-dispersed adventive and the data suggest that it establishes most readily in 'open' turf associated with scree conditions, cattle trampling or burning.

B.S.B.I. Atlas   Ubiquitous.

Biological Flora   Harper and Wood (1957).

			Geological formation			
	TS	CL	MG	CM	ML	BS
pH (0–3 cm)						
3.0–4.0	—	—	—	—	—	—
4.1–5.0	—	9	—	—	—	—
5.1–6.0	5	23	—	—	1	—
6.1–7.0	3	14	—	—	1	—
7.1–8.0	1	19	—	—	14	—
pH (9–12 cm)						
2.8–4.0	—	—	—	—	—	—
4.1–5.0	4	4	—	—	—	—
5.1–6.0	4	15	—	—	—	—
6.1–7.0	1	16	—	—	2	—
7.1–8.1	—	31	—	—	14	—
Constancy (%)	24	**37**	*0*	*0*	19	0
Ungrazed, unburned	—	26	0	0	—	0
Grazed, unburned	33	22	0	0	60	—
Ungrazed, burned	13	59	—	0	15	—
Grazed, burned	—	71	—	—	—	—

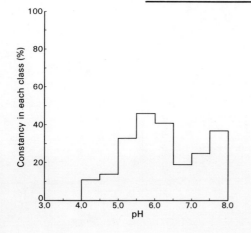

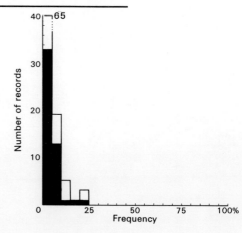

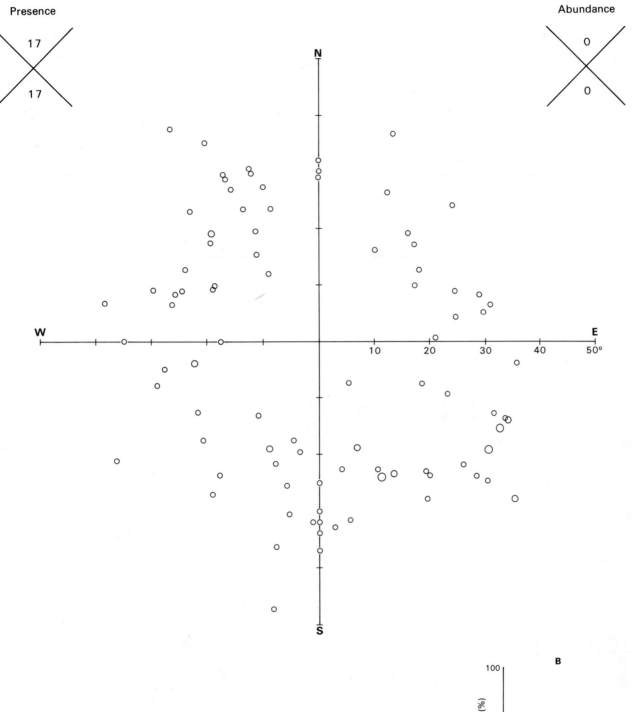

Presence

17

17

Abundance

0

0

N

W ——————————————————— E
10   20   30   40   50°

S

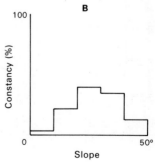

B

100

Constancy (%)

0   50°

Slope

Sieglingia decumbens Heath-grass

Tufted perennial grass, 10–40 cm.

Occurrence 7%

Grassland and heathland

Substratum   An infrequent constituent of grassland on the Carboniferous Limestone and Toadstone with scattered occurrences on other strata. Fairly wide ranging with respect to soil pH. The pattern on the Carboniferous Limestone and Toadstone suggests that the species is most common on mildly acidic soils. On the Magnesian Limestone, however, the species occurs on unleached calcareous soils (cf. *Betonica officinalis*).

Slope and aspect   Frequent only in the slope range 20–30°. No aspect preference.

Grazing and burning   Insufficient records for meaningful comparison. The species occurs most frequently in lightly grazed and occasionally burned sites on the Carboniferous Limestone.

Frequency distribution   Class 2.

B.S.B.I. Atlas   Widespread but mainly in the west.

			Geological formation			
	TS	CL	MG	CM	ML	BS
pH (0–3 cm)						
3.0–4.0	1	1	3	2	—	1
4.1–5.0	3	6	—	—	—	—
5.1–6.0	3	8	—	—	1	—
6.1–7.0	—	7	—	—	—	—
7.1–8.0	—	3	—	—	5	—
pH (9–12 cm)						
2.8–4.0	—	—	1	2	—	1
4.1–5.0	4	4	2	—	1	—
5.1–6.0	2	6	—	—	1	—
6.1–7.0	1	9	—	—	4	—
7.1–8.1	—	6	—	—	—	—
Constancy (%)	**18**	**14**	2	2	7	3
Ungrazed, unburned	—	0	0	0	—	3
Grazed, unburned	7	12	2	0	20	—
Ungrazed, burned	25	14	—	10	5	—
Grazed, burned	—	43	—	—	—	—

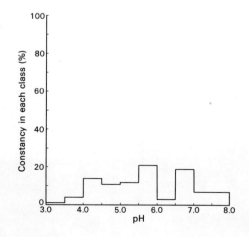

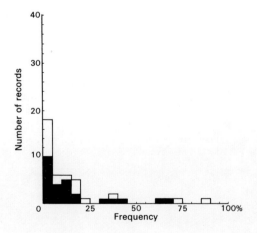

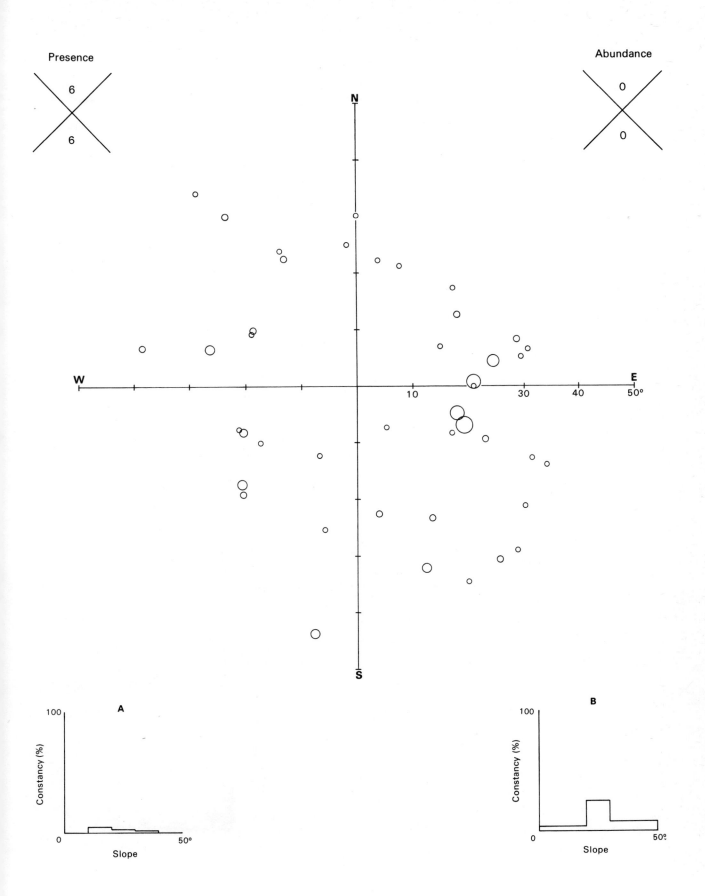

Presence

6

6

Abundance

0

0

N

W   10   20   30   40   50°   E

S

100

Constancy (%)

A

0   50°

Slope

100

Constancy (%)

B

0   50°

Slope

Succisa pratensis Devil's-bit Scabious

Perennial herb, 15–100 cm, with a rosette of ascending leaves.

Occurrence 6%

Marshland and grassland

Substratum   Restricted to the Carboniferous Limestone and Toadstone. The pH distribution is calcicolous with maximum frequency in the pH range 6.0–6.5. There are, however, some records from leached brown earths on the Carboniferous Limestone.

Slope and aspect   Most of the sites at which *S. pratensis* occurs are situated on 20–35° slopes of northern aspect. The preference for north-facing slopes is not surprising in view of the known occurrence of the species in open woods, fens and marshes (Adams 1955).

Grazing and burning   Absent from burned sites and displaying a strong association with grazing on the Toadstone.

Frequency distribution   Class 2.

B.S.B.I. Atlas   Ubiquitous.

Biological Flora   Adams (1955).

			Geological formation			
	TS	CL	MG	CM	ML	BS
pH (0–3 cm)						
3.0–4.0	—	—	—	—	—	—
4.1–5.0	1	2	—	—	—	—
5.1–6.0	4	9	—	—	—	—
6.1–7.0	4	7	—	—	—	—
7.1–8.0	2	9	—	—	—	—
pH (9–12 cm)						
2.8–4.0	—	—	—	—	—	—
4.1–5.0	8	2	—	—	—	—
5.1–6.0	3	3	—	—	—	—
6.1–7.0	—	8	—	—	—	—
7.1–8.1	—	14	—	—	—	—
Constancy (%)	**29**	**15**	*0*	*0*	*0*	0
Ungrazed, unburned	—	16	0	0	—	0
Grazed, unburned	53	21	0	0	0	—
Ungrazed, burned	0	0	—	0	0	—
Grazed, burned	—	10	—	—	—	—

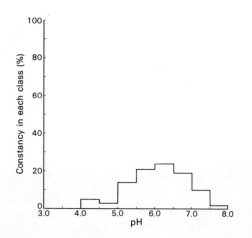

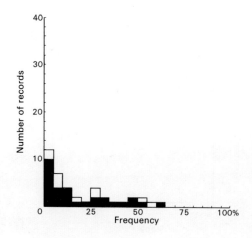

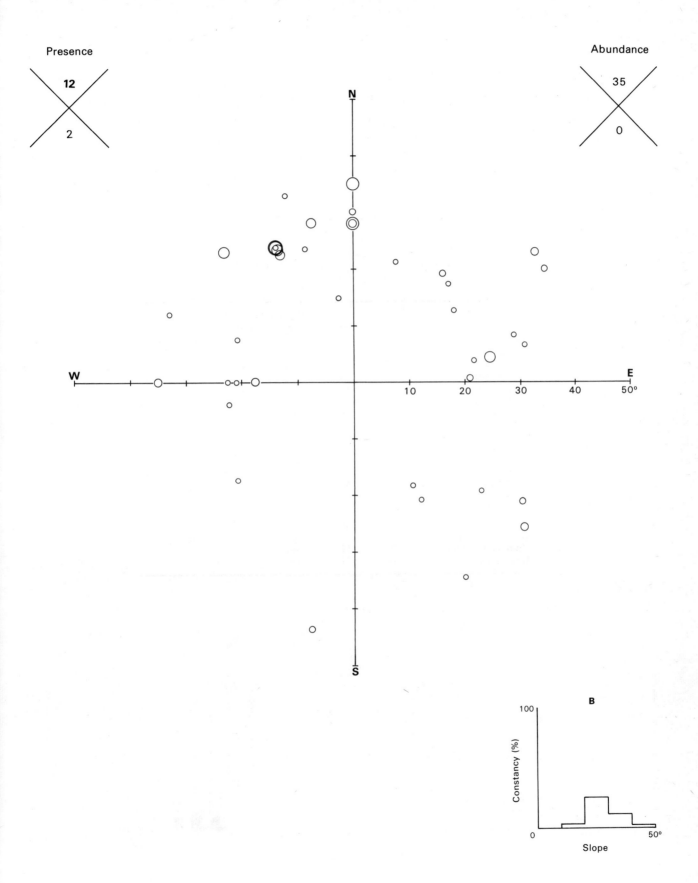

Teucrium scorodonia Wood Sage

Strongly rhizomatous perennial herb, 15–30 cm.

Occurrence 8%

Woodland, scrub and waste places

Substratum   In the present survey, *T. scorodonia* was encountered only on soils of high base-status on the limestones, although it occurs widely in other habitats. In contrast with several species with a comparable range in soil pH (e.g. *Poterium sanguisorba*) the species shows a high frequency of occurrence in the pH range 7.5–8.0. This probably reflects its success in screes. Edaphic ecotypes occur (Hutchinson 1967).

Slope and aspect   Confined to steep slopes (20–45°). Occurs most often and with higher frequency values on south-facing slopes.

Grazing and burning   *T. scorodonia* has a low constancy in pastures. The species is common on screes, a habitat which is usually inaccessible to grazing animals.

Frequency distribution   Class 2.

B.S.B.I. Atlas   Ubiquitous except for East Anglia and the South Midlands.

	TS	CL	MG	CM	ML	BS
			Geological formation			
pH (0–3 cm)						
3.0–4.0	—	—	—	—	—	—
4.1–5.0	—	7	—	—	—	—
5.1–6.0	—	11	—	—	—	—
6.1–7.0	—	10	—	—	—	—
7.1–8.0	—	20	—	—	2	—
pH (9–12 cm)						
2.8–4.0	—	—	—	—	—	—
4.1–5.0	—	4	—	—	—	—
5.1–6.0	—	8	—	—	—	—
6.1–7.0	—	8	—	—	—	—
7.1–8.1	—	29	—	—	2	—
Constancy (%)	0	**27**	*0*	*0*	2	0
Ungrazed, unburned	—	45	0	0	—	0
Grazed, unburned	0	2	0	0	0	—
Ungrazed, burned	0	65	—	0	3	—
Grazed, burned	—	38	—	—	—	—

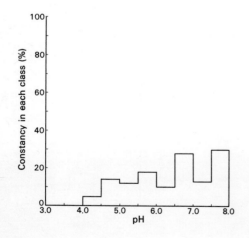

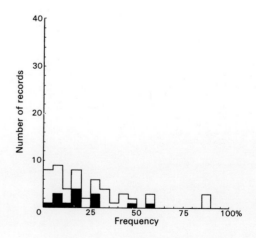

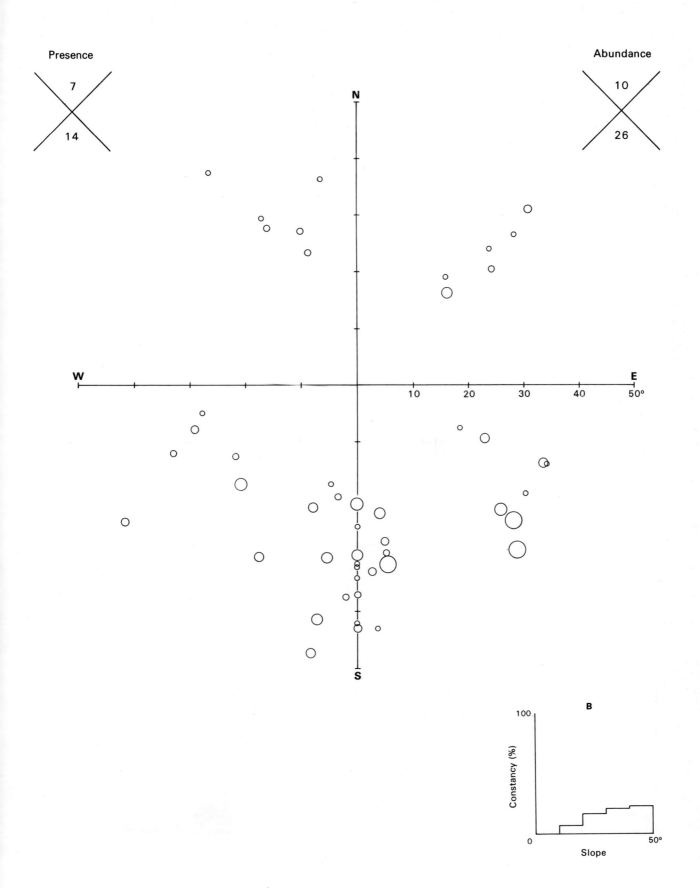

Thymus drucei Thyme

Small mat-forming undershrub, up to 7 cm.

Grassland and open rocky or sandy places

Substratum　A calcicole common only on the Carboniferous Limestone and frequently occurring in association with *Helianthemum chamaecistus*.

Slope and aspect　Strictly confined to sites on steep slopes (20–50°). No aspect preference apparent.

Grazing and burning　Insufficient records. Most frequent in grazed, unburned grassland.

Frequency distribution　Class 2.

B.S.B.I. Atlas　Predominantly western. In SE England confined to calcareous substrata.

Biological Flora　Pigott (1955).

			Geological formation			
	TS	CL	MG	CM	ML	BS
pH (0–3 cm)						
3.0–4.0	—	—	—	—	—	—
4.1–5.0	—	—	—	—	—	—
5.1–6.0	1	14	—	—	—	—
6.1–7.0	1	13	—	—	—	—
7.1–8.0	—	23	—	—	2	—
pH (9–12 cm)						
2.8–4.0	—	—	—	—	—	—
4.1–5.0	—	—	—	—	—	—
5.1–6.0	1	5	—	—	—	—
6.1–7.0	1	19	—	—	—	—
7.1–8.1	—	25	—	—	2	—
Constancy (%)	5	**28**	*0*	*0*	2	*0*
Ungrazed, unburned	—	16	0	0	—	0
Grazed, unburned	7	35	0	0	20	—
Ungrazed, burned	0	30	—	0	0	—
Grazed, burned	—	14	—	—	—	—

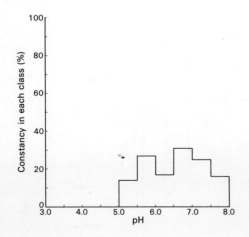

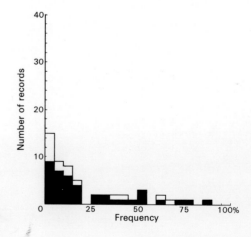

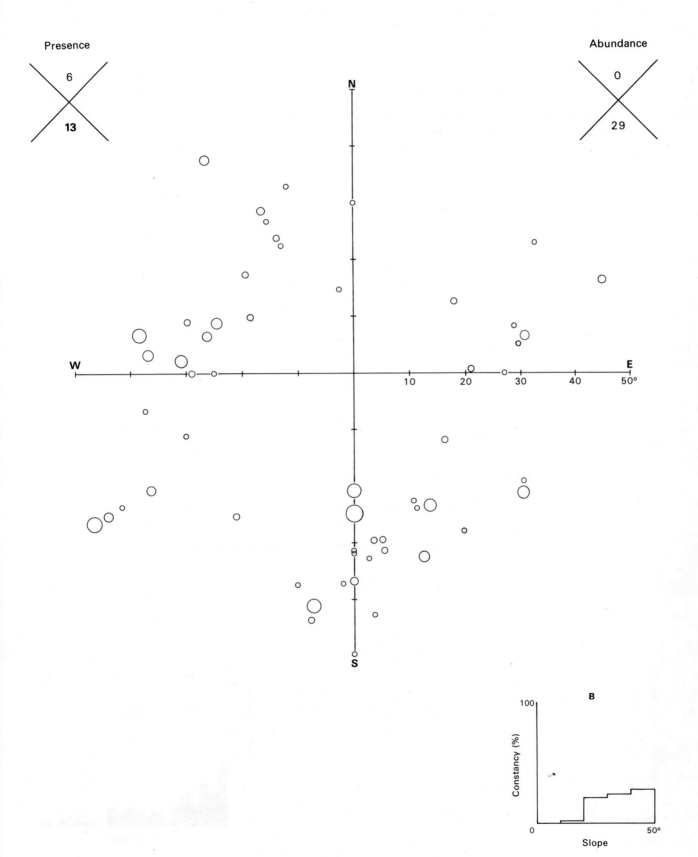

Presence
6
13

Abundance
0
29

N

W   E
10   20   30   40   50°

S

Constancy (%)

100

B

0   50°
Slope

Trifolium repens White Clover

Creeping perennial herb, up to 50 cm.

Occurrence 13%

Grassland and grassy paths

Substratum Wide-ranging with respect to soil pH but common only on soils of intermediate pH. Scarce on substrata giving rise to acidic soils. Edaphic ecotypes are known to occur (Snaydon 1962).

Slope and aspect Widespread over all aspects and slopes but most frequent in occurrence over the range in slope 0–30°.

Grazing and burning Characteristic of cattle pasture and intolerant of conditions associated with frequent burning.

Frequency distribution Class 2.

B.S.B.I. Atlas Ubiquitous.

		Geological formation				
	TS	CL	MG	CM	ML	BS
pH (0–3 cm)						
3.0–4.0	—	—	—	1	—	—
4.1–5.0	1	9	1	3	—	—
5.1–6.0	10	16	1	1	1	—
6.1–7.0	4	9	—	—	2	—
7.1–8.0	—	13	—	—	11	—
pH (9–12 cm)						
2.8–4.0	—	1	—	2	—	—
4.1–5.0	9	5	2	2	—	—
5.1–6.0	3	9	—	1	—	—
6.1–7.0	3	13	—	—	2	—
7.1–8.1	—	18	—	—	12	—
Constancy (%)	**40**	**26**	*1*	*4*	17	*0*
Ungrazed, unburned	—	3	0	3	—	0
Grazed, unburned	93	33	2	8	90	—
Ungrazed, burned	0	38	—	0	6	—
Grazed, burned	—	10	—	—	—	—

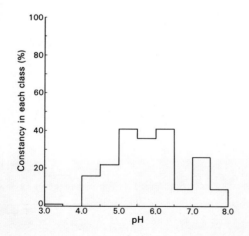

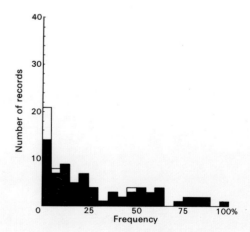

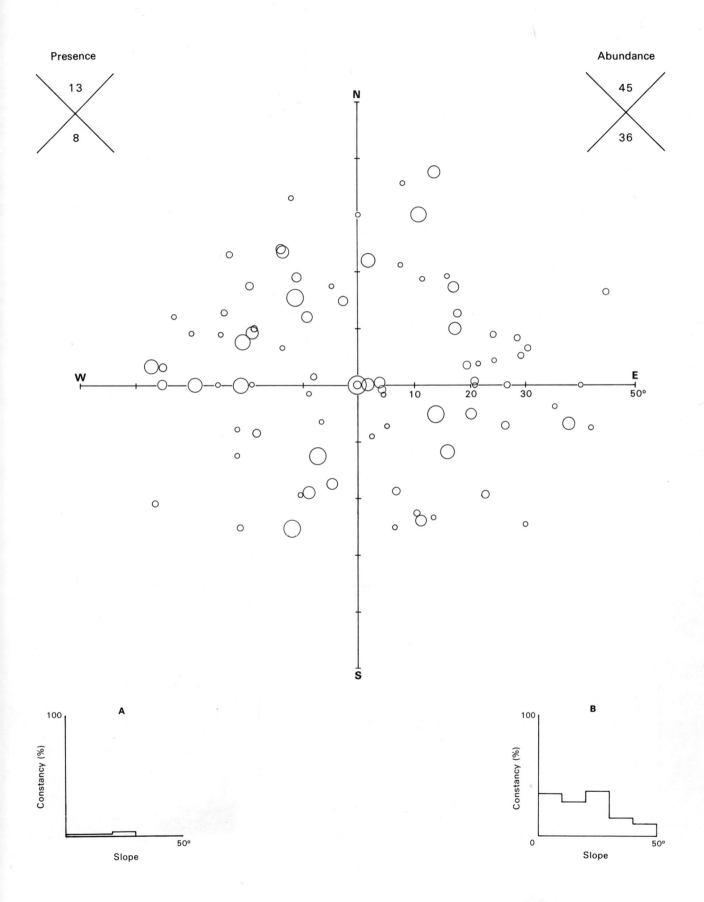

Presence

13

8

Abundance

45

36

N

S

W

E

10   20   30   50°

A

100

Constancy (%)

Slope

50°

B

100

Constancy (%)

Slope

0   50°

Trisetum flavescens Yellow Oat

Occurrence 18%

Erect stoloniferous perennial grass, 20–50 cm.

Grassland

Substratum   A common plant of limestone and Toadstone. Occurring on mildly acidic and base-rich soils but showing a well-defined optimum at about pH 6.5.

Slope and aspect   Found over the range 10–50°. Occurrences on south-facing slopes twice as numerous as those on north-facing slopes.

Grazing and burning   On the Toadstone and Carboniferous Limestone the species is most common in burned, ungrazed grassland. On the Magnesian Limestone, the records are proportionately fewer in burned than in grazed sites. It is perhaps significant that burned sites on the Magnesian Limestone differ from those on other strata in the presence of *Brachypodium pinnatum*.

Frequency distribution   Class 1–2.

B.S.B.I. Atlas   Of common occurrence in SE Britain.

	TS	CL	MG	CM	ML	BS
			Geological formation			
pH (0–3 cm)						
3.0–4.0	—	—	—	—	—	—
4.1–5.0	2	3	—	1	1	—
5.1–6.0	9	14	—	1	4	—
6.1–7.0	5	18	—	—	5	—
7.1–8.0	—	29	—	—	19	—
pH (9–12 cm)						
2.8–4.0	—	—	—	—	—	—
4.1–5.0	1	—	—	—	—	—
5.1–6.0	9	10	—	1	—	—
6.1–7.0	5	14	—	—	8	—
7.1–8.1	1	36	—	1	21	—
Constancy (%)	**42**	**36**	*0*	*2*	**34**	*0*
Ungrazed, unburned	—	10	0	3	—	0
Grazed, unburned	13	37	0	0	50	—
Ungrazed, burned	69	51	—	0	30	—
Grazed, burned	—	33	—	—	—	—

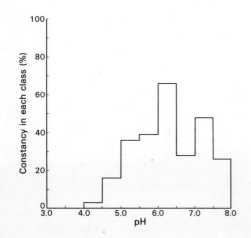

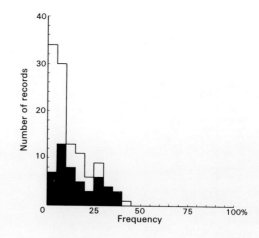

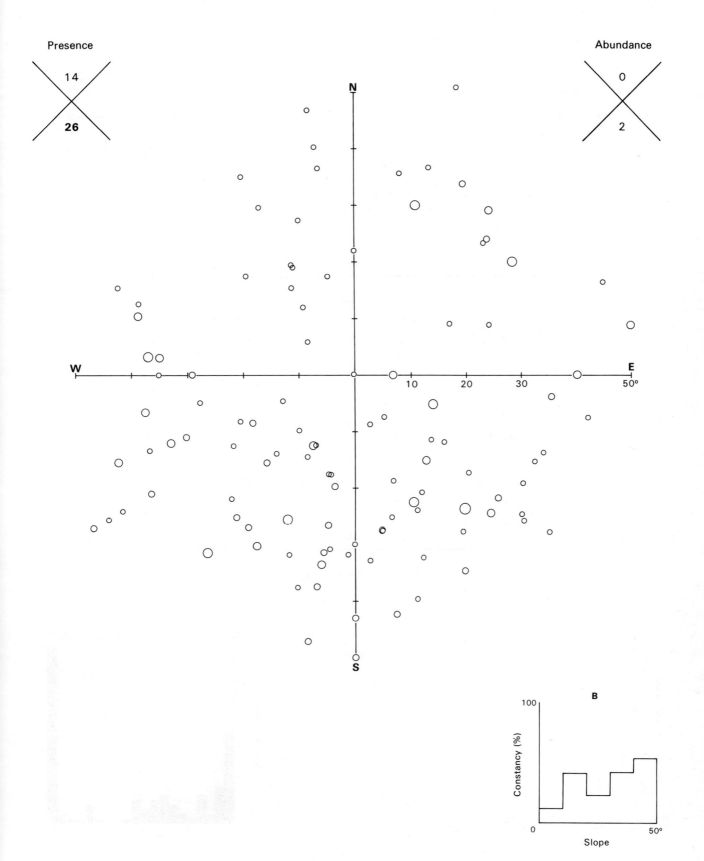

Vaccinium myrtillus Bilberry

Dwarf shrub, up to 60 cm, with creeping rhizomes.

Occurrence 21%

Open woods and moorland

Substratum   Widespread on the Millstone Grit but infrequent or absent elsewhere. Strongly calcifuge.

Slope and aspect   On acidic substrata, frequent over the range in slope 0–40°, but showing maximum constancy of occurrence on gentle slopes. Over limestone the species is virtually confined to leached plateaux.

Grazing and burning   No consistent pattern. Under intensive grazing by sheep, *V. myrtillus* forms a dense mat of short erect shoots; the results for the Millstone Grit confirm that the species is resistant to grazing.

Frequency distribution   Class 3, but often a subsidiary component.

B.S.B.I. Atlas   Widespread, but scarce in southern and eastern England and central Ireland.

Biological Flora   Ritchie (1956).

	TS	CL	MG	CM	ML	BS
			Geological formation			
pH (0–3 cm)						
3.0–4.0	1	4	113	8	—	—
4.1–5.0	2	1	2	1	—	—
5.1–6.0	—	—	1	—	—	—
6.1–7.0	—	1	—	—	—	—
7.1–8.0	—	—	—	—	—	—
pH (9–12 cm)						
2.8–4.0	—	3	114	8	—	—
4.1–5.0	3	2	2	1	—	—
5.1–6.0	—	—	—	—	—	—
6.1–7.0	—	—	—	—	—	—
7.1–8.1	—	1	—	—	—	—
Constancy (%)	8	3	70	7	0	0
Ungrazed, unburned	—	0	57	5	—	0
Grazed, unburned	0	5	73	11	0	—
Ungrazed, burned	19	0	—	14	0	—
Grazed, burned	—	0	—	—	—	—

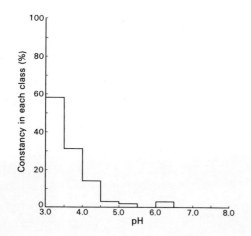

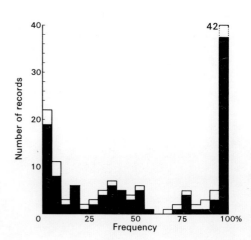

164

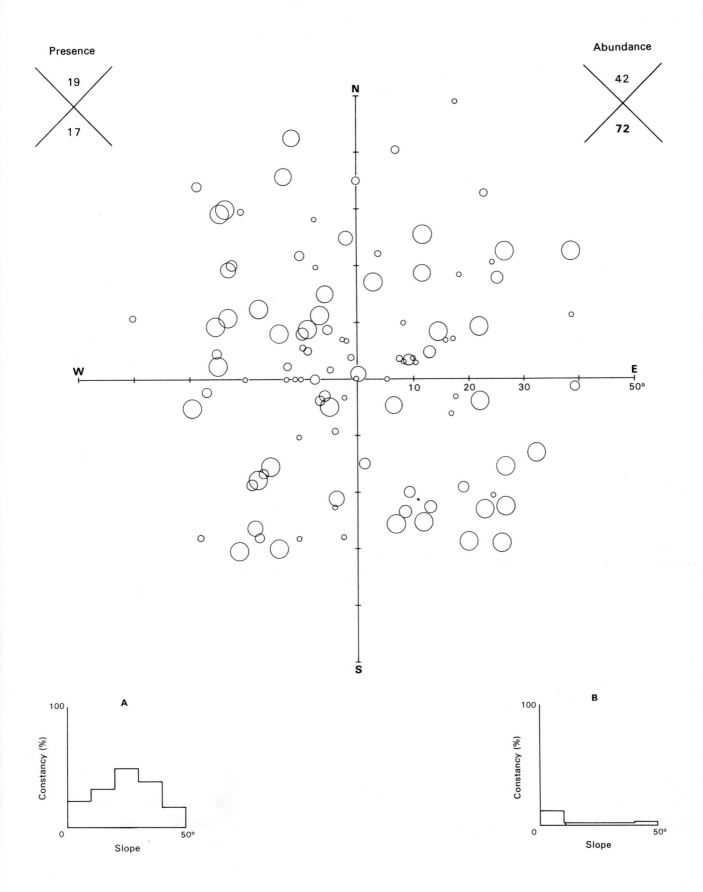

Presence

19
17

Abundance

42
72

N

W   10   20   30   50°   E

S

A

Constancy (%)

100

0   50°

Slope

B

Constancy (%)

100

0   50°

Slope

Veronica chamaedrys Germander Speedwell

Prostrate perennial herb, 20–40 cm.

Occurrence 7%

Grassland, scrub and waste places

Substratum An infrequent component of grassland except on the Toadstone and Carboniferous Limestone. The records are normally distributed over the pH range 4.0–8.0.

Slope and aspect Occurrences widely scattered with respect to slope. No marked pattern in relation to aspect.

Grazing and burning Abundant in or restricted to grazed grassland on each of the five strata on which the species was recorded.

Frequency distribution Class 2.

B.S.B.I. Atlas Ubiquitous.

			Geological formation			
	TS	CL	MG	CM	ML	BS
pH (0–3 cm)						
3.0–4.0	—	—	—	—	—	—
4.1–5.0	2	2	1	1	—	—
5.1–6.0	5	6	—	—	—	—
6.1–7.0	4	9	—	—	1	—
7.1–8.0	1	10	—	—	2	—
pH (9–12 cm)						
2.8–4.0	—	—	—	—	—	—
4.1–5.0	4	1	—	1	—	—
5.1–6.0	6	1	1	—	—	—
6.1–7.0	2	8	—	—	1	—
7.1–8.1	—	15	—	—	2	—
Constancy (%)	**32**	**15**	*1*	*1*	4	0
Ungrazed, unburned	—	7	0	0	—	0
Grazed, unburned	60	26	1	3	20	—
Ungrazed, burned	6	2	—	0	1	—
Grazed, burned	—	0	—	—	—	—

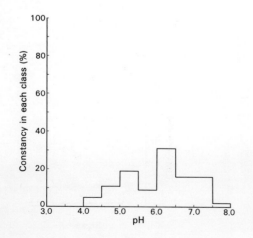

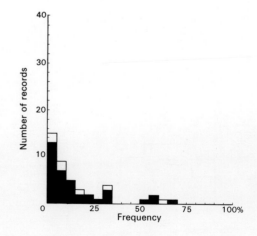

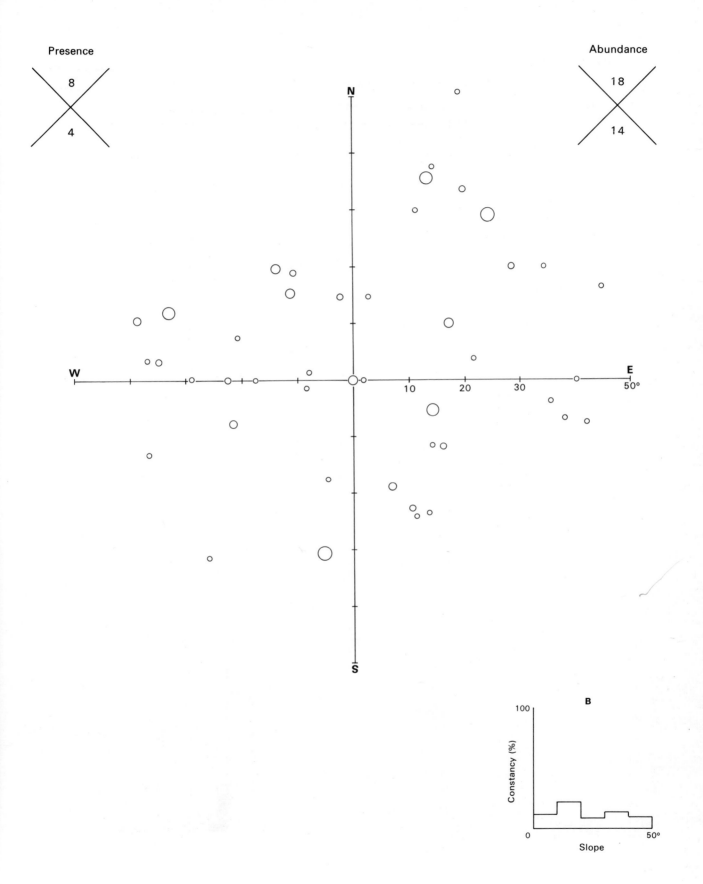

Presence

8

4

Abundance

18

14

N

W   E
        10   20   30   50°

S

B

100

Constancy (%)

0   50°
          Slope

Viola hirta Hairy Violet

Perennial herb, 4–20(–40) cm, with petiolate rosettes.

Occurrence 6%

Grassland and scrub

Substratum   With one exception the records are from limestone. The distribution is calcicolous.

Slope and aspect   Absent from grassland on flat ground. In marked contrast to *V. riviniana* the species is strongly associated with southern aspects.

Grazing and burning   No obvious correlations.

Frequency distribution   Class 2.

B.S.B.I. Atlas   Most frequent in SE Britain and mainly restricted to calcareous substrata.

			Geological formation			
	TS	CL	MG	CM	ML	BS
pH (0–3 cm)						
3.0–4.0	—	—	—	—	—	—
4.1–5.0	—	2	—	—	—	—
5.1–6.0	1	3	—	—	4	—
6.1–7.0	—	6	—	—	2	—
7.1–8.0	—	13	—	—	7	—
pH (9–12 cm)						
2.8–4.0	—	—	—	—	—	—
4.1–5.0	—	2	—	—	—	—
5.1–6.0	1	3	—	—	1	—
6.1–7.0	—	3	—	—	6	—
7.1–8.1	—	16	—	—	6	—
Constancy (%)	3	**14**	*0*	*0*	**15**	0
Ungrazed, unburned	—	13	0	0	—	0
Grazed, unburned	0	9	0	0	20	—
Ungrazed, burned	6	19	—	0	16	—
Grazed, burned	—	24	—	—	—	—

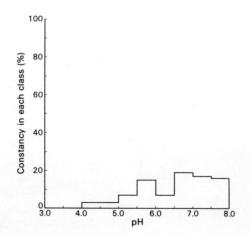

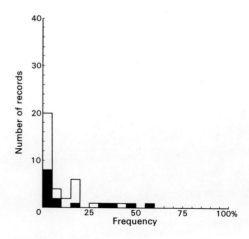

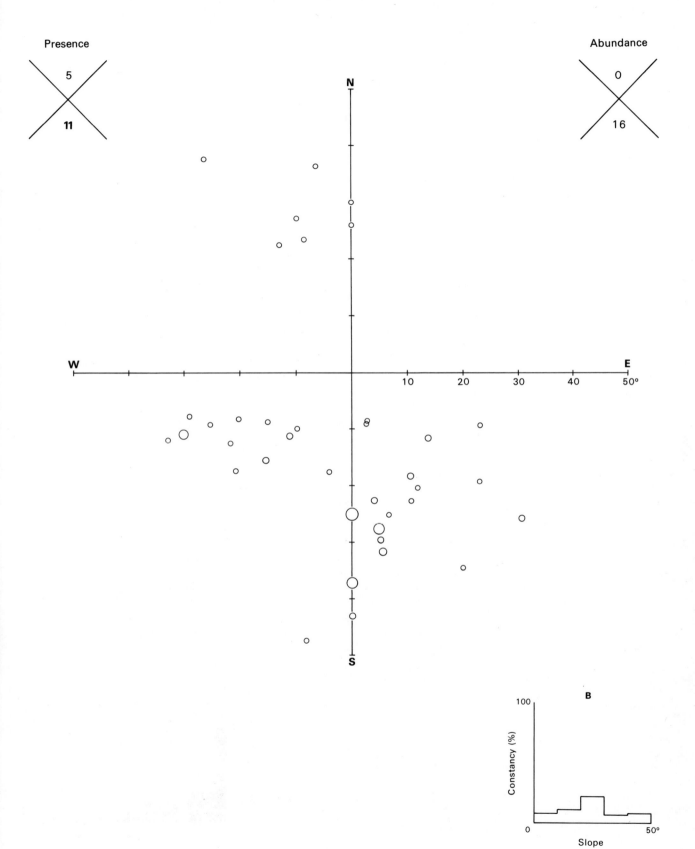

Presence
5
11

Abundance
0
16

N

W   10   20   30   40   50°   E

S

B

100

Constancy (%)

0   50°

Slope

Viola riviniana Common Violet

Perennial herb, 2–20(–40) cm, with petiolate rosettes.

Occurrence 16%

Woodland, scrub, hedgebanks and grassland

Substratum   Abundant only on the Carboniferous Limestone and Toadstone. Frequent in the pH range 4.0–8.0. *V. riviniana* is common on stabilized limestone screes; this fact probably explains the second peak in the pH histogram in the range 7.5–8.0 (cf. *Senecio jacobaea*).

Slope and aspect   Occurs commonly over the range in slope 15–40°. The species is rather more frequent on slopes of northern (especially north-western) aspect and here it attains higher frequency values and appears to extend further on to steeply sloping ground. In its association with scree slopes of northern aspect *V. riviniana* resembles *Oxalis acetosella* and *Geranium robertianum* and again like these two species it is to be found in damp open woods. However, the populations of *V. riviniana* in woodlands are different genetically and physiologically from those occurring in the open (Valentine 1941).

Grazing and burning   No consistent pattern. Apparently resistant to both factors.

Frequency distribution   Class 2.

B.S.B.I. Atlas   Ubiquitous.

	TS	CL	MG	CM	ML	BS
			Geological formation			
pH (0–3 cm)						
3.0–4.0	—	1	—	—	—	—
4.1–5.0	2	13	1	1	—	—
5.1–6.0	8	21	—	—	2	—
6.1–7.0	4	14	—	—	2	—
7.1–8.0	—	25	—	—	3	—
pH (9–12 cm)						
2.8–4.0	—	—	—	1	—	—
4.1–5.0	6	8	—	—	—	—
5.1–6.0	6	14	1	—	—	—
6.1–7.0	2	16	—	—	3	—
7.1–8.1	—	37	—	—	4	—
Constancy (%)	**37**	**42**	*1*	*1*	9	*0*
Ungrazed, unburned	—	45	0	0	—	0
Grazed, unburned	27	38	1	3	0	—
Ungrazed, burned	44	22	—	0	10	—
Grazed, burned	—	86	—	—	—	—

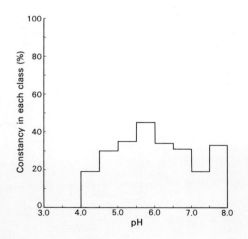

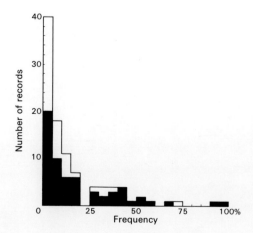

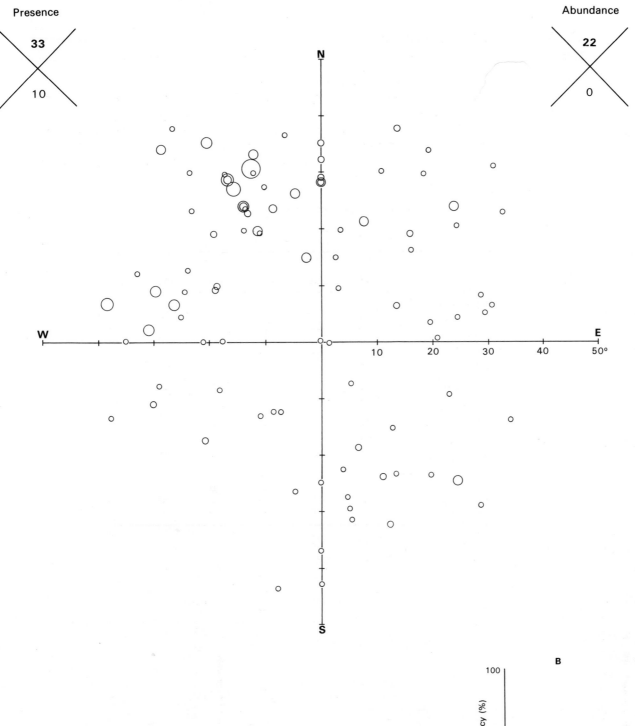

Presence

33

10

Abundance

22

0

N

W

E

10   20   30   40   50°

S

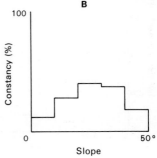

B

100

Constancy (%)

0   50°

Slope

Zerna erecta Upright Brome

Tufted perennial grass, 60–100 cm.

Substratum Recorded only on the Magnesian Limestone, although isolated colonies are known to occur on the Carboniferous Limestone. A strict calcicole, differing from *Brachypodium pinnatum*, with which it is frequently associated, in its lower constancy of occurrence on surface leached soils.

Slope and aspect Widely distributed but showing a slight bias towards southern aspects. In contrast to *Brachypodium pinnatum, Z. erecta* is commonly found on shallow soils.

Grazing and burning Less frequent at burned sites where it appears to be replaced by *Brachypodium pinnatum.*

Frequency distribution Class 2.

B.S.B.I. Atlas SE England, mostly on chalk or limestone.

	TS	CL	MG	CM	ML	BS
			Geological formation			
pH (0–3 cm)						
3.0–4.0	—	—	—	—	—	—
4.1–5.0	—	—	—	—	2	—
5.1–6.0	—	—	—	—	6	—
6.1–7.0	—	—	—	—	10	—
7.9–8.0	—	—	—	—	38	—
pH (9–12 cm)						
2.8–4.0	—	—	—	—	—	—
4.1–5.0	—	—	—	—	—	—
5.1–6.0	—	—	—	—	2	—
6.1–7.0	—	—	—	—	4	—
7.1–8.1	—	—	—	—	49	—
Constancy (%)	*0*	*0*	*0*	*0*	**66**	*0*
Ungrazed, unburned	—	0	0	0	—	0
Grazed, unburned	0	0	0	0	90	—
Ungrazed, burned	0	0	—	0	58	—
Grazed, burned	—	0	—	—	—	—

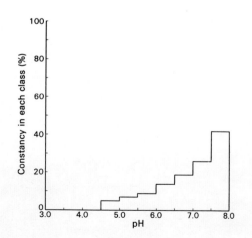

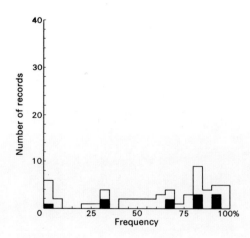

172

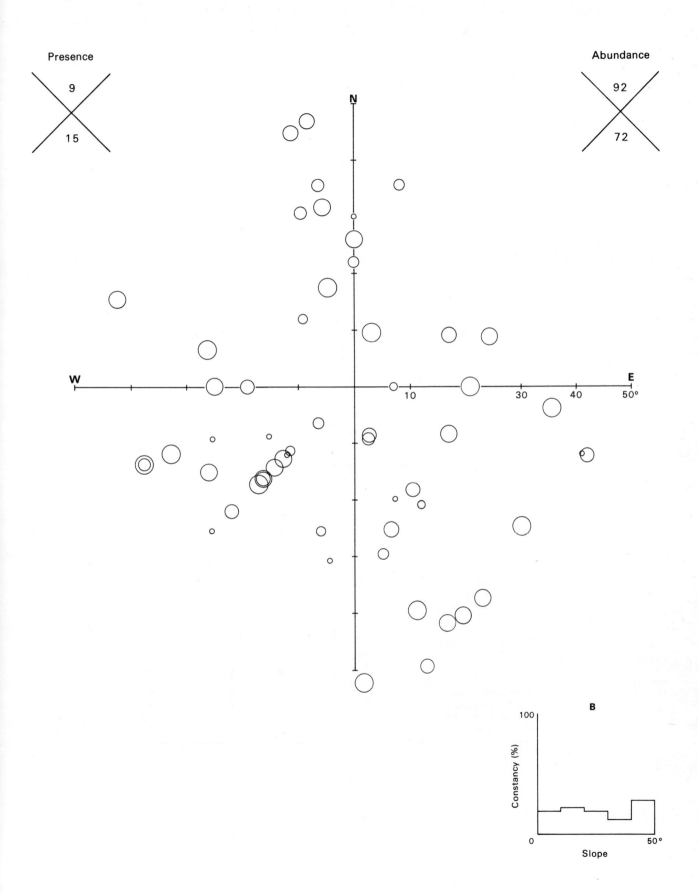

Presence
9
15

Abundance
92
72

N

W   10   30   40   50° E

B

100

Constancy (%)

0   50°

Slope

1 *Carex nigra*   Common Sedge

Occurrence 2%

Tufted or rhizomatous perennial sedge, 7–70 cm.   Marshes, wet moorland and blanket peat

Substratum   Local occurrences in acidic grassland on the Millstone Grit, Coal Measures and Carboniferous Limestone. Calcifuge.

Slope and aspect   Most of the sites at which *C. nigra* occurred were on flat (probably waterlogged) ground.
Grazing and burning   Insufficient records.
Frequency distribution   Class 2.
B.S.B.I. Atlas   Widespread in Britain but concentrated in northern and western areas.

2 *Carex panicea*   Carnation-grass

Occurrence 3%

Creeping perennial sedge, 10–40(–60) cm.   Fens and wet grassy places

Substratum   Recorded only from Carboniferous Limestone where the species is present on base-rich and calcareous soils but shows no clear optimum with respect to soil pH.

Slope and aspect   All occurrences are within the range 15–35° and are concentrated on north-facing slopes. Like *Carex flacca* and *C. pulicaris*, which also occur in north-facing calcareous grassland, *C. panicea* is a well-known constituent of eutrophic mire which is indeed its main habitat.
Grazing and burning   Not recorded from burned grassland.
Frequency distribution   Class 2.
B.S.B.I. Atlas   Very similar to that of *Carex nigra*.

	Geological formation				
	1 CL	MG	CM	**2**	CL
pH (0–3 cm)					
3.0–4.0	—	6	—		—
4.1–5.0	2	—	5		4
5.1–6.0	1	—	1		5
6.1–7.0	—	—	—		4
7.1–8.0	—	—	—		3
pH (9–12 cm)					
2.8–4.0	1	6	6		—
4.1–5.0	1	—	—		2
5.1–6.0	1	—	—		2
6.1–7.0	—	—	—		4
7.1–8.1	—	—	—		8
Constancy (%)	2	4	5		9
Ungrazed, unburned	0	11	0		10
Grazed, unburned	3	2	16		14
Ungrazed, burned	0	—	0		0
Grazed, burned	0	—	—		0

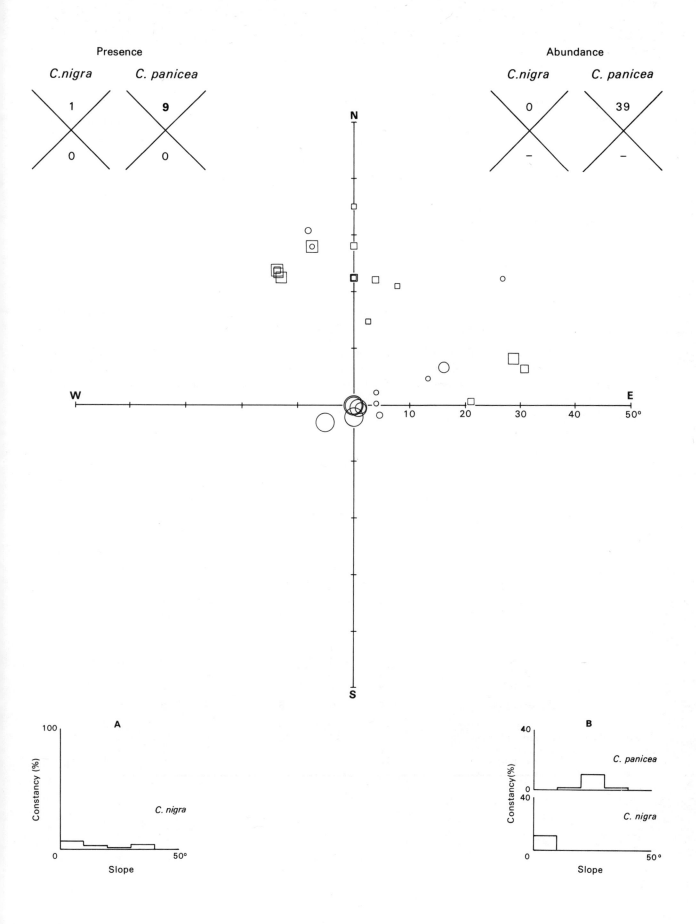

Presence

C.nigra   C. panicea

1   9

0   0

Abundance

C.nigra   C. panicea

0   39

−   −

N

W   E

10   20   30   40   50°

S

Constancy (%)   A
100

C. nigra

0   50°
Slope

Constancy(%)   B
40

C. panicea
0
40

C. nigra

0   50°
Slope

1 *Cynosurus cristatus* Crested Dog's-tail

Tufted perennial grass, 15–75 cm.

Occurrence 3%

Pastures, lawns and grassy paths

Substratum Only on the limestones and the Toadstone and absent from soils below pH 4.0. Primarily a species of agricultural land, and found on other strata in that habitat.

Slope and aspect Confined to the range in slope 20–30°.

Grazing and burning Restricted to grazed turf, particularly the close-knit turf of cattle pasture. Frequently associated with *Lolium perenne* and *Trifolium repens*.

Frequency distribution Class 2.

B.S.B.I. Atlas Ubiquitous.

Biological Flora Lodge (1959).

2 *Poa trivialis* Rough Meadow-grass

Lax tufted perennial grass, 20–60 cm.

Occurrence 3%

Meadows, cattle pastures and moist, often shady, places

Substratum Recorded only from limestone and Toadstone. Most frequent on circum-neutral soils.

Slope and aspect Most of the sites are north-facing, some on steep slopes. *P. trivialis* usually occurred as an inconspicuous under-storey component of taller vegetation types, some of which tend to be more frequent on north-facing slopes.

Grazing and burning Insufficient data.

Frequency distribution Class 2.

B.S.B.I. Atlas Ubiquitous.

	Geological formation						
	1 TS	CL	ML	**2** TS	CL	ML	
pH (0–3 cm)							
3.0–4.0	—	—	—	—	—	—	
4.1–5.0	—	2	—	—	—	—	
5.1–6.0	2	7	—	1	1	1	
6.1–7.0	—	4	1	—	6	1	
7.1–8.0	—	—	3	—	7	1	
pH (9–12 cm)							
2.8–4.0	—	—	—	—	—	—	
4.1–5.0	2	1	—	1	—	—	
5.1–6.0	—	4	—	—	2	—	
6.1–7.0	—	6	1	—	1	2	
7.1–8.1	—	2	3	—	12	1	
Constancy (%)	5	7	5	3	8	3	
Ungrazed, unburned	—	0	—	—	3	—	
Grazed, unburned	13	14	40	7	15	20	
Ungrazed, burned	0	0	0	0	0	1	
Grazed, burned	—	0	—	—	0	—	

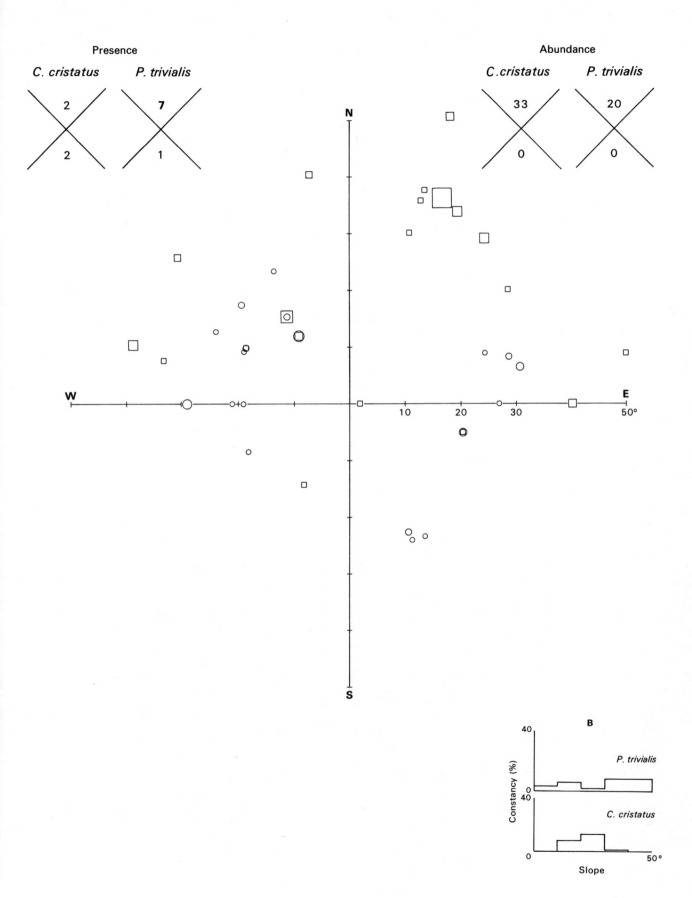

Presence

C. cristatus   P. trivialis

Abundance

C. cristatus   P. trivialis

1 *Fragaria vesca* Wild Strawberry

Perennial herb, 5–30 cm, with rosettes and long stolons.

Occurrence 4%

Scrub, hedgebanks and grassland

Substratum Only on the limestones and the Toadstone but found throughout the range of pH 4.0–8.0.

Slope and aspect Mainly on slopes of 15–35° with a slight bias to southern aspects. Often associated with broken turf.

Grazing and burning Tendency to be less common in grazed than in ungrazed communities.

Frequency distribution Class 1.

B.S.B.I. Atlas Widespread, but relatively scarce in north Scotland.

2 *Potentilla sterilis* Barren Strawberry

Perennial herb, 5–15 cm, with rosettes and prostrate stolons.

Occurrence 3%

Scrub, hedgebanks and grassland

Extraordinarily similar to *F. vesca* in morphology, ecology and distribution. The only points of difference suggested by the data are that *P. sterilis* is perhaps more restricted than *F. vesca* in its pH range, and that it is more tolerant of grazing.

	1	TS	CL	ML	**2**	TS	CL	ML
					Geological formation			
pH (0–3 cm)								
3.0–4.0		—	—	—		—	—	—
4.1–5.0		—	1	—		—	2	—
5.1–6.0		1	5	—		1	8	—
6.1–7.0		—	3	—		1	4	—
7.1–8.0		—	8	4		—	2	1
pH (9–12 cm)								
2.8–4.0		—	—	—		—	—	—
4.1–5.0		—	—	—		1	—	—
5.1–6.0		1	4	—		—	7	—
6.1–7.0		—	2	1		1	6	—
7.1–8.1		—	11	3		—	3	1
Constancy (%)		3	**10**	5		5	**9**	1
Ungrazed, unburned		—	19	—		—	7	—
Grazed, unburned		7	3	0		13	11	0
Ungrazed, burned		0	19	6		0	5	1
Grazed, burned		—	5	—		—	10	—

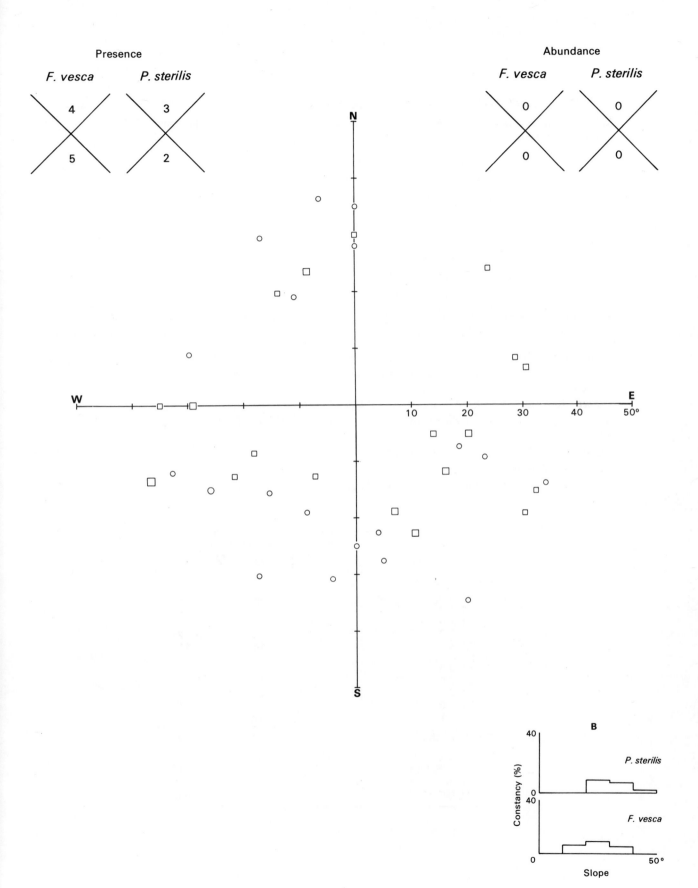

Presence

F. vesca

P. sterilis

Abundance

F. vesca

P. sterilis

N

W

E

10   20   30   40   50°

S

B

P. sterilis

F. vesca

40

40

0

50°

Constancy (%)

Slope

1 *Geranium robertianum* Herb-Robert

Occurrence 3%

Annual or biennial herb, 10–50 cm, with decumbent or ascending shoots.

Damp, usually shaded habitats, open woods and river shingle

Substratum Confined to the Carboniferous Limestone, but as a plant of open woods and streamsides *G. robertianum* occurs on other strata in the region.

Slope and aspect The records for *G. robertianum* are exclusively from daleside screes. This explains the concentration of the sites in the slope range 20–40°.

Grazing and burning The sparsely colonized scree sites are likely to escape both grazing and burning.

Frequency distribution Class 1.

B.S.B.I. Atlas Ubiquitous except in north Scotland.

2 *Oxalis acetosella* Wood Sorrel

Occurrence 2%

Rhizomatous perennial herb, 5–15 cm.

Woods and shaded places

Substratum Recorded only from the Carboniferous Limestone. The apparently calcicolous distribution arises from the confinement of the species to limestone scree. In woodlands, *O. acetosella* occurs on both calcareous and non-calcareous substrata.

Slope and aspect Restricted to steep scree slopes of northern aspect. In this situation it seems likely that the species will encounter conditions of light and moisture supply similar to those experienced in woodland habitats.

Grazing and burning See *G. robertianum*.

Frequency distribution Class 2.

B.S.B.I. Atlas Ubiquitous except in East Anglia and central Ireland.

	Geological formation			
	1	CL	**2**	CL
pH (0–3 cm)				
3.0–4.0		—		—
4.1–5.0		—		—
5.1–6.0		—		—
6.1–7.0		2		2
7.1–8.0		14		11
pH (9–12 cm)				
2.8–4.0		—		—
4.1–5.0		—		—
5.1–6.0		—		—
6.1–7.0		1		1
7.1–8.1		12		12
Constancy (%)		9		7
Ungrazed, unburned		29		19
Grazed, unburned		2		1
Ungrazed, burned		2		0
Grazed, burned		24		33

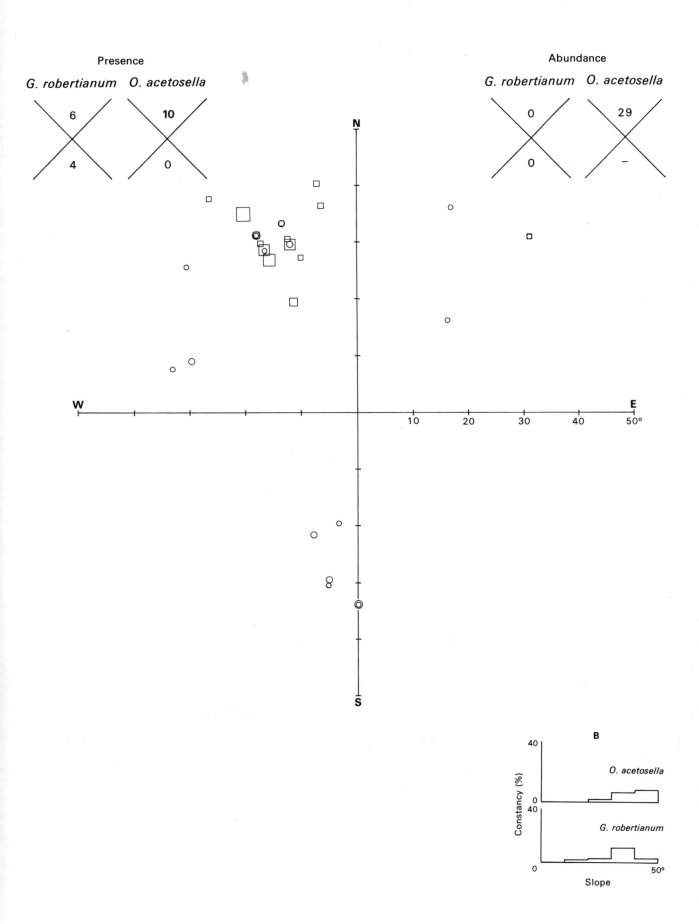

Presence

G. robertianum

6
4

O. acetosella

10
0

Abundance

G. robertianum

0
0

O. acetosella

29
–

N

W

10   20   30   40   50°

E

S

B

O. acetosella

40

Constancy (%)

40

G. robertianum

0

50°

Slope

1 *Hypericum montanum* Mountain St. John's Wort *Occurrence* 2%
Erect perennial herb, 40–80 cm. Grassland and scrub

Substratum Magnesian Limestone. *H. montanum* also occurs locally (but was not recorded) on the Carboniferous Limestone. A calcicole.
Slope and aspect Recorded only on slopes greater than 20°.
Grazing and burning All the sites at which the species occurred were subject to burning.
Frequency distribution Class 2.
B.S.B.I. Atlas Local on calcareous substrata in England and Wales. Absent elsewhere and number of sites declining rapidly.

2 *Hypericum perforatum* Common St. John's Wort *Occurrence* 3%
Erect rhizomatous perennial herb, 30–90 cm. Open woods, scrub and derelict grassland

Substratum Frequent on the Toadstone, scattered occurrences on the two limestones. Most common on soils of intermediate base-status.
Slope and aspect Scattered occurrences over the slope range 15–45°. Clear concentration of sites in grassland of southern aspect.
Grazing and burning On the Toadstone and Magnesian Limestone the species is confined to burned, ungrazed sites.
Frequency distribution Class 2.
B.S.B.I. Atlas Throughout southern England, becoming less common in the north and west.

			Geological formation			
	1	ML	**2**	TS	CL	ML
pH (0–3 cm)						
3.0–4.0		—		—	—	—
4.1–5.0		—		—	—	—
5.1–6.0		2		4	—	4
6.1–7.0		2		3	3	—
7.1–8.0		9		—	—	5
pH (9–12 cm)						
2.8–4.0		—		—	—	—
4.1–5.0		—		—	—	—
5.1–6.0		1		4	—	—
6.1–7.0		—		2	1	5
7.1–8.1		12		1	2	4
Constancy (%)		15		18	2	11
Ungrazed, unburned		—		—	3	—
Grazed, unburned		0		0	2	0
Ungrazed, burned		19		44	0	13
Grazed, burned		—		—	0	—

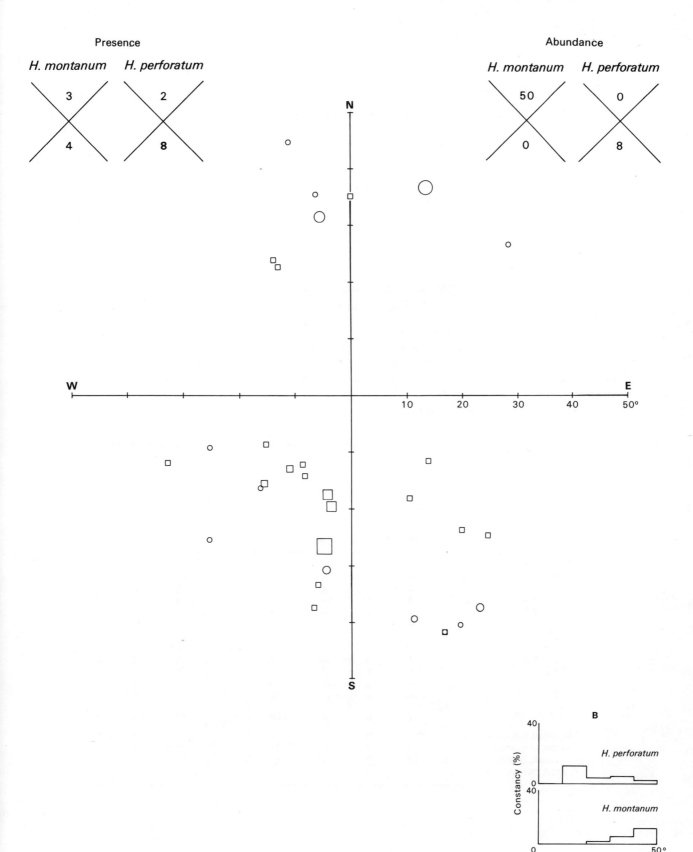

Presence

H. montanum

3
4

H. perforatum

2
8

Abundance

H. montanum

50
0

H. perforatum

0
8

N

W

E

10 20 30 40 50°

S

B

40

Constancy (%)

H. perforatum

0

40

H. montanum

0

50°

Slope

1 *Lathyrus pratensis* Meadow Vetchling

Perennial herb, 30–120 cm, with ascending shoots and tendrils.

Occurrence 4%

Meadows, hedgerows and
grassy wasteland

Substratum Scattered occurrences on four strata. Absent from Millstone Grit and Bunter Sandstone; most frequently found over limestone on soils of intermediate pH.

Slope and aspect Found more commonly on gently sloping ground. No aspect preference apparent.

Grazing and burning Insufficient records.

Frequency distribution Class 2.

B.S.B.I. Atlas Ubiquitous except in north Scotland.

2 *Lathyrus montanus* Bitter Vetch

Erect perennial herb, 15–40 cm, with creeping tuberous rhizome.

Occurrence 3%

Grassland and heathland

Substratum A common plant on the Toadstone but scarce elsewhere. With the exception of a small number of calcareous sites, the species is confined to soils of intermediate base-status (cf. *Potentilla erecta*).

Slope and aspect Sites occur mainly on gentle (10–25°) slopes of north-western aspect. On the Carboniferous Limestone the species is often confined to plateau edges, where there is a transition between calcareous and acidic soils.

Grazing and burning Insufficient records.

Frequency distribution Class 2.

B.S.B.I. Atlas Widespread except in East Anglia, the SE Midlands and central Ireland where the species is virtually absent.

	1	TS	CL	CM	ML	2	TS	CL	ML
					Geological formation				
pH (0–3 cm)									
3.0–4.0		—	—	—	—		—	—	—
4.1–5.0		2	1	2	2		2	4	—
5.1–6.0		3	1	—	4		3	—	1
6.1–7.0		—	2	—	2		4	—	—
7.1–8.0		—	1	—	5		2	1	—
pH (9–12 cm)									
2.8–4.0		—	—	—	—		—	—	—
4.1–5.0		1	—	—	1		8	2	—
5.1–6.0		4	1	2	1		3	—	1
6.1–7.0		—	2	—	5		—	1	—
7.1–8.1		—	2	—	6		—	2	—
Constancy (%)		13	3	2	**15**		29	3	1
Ungrazed, unburned		—	0	3	—		—	7	—
Grazed, unburned		7	5	0	20		33	0	0
Ungrazed, burned		19	0	0	13		13	8	1
Grazed, burned		—	0	—	—		—	0	—

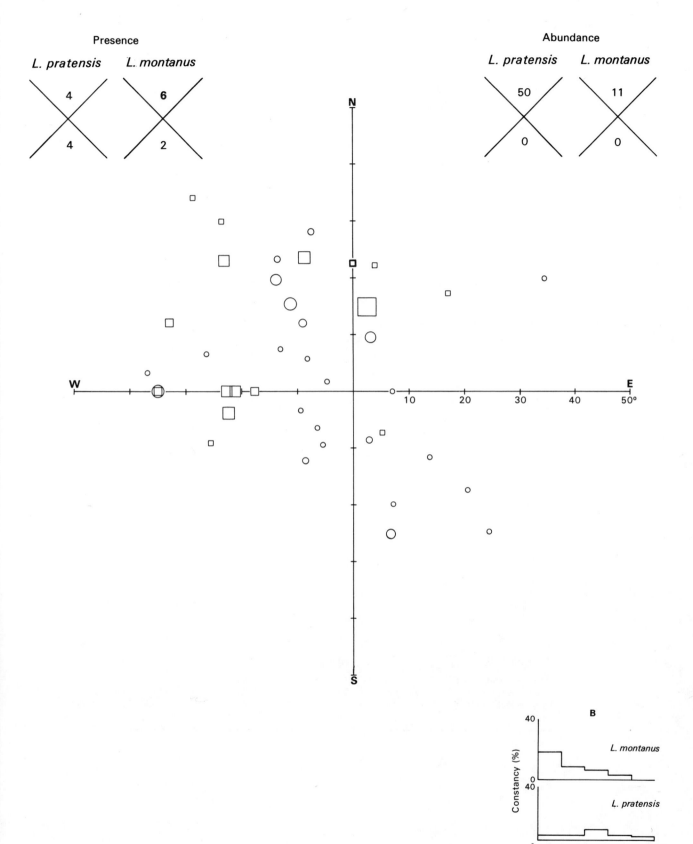

Presence

L. pratensis   *L. montanus*

Abundance

L. pratensis   *L. montanus*

B

Constancy (%)

L. montanus

L. pratensis

Slope

1 *Taraxacum officinale* s.l. Common Dandelion   Occurrence 9%

Perennial herb, up to 40 cm, with rosette of ascending leaves.   Fertile grassland and waste places

Substratum   Recorded frequently only on the Magnesian Limestone where it is confined to base-rich and calcareous soils.

Slope and aspect   Scattered occurrences on slopes of all aspect. Rather more records in the slope range 20–30°.

Grazing and burning   On the Magnesian Limestone *T. officinale* is of very common occurrence in pasture.

Frequency distribution   Class 1.

B.S.B.I. Atlas   Ubiquitous.

2 *Taraxacum laevigatum* s.l. Lesser Dandelion   Occurrence 5%

Perennial herb, up to 15 cm, with rosette of prostrate leaves.   Dry grassland, walls and rock outcrops

Substratum   Confined to calcareous soils on the two limestones.

Slope and aspect   Scattered occurrences over the range in slope 10–50°. The species is most commonly found on shallow soils with broken turf, frequently on southern aspects.

Grazing and burning   No clear-cut differences.

Frequency distribution   Class 1.

B.S.B.I. Atlas   Mainly in SE England and in coastal localities (Perring 1968).

	1	TS	CL	CM	ML	2	CL	ML
				Geological formation				
pH (0–3 cm)								
3.0–4.0		—	—	—	—		—	—
4.1–5.0		—	—	2	—		—	1
5.1–6.0		1	7	1	1		4	1
6.1–7.0		1	11	—	1		4	1
7.1–8.0		—	10	—	21		14	6
pH (9–12 cm)								
2.8–4.0		—	—	—	—		—	—
4.1–5.0		—	—	1	1		—	—
5.1–6.0		—	3	2	—		2	1
6.1–7.0		2	9	—	2		4	1
7.1–8.1		—	14	—	20		15	7
Constancy (%)		5	**16**	2	**27**		**12**	**11**
Ungrazed, unburned		—	10	5	—		3	—
Grazed, unburned		7	20	0	70		12	10
Ungrazed, burned		0	14	0	22		24	10
Grazed, burned		—	5	—	—		5	—

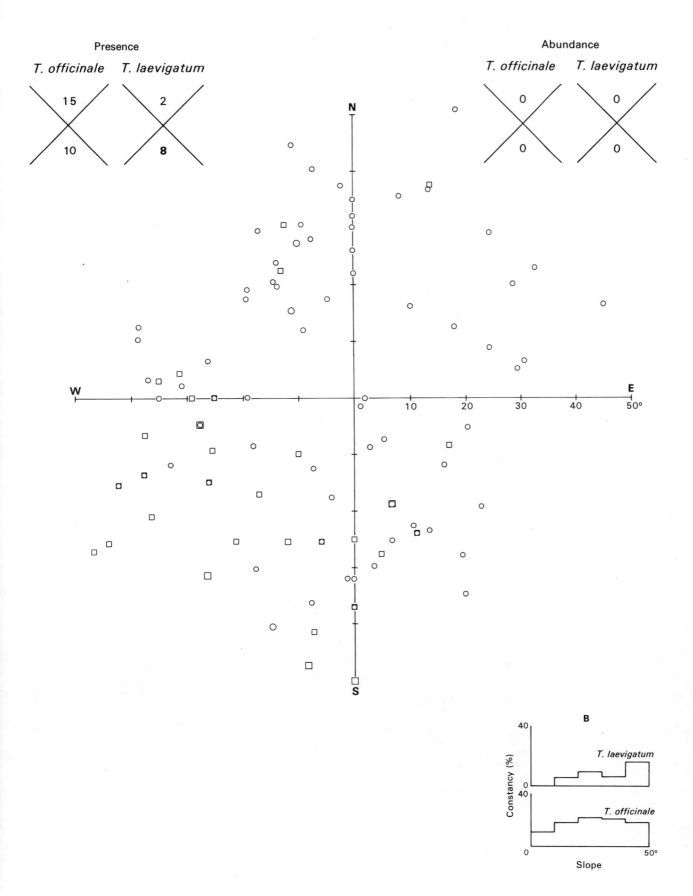

Presence

T. officinale   *T. laevigatum*

15 / 2

10 / **8**

Abundance

T. officinale   *T. laevigatum*

0 / 0

0 / 0

N

W   E
10   20   30   40   50°

S

B

40

Constancy (%)

T. laevigatum

0

40

T. officinale

0   50°

Slope

1 *Trifolium medium* Zigzag Clover

Rhizomatous perennial herb, up to 50 cm.

Occurrence 3%

Grassy places

Substratum   With one exception, the sites at which the species occurs are on the Magnesian Limestone, on which *T. medium* shows a shallow normal pH distribution, being rather more common in the range pH 5.5–7.0.

Slope and aspect   No clear relationship with slope but a distinct association with southern aspects.

Grazing and burning   Unlike *Trifolium repens* and *T. pratense*, this species has robust ascending shoots and is often observed in tall grassland dominated by *Brachypodium pinnatum*. Most of the records are from burned, ungrazed grassland.

Frequency distribution   Class 2.

B.S.B.I. Atlas   Widespread in England except in East Anglia, scarcer in the north and west.

2 *Trifolium pratense* Red Clover

Perennial herb, up to 60 cm.

Occurrence 3%

Meadows and fertile grassy places

Substratum   *T. pratense* is infrequent as a constituent of natural or semi-natural grassland, and was encountered as a minor component of grassland on limestone and Toadstone. Present on soils of intermediate base-status and on calcareous soils.

Slope and aspect   Scattered occurrences over a wide range of slope and aspect.

Grazing and burning   Particularly on the Magnesian Limestone, the species is most often found in pasture.

Frequency distribution   Class 1.

B.S.B.I. Atlas   Ubiquitous.

	1	TS	ML	2	TS	CL	ML
				Geological formation			
pH (0–3 cm)							
3.0–4.0		—	—		—	—	—
4.1–5.0		—	1		—	1	—
5.1–6.0		—	6		1	2	1
6.1–7.0		1	4		1	5	2
7.1–8.0		—	7		—	2	6
pH (9–12 cm)							
2.8–4.0		—	—		—	—	—
4.1–5.0		1	—		2	1	—
5.1–6.0		—	—		—	1	3
6.1–7.0		—	6		—	3	6
7.1–8.1		—	12		—	5	—
Constancy (%)		3	21		5	6	11
Ungrazed, unburned		—	—		—	0	—
Grazed, unburned		7	0		13	11	40
Ungrazed, burned		0	25		0	0	7
Grazed, burned		—	—		—	0	—

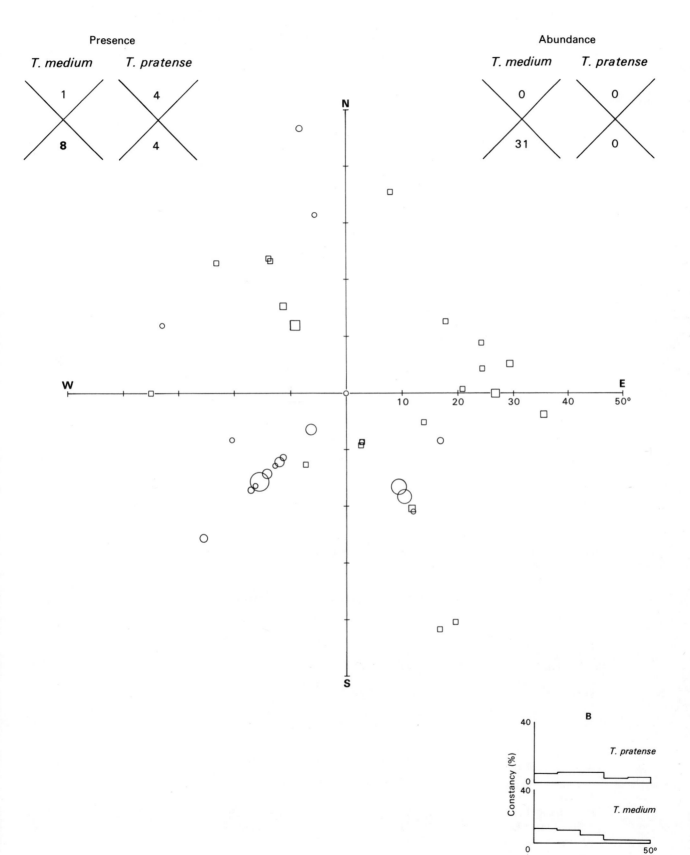

N

W　　　　　　　　　　　　　　　　10　　20　　30　　40　　50°　E

S

B

T. pratense

T. medium

Constancy (%)

40

40

0　　　　　　　　　　　　　50°

Slope

Index and ecological synopsis of species

Aspect distributions are statistically significant (or nearly so if in parenthesis); other distributions are subjectively assessed.

    * Species marked B show a slope bias on basic but not acidic substrata.

  ** Cf: strongly calcifuge distribution.

      I: intermediate distribution, scarce on soils with pH < 4.0.

    Cc: strongly calcicole distribution.

	Page	Aspect N	Aspect S	Slope* Flat	Slope* Steep	pH Hist. Cf	pH Hist. I	pH Hist. Cc	Freq. 1	Freq. 2	Freq. 3
Achillea millefolium L.	18			+			+		+		
Agrostis canina L.	20	(+)					+			+	
Agrostis tenuis Sibth.	22	+		B			+				+
Anemone nemorosa L.	24	+					+		+		
Anthoxanthum odoratum L.	26	+					+			+	
Arabis hirsuta (L.) Scop.	28		+		+			+	+		
Arenaria serpyllifolia L.	30		+		+			+	+		
Arrhenatherum elatius (L.) J. & C. Presl	32	(+)		B			+			+	
Bellis perennis L.	34						+				
Betonica officinalis L.	36						+			+	
Brachypodium pinnatum (L.) Beauv.	38		+					+			+
Brachypodium sylvaticum (Huds.) Beauv.	40				+		+			+	
Briza media L.	42	+			+		+				
Calluna vulgaris (L.) Hull	44			B		+				+	
Campanula rotundifolia L.	46						+		+		
Carex caryophyllea Latour.	48				+		+			+	
Carex flacca Schreb.	50	+			+		+			+	
Carex nigra (L.) Reichard	174			B						+	
Carex panicea L.	174	+			+					+	
Centaurea nigra L.	52							+	+		
Centaurea scabiosa L.	54		(+)					+	+		
Cerastium holosteoides Fr.	56						+		+		

	Page	Aspect N	Aspect S	Slope Flat	Slope Steep	pH Histogram Cf	pH Histogram I	pH Histogram Cc	Frequency Class 1	Frequency Class 2	Frequency Class 3
Chamaenerion angustifolium (L.) Scop.	58						+		+		
Chrysanthemum leucanthemum L.	60	(+)			+			+			
Cirsium arvense (L.) Scop.	62		(+)				+		+		
Cirsium palustre (L.) Scop.	64	+					+		+		
Conopodium majus (Gouan) Loret	66	(+)					+			+	
Cynosurus cristatus L.	176									+	
Dactylis glomerata L.	68		+				+			+	
Deschampsia cespitosa (L.) Beauv.	70	+					+			+	
Deschampsia flexuosa (L.) Trin.	72			B		+					+
Euphrasia officinalis agg.	74				+			+			
Festuca ovina L.	76						+				+
Festuca rubra L.	78	+					+				
Fragaria vesca L.	178								+		
Galium saxatile L.	80	+		B		+				+	
Galium sterneri Ehrendorf.	82				+			+			
Galium verum L.	84						+			+	
Geranium robertianum L.	180				+			+	+		
Helianthemum chamaecistus Mill.	86		(+)		+			+		+	
Helictotrichon pratense (L.) Pilger	88							+		+	
Helictotrichon pubescens (Huds.) Pilger	90	(+)					+			+	
Heracleum sphondylium L.	92						+		+		
Hieracium pilosella L.	94		+		+		+				
Holcus lanatus L.	96	+					+				
Holcus mollis L.	98					+					
Hypericum montanum L.	182									+	
Hypericum perforatum L.	182		+							+	
Hypochoeris radicata L.	100							+	+		
Koeleria cristata (L.) Pers.	102						+			+	
Lathyrus montanus Bernh.	184	+								+	
Lathyrus pratensis L.	184			+						+	
Leontodon hispidus L.	104	(+)						+		+	
Linum catharticum L.	106				+			+		+	
Lotus corniculatus L.	108		+		+		+			+	
Luzula campestris (L.) DC.	110	+					+			+	
Medicago lupulina L.	112		+		+			+		+	
Mercurialis perennis L.	114	+			+			+		+	

	Page	Aspect		Slope		pH Histogram			Frequency Class		
		N	S	Flat	Steep	Cf	I	Cc	1	2	3
Molinia caerulea (L.) Moench	116	+		+		+				+	
Nardus stricta L.	118		+	B		+				+	
Origanum vulgare L.	120		+					+			
Oxalis acetosella L.	180	+			+			+		+	
Pimpinella saxifraga L.	122				+		+				
Plantago lanceolata L.	124		+								
Poa pratensis ssp. *pratensis* L.	126		+				+			+	
ssp. *angustifolia* (L.) Gaud.	126		+					+		+	
Poa trivialis L.	176	+								+	
Polygala vulgaris L.	128				+		+		+		
Potentilla erecta (L.) Räusch.	130	+					+				
Potentilla sterilis (L.) Garcke	178								+		
Poterium sanguisorba L.	132						+			+	
Primula veris L.	134						+		+		
Prunella vulgaris L.	136	+					+		+		
Pteridium aquilinum (L.) Kuhn	138		+			+					
Ranunculus acris L.	140						+				
Ranunculus bulbosus L.	142						+		+		
Rumex acetosa L.	144	(+)					+				
Rumex acetosella L.	146	+				+				+	
Scabiosa columbaria L.	148		(+)		+			+		+	
Senecio jacobaea L.	150				+		+		+		
Sieglingia decumbens (L.) Bernh.	152						+			+	
Succisa pratensis Moench	154	+			+		+			+	
Taraxacum laevigatum (Willd.) DC.	186		+		+				+		
Taraxacum officinale Weber	186								+		
Teucrium scorodonia L.	156		(+)		+			+		+	
Thymus drucei Ronn.	158		+		+			+		+	
Trifolium medium L.	188		+							+	
Trifolium pratense L.	188								+		
Trifolium repens L.	160						+			+	
Trisetum flavescens (L.) Beauv.	162		+		+	+					
Vaccinium myrtillus L.	164		+			+					+
Veronica chamaedrys L.	166						+			+	
Viola hirta L.	168		+					+		+	
Viola riviniana Rchb.	170	+			+		+			+	
Zerna erecta (Huds.) S. F. Gray	172							+		+	